Do you know Derry Kissack?

No! But I know a fella who does!

The life and times of Derry Kissack

written by Derry Kissack

Acknowledgements

With many thanks to the following good people:

A. J. Thompson and Keith Marshall.

To Alice Corrin for all her enthusiasm and for typing the text for me - often encouraging me to continue writing when I was on the point of quitting.

To Dot Tilbury, MBE, for all her help and advice.

Also to my wife Tricia for putting up with me, and for help from Bill Snelling, my brother Howard and the Copy Shop.

A special mention to my friends Phil Quayle and Steve "Sparkey" Parkinson, my postman, for patiently listening to my readings of this drivel over the past years!

Also to Steve Murzell and Dave Walker.

My sincere appreciation to Ian Macfadyen CB OBE for taking the time from his busy schedule as Master of Windsor Castle to write a foreword for me.

Thank you all and to anyone and everyone who has helped me along the way so far.

Published by: Derry Kissack

© Derry Kissack 2009

ISBN No. 978-0-9564412

Printed by The Copy Shop - 01624 622697

Contents

Introduction	5
Early memories	6
The Collegiate School	9
Crosby village and its motor cars	11
The Bungalow and TV	15
John 'Smell' - Douglas Carnival - Steam Sawmills	17
Braddan School - Winter Hill disaster	20
Our first car - motorbikes and Hondas!	23
Petrol rationing - Woolworths fire	25
The Austin Sevens	27
Real motorbikes and a drive on the road	32
Ballakermeen	35
Some mischief - Youth Club	37
Bikes and St Ninians	39
Ballavitchel - Ronague Mountain	41
Tough times - Emigration?	44
Real trials and competition	47
First job	53
My first road accident - sidecar trials	54
Yorkshire	57
From engineer to joiner	59
Peveril Club and Knock Froy	62
An apprentice in the sixties	66
The 'Tech' at Hannover Street - characters at work	76
Scrap dealer then disaster	79
Stockcars, the wedding and three funerals	82
Back home to Crosby and Kissack Bros	87
"Go back when I tell you"	90
Rover the dog 'Pine Lodge' Dad!	91
The TT Course job and driving coaches and wagons	94
Greeba Castle - lager and a chaser!	96
The Clelland adjustable wheel! Club dinners	97
Kawasaki days - Southern MCC	100
Rover at the MSPCA	103
Derry Kissack Ltd	105
The 'Hot Dogs'	110
Wensleydale and The Cover Bridge Inn	112
New business - new workforce	114
The summer cabarets	116
Another scrap digger	117
On my own now at work - Joe Cain	120
Buying a farm	121
Tarmac, reclamation and motorbikes	124
The bombs	129
No going back	131
Steve Colley and the Purple Helmets	132
Big Thomas - shire horse	136
Honda at the farm	137
The birth of the pub doughnut	139
Good neighbours and Thomas at the Show	140
New girlfriend! Things are looking up	142
Live on stage! A busy year for the 'Helmets'	144
2002 and disaster in the mist	145
The end of an era. Prince William, Steve Hislop	149
More trouble and the 'Helmets' get the sack	151
Could this be the last supper?	152
Mares, foals, our lovely wedding and Norman Wisdom	153
New DVD and farewell to the Macfadyens	155

The Kissack Malt

YEARS 60 OLD

THE PASSING YEARS HAVE
CREATED A WELL ROUNDED
CHARACTER - ASTONISHING
AND ROBUST, YET MELLOW,
WITH A WARMTH AND
SWEETNESS THAT LINGERS
LONG IN THE MEMORY.

70cl   PRODUCE OF THE ISLE OF MAN   40%vol

Do you know the famous Derry?
Prefers his pint to a glass of sherry
His curtains are falling off the pelmets
But he's far more worried about the Purple
Helmets
Old Kissack's made it to the big six o
And his busy life is like a travelling show
Now he's writing his Manx memoirs
And in them he remembers all the cars
Old Decker's stories always thrill
With his mischievous grin like Benny Hill
As a biker, horseman and a builder
He's a rock solid currency like the guilder
Derry the legend is famous and real
He's known world wide from Thailand to Peel
So as you cuddle up to the lovely Trish
Here is our special and heartfelt wish

4

Foreword

I first met Derry Kissack in the grounds of Government House on the Isle of Man when he was doing some contract work there. I had absolutely no idea what I was letting myself in for when I invited him to bring the Purple Helmets display team to Government House. I soon found out!

The Isle of Man is synonymous with motor bikes. Derry Kissack got the bug at an early age and, inevitably, this book is full of tales of bikes, many long since forgotten. His early life was during a time when many on the island suffered hardship, but in his later years he has been a part of the success story that is the Isle of Man today.

Derry Kissack's own very special humour comes across well in this readable and amusing book. It is a story of the lives of good Manx folk, of hardship and of good times, of machinery of all kinds that covers it seems most of the Manx vehicle register! It is also a tale of a most likeable man who has lived life to the full.

During my time at Government House, the Purple Helmets gave a number of memorable displays for visitors there, including Royalty. One member of the Royal Family turned to me afterwards and said he had not laughed so much in years. It is difficult enough to clown about on bikes, but their extraordinary display is all the more remarkable for the wonderful dry humour of Derry's commentary. That seems to me to sum up the spirit of this book. It is full of mischief, laughter and fun.

I therefore commend this bit of Manx magic to you, whether you are a motor cycle enthusiast or not.

I. D. Macfadyen

Windsor Castle October 2009

Air Marshal Sir Ian Macfadyen CB OBE
at Government House

The Kissack Family in 1950

*My first ride on a motor bike.
Mr. Napier's Morris 10 in the
background*

6

Early memories

Early memories - I was born in 1948 - my Mum nearly died in childbirth but thanks to Dr Stuart we both survived! My mum always swore by him as a doctor and got to know him well. I later learned that I was named after his son Derek who was killed in the war by a tank wire. Anyway, after a somewhat shaky start which included pneumonia and a hernia, I reached the age of two when I broke my collarbone. This injury was probably the first of many and I remember it happening. My brother Howard, who is one and a half years older than me, was having a rough and tumble with me one Sunday morning when I fell off the bed and something went 'snap'. There followed a trip to Nobles' Hospital in the Morris Major car that my Dad had at the time.

In 1950, cars were very scarce in the Island and the 'Major' as it was known was the first one I remember. It was of 1932 vintage and instead of its original 6-cylinder engine; Dad had fitted, as a replacement, a Morris 12/4 cylinder unit. It was a big, black (as most cars were) saloon with leather upholstery and it always seemed to smell of petrol! Its registration number was MN 7682 and I mention this because I can remember most of the registration numbers from round the Crosby area in those early days.

A very early memory is that of the Napier family who lived in a caravan behind our builders yard in the market garden and ran the greenhouses there. Roland and Jean, I think their names were, and they kept hens, they had a Morris car too and I think it was a 10/4 from about 1934. They were nice people and I have happy memories of biscuits and milk in the caravan where they lived. They didn't stay long and I think it was because the Manx Government banned caravans! The nursery was then taken over by Ernie and Harold Leece and run very successfully by them until Howard and I bought the land in the mid '70's.

One of the really great things about those years was the closeness and love shared by good neighbours. No one had better neighbours than we did and to this day I am grateful to the Gelling family who lived next door in 'Woodlea'.

'Woodlea' was home from home for me with Mrs Gelling and her husband Tom or T.W. as he was sometimes known, two sons John and George, three daughters - Maisie (who I didn't know so well as she went to London to live), Voirrey and Joice.

They were all very kind to us and good fun as well. Voirrey and Joice looked after us on countless days, as did their Mum who always had a nice coal fire in the big black range in their kitchen. Many a wet day would be spent in there playing the Pianola or managing fruitless attempts at the many other instruments in the front room of this very musical family.

Johnny worked with his father in their building business and he had a bull nosed Morris Oxford Cabriolet MN 4337. George was at that time an apprentice motor mechanic with my uncle Henry Kissack in his business on part of our yard. George was (and still is) a brilliant mechanic and even in those days built himself a car out of many bits and pieces salvaged from the scrap and restored to perfection. The car was based on a 1930's Riley Nine with a gate change, crash gearbox rather than the later type pre-select box. The bodywork was entirely home made with some guidance from my Dad who was very good at making 'something out of nothing'. I well remember George painting it green and with the registration number OMN 100. It had no doors at that time and some years later it had a roof added along with two front doors.

My mum Ella, Dad, Howard and I lived in the cottage 'West Lynne' in the lane named 'Kissacks Lane' after our family who have occupied our yard, sawmill, joiners shop and smithy since the early 1700's.

My dad Reg was a joiner and builder in the family tradition and worked for his father Harry who was also a joiner by trade but spent most of his working life in our smithy as a blacksmith. Grandad Harry and granny Katie lived about 30 yards from our house in Rosevilla, the main house on our yard, along with Auntie Mary, their daughter and her son, my cousin Norman or 'Pally' as we called him.

Pally's dad Jack Pallister had just died, and he was also dealt a cruel blow as it was discovered that at the age of just two, he had T.B. of the spine, resulting in the next two years of his life being spent in the children's ward at Nobles' Hospital.

My uncle Henry, his wife Eileen and their two children Ralph and Wendy lived nearby in 'Rosebank' on the main road in Crosby village. As mentioned, Henry ran the motor garage on our yard for some years, I remember him as a bit of a character and the yard was always 'buzzing' with people and vehicles of all descriptions.

As well as customers there would be such as the Reliant 3 wheeler bread vans of C.A. Kermode's of Onchan, driven by Alan Burgess I think his name was (they had lovely yellow iced lemon cake which was my favourite). There would be Bob Lewin or Robbie Willie Kelly the postmen with their red bicycles, Jack Callister the milk man in his Jowett Bradford Van GMN 606 or Bobby Fargher also with milk in his similar Bradford. In fact lots of farmers seemed to like the twin cylinder Bradford - Elmer Quirk at the Braaid, Willie Quirk at Corvalley, Laurie Gerrard at Ballaharry as well as our own van GMN 648 and slightly later on the last and newest one I remember at Crosby Wholesalers RMN 261.

Also calling would be travelling shops which were quite common then - the Co-op would be the main one but I also remember an old bus or converted charabanc coming round.

As and when required Dad would order a load of sand from Harold and Alfie Craine from Foxdale who would deliver the five ton load in one of the 'O' type Bedford Tippers and sometimes they would have a real old character with them 'riding shotgun'. His name was Gerra Senogles and his stories of rabbit breeding used to amuse us as little boys.

Frequent visitors to the yard would also be the green Austin K4 lorries of Fred Leece, either in for repairs to bodywork or maybe just for a cuppa and a chat. My father built the first livestock lorry body for Fred (a cousin) in the mid 1930's on a Chevrolet chassis and the family friendship continues through the generations to the present day.

Characters such as Fred himself, Victor Clarke, Ken Leece and Eric Leece in the 1950's and many more through the years, like Albert Crellin, Lenny Kerruish and Freddie Clague, to mention just a few, all passed through our yard. There would be many farmers bringing implements and things in for welding and general repairs as well as for collecting newly made trailers and wooden wheelbarrows, in fact anything that could be made or repaired! Jack Callister from Ballavitchel got a new David Brown 'Cropmaster' PMN 658 and I remember Robbie Gelling bringing it on the yard and extolling it's virtues and saying' it was six speed and ran on paraffin!'

In those days of 'make do and mend' in the early '50's, my father and mother worked very hard as I remember, to keep house and home together. I remember an old wash boiler (gas) and a poss stick next to a big mangle, and clothes airing on the clothes horse or maiden in front of the coal fire. They were very happy days for me in that little cottage which was always warm and cosy - nice coal fires, sometimes upstairs in the little bedroom grates as well on snowy winter evenings. We seemed to get deep snow every winter then and on one occasion I remember Crosby Silver Band standing outside in the snow and playing a wonderful selection of Christmas carols and hymns - magical!

In Crosby village at that time, there were two shops, one on the north side of the crossroads at the foot of Eyreton Road, owned and run by Mrs Daisy Hill which was very small and sold mainly foodstuffs, whilst opposite this was the Post Office and shop run by one of Mrs Hill's brothers - Len Gelling. This sold all manner of merchandise and hardware - in fact anything from bicycle spares and puncture repair kits, Wellington boots, lamp wicks, Thermos flasks and brushes and shovels to the famous Green Final, which as children we would be sent to collect on Saturday evenings when the bus from Douglas dropped off the bundle of green coloured newsprint. This was very important apparently as nearly everyone seemed to 'do the Pools' and eagerly awaited the football results to check their 'coupons'. Len owned a Bedford van HMN 460.

I vaguely remember ration books and bottles of orange juice with a cork in the top which was supposed to 'do you good', as were many things like buttermilk, pin jane or castor oil! I can never recall going **hungry** or indeed 'wanting' for anything and even when it was rumoured that maybe butter or sugar or such like was scarce, we always seemed to manage. In the circles in which I travelled in fact I suppose if anything I was over fed, what with my mum's good food, Mrs Gelling's kindness and my granny Kissack's wonderful gingerbread men, I certainly knew which houses to visit!

Crosby was a friendly place where everyone knew everyone else by name and neighbours were home from home in each others houses, small gangs of children played together sharing toys, of which there were a lot less than today's children seem to have, but were probably treasured even more in the absence of T.V. sets.

My auntie Mary had trained as a nurse and very good she was too, being called on often to patch up cuts and abrasions. I well remember running headlong into the back of our old Morris one ton lorry (MN 7234) and gashing my forehead open - my uncle Henry rushed me in the house and I was patched up expertly by Mary. I still have the scar today and feel sure that, not only would I have needed stitches but by the time I would have reached hospital I would have lost a lot of blood. No panic in those days but I wonder how many injections, stitches and antibiotics would be needed nowadays to achieve the same healing?

My mum and dad, always tried their best for us and looking back, I'm sure they did without themselves on occasions to try and give Howard and I the best possible start in life. Nowadays, 50 years on, I appreciate what they endeavoured to do for us but one decision they made when I was four years old definitely wasn't appreciated at the time! Howard had already started the year previously and now it was my turn to join him at the Collegiate School! All I knew was that my dad and his brothers Henry and Ralph had attended in their youth and Howard and I were to follow family tradition.

The Collegiate School

The Collegiate school was a private school at the junction of Mount Bradda and Hawarden Avenue in upper Douglas. I remember three classrooms, one upstairs (which was my favourite) and two downstairs. Also downstairs was a back room with a big display cabinet full of trophies won by the great Geoff Duke who was married to Pat, a niece of the Misses Reid who were the proprietors or joint principals along with their mother. Run very strictly in the old Victorian manner and with only lady teachers, it wasn't my cup of tea at all! It was probably more suited to young ladies than little boys who loved the open air and the countryside so it was all a bit of a culture shock to be cooped up all day without playtimes but with liberal doses of the English grammar and literature involving lots of William Shakespeare! Very heavy stuff for a four year old.

In the summer months I can rememberss trips to 'Woodlands', that fine house at Brown's Hill owned then by the Crookall family, where we would perform a play in the lovely gardens and yes, as you probably guessed it was Midsummer Nights Dream by William Shakespeare! On these somewhat rare outings we would walk in pairs on our very best behaviour and touch our caps in respect to adults. We would also visit the old All Saints tin Church and All Saints Hall on the opposite side of Selborne Drive for events such as the Christmas party. I still have some of my school reports which say that 'if Derek concentrated harder he could do much better!' - not much chance of that I'm afraid, my mind was miles away - at home on Kissacks yard! Probably the highlight of going to school for me, was the mode of travel to and from Douglas, and coming home at night especially. This could vary from day to day. My earliest memory was that of mother taking us in the Morris Major but I also remember waiting for the bus in the care of Joice Gelling who was still attending the Girls High School at the time. Joice was like 'family' to us, as were all her family in 'Woodlea' and fond memories of their kindness will stay with me all my life. On leaving the Road Services bus in Lord Street, we would walk past the hoarding around the site that was to become the Co-op, along Duke Street, past Gilbert Harding's bike shop and Tod Hunters with a display of new Dinky toys in the window, round Boots corner and wait there for the yellow Corporation bus which would take us up Prospect Hill and Bucks Road to our stop at Woodbourne Square. This bus would nearly always be one of the old Leyland Cubs or sometimes one of the new Leyland Comets (KMN 518). Alighting at Woodbourne Square I remember walking up Hawarden Avenue with Howard and past 'Oates and Quayle's' shop on the left hand side. This was situated in the front room of the house and was a real 'cottage industry' with delicious pastries of all kinds and fancy cakes as well as bread and buns.

In later years we were fortunate enough to get lifts on many days as cars became more available. We had a good friend in Graham Glover who came to live in Woodlea Villas on the main road in Crosby and when he too started at the Collegiate, we had a lift each morning with his dad Cecil, an insurance agent, who had a brand new Morris Minor with the Austin A30 O.H.V. engine.

Also living in Woodlea Villas (houses built by 'T.W.' Tom Gelling and named after his own house Woodlea) were the Kelly's - Stanley and Lou and their three sons Brian (Horace), Mike (later M.G.P. rider) and Juan. Stanley had a little green Standard 8hp MMN 332 and kindly gave us a lift on many occasions.

Coming home from school would be different altogether as it could be different every day. Often, I can remember a long and (at four years old) very

Derry & Howard Kissack

tiring walk down Mount Bradda turning right along Brighton Terrace to the hospital and Westmoreland Road, down Hillside Avenue along Belmont Terrace to the Brown Bobby to catch the bus. I clearly remember the Nurses Home being built and watching in awe as the hod carriers went up the maze of ladders and scaffolding with the bricks and cement - not a crane in sight. Just a bit further along on the hospital side, the first on the right of a pair of semi-detached houses had a wooden shop in the garden and this was run by a Mr Christian - the blind man. He seemed to know where everything was and we would sometimes buy sweets if we had a penny or two

Quite often my mum would collect us and if we were lucky we might go to the Terrace shops - maybe to Quirks the bakers for an iced fancy cake - pink was my favourite! and maybe to Loweys' for a 'Dandy' or 'Beano' comic, always a nice treat. On one of these trips in an Austin 8 van DMN 883, we had

Derry   Graham   Howard   Pally

just turned into Alexander Drive from Woodbourne Road when the 'alligator' type bonnet suddenly flew up in the wind totally blocking the forward vision. Mother jumped on the brakes, such as they were, and we came to rest against the wall of Dick Cubbon the butcher's shop! Mum was used to driving old 'nails' and she calmly shut the bonnet and off we went!

Another time we were collected in an old open box sidecar by George Gelling in his oily boiler suit and his old beret. It was a pre war Rudge belonging to Mr John Greenwood and the box sidecar was normally used for his market garden produce or to carry his rotavator - great fun for two little boys who had spent the day in such a quiet and subdued atmosphere. I seem to remember some sarcasm from the Misses Reid the next morning - they were quite snobby and thought that the reputation of the school had been compromised by our mode of transport!.

We stayed at the Collegiate school till about 1956 and I can say that it certainly wasn't a happy experience for me. We would have sandwiches every day except for a time when we got a nice dinner down at Raphael Road at the home of 'Aunt' Edith Lightfoot, her sons John and Roy, her step son John Stott and her husband Walter. They were nice people and I remember laughter there and a welcome break from the school. It was a time for great celebration when we left the Collegiate and went to Braddan School but years later I have come to appreciate the discipline and English teaching of the Misses Reid.

Crosby village & its motor cars

Meanwhile back in Crosby things were slowly changing with the march of time. At the yard I think the business just 'ticked over' as with many of that time and a lot of Manx tradesman left the Island seeking work elsewhere. My father's workforce varied up and down as and when the work came in but the main 'man' and undoubtedly a cornerstone of Kissack Bros, was 'Jacko' Gelling, who started with my granddad Harry on his being demobbed n 1945 and stayed on for close on 50 years. In all this time he hardly had a day off with the exception of the agricultural shows and later on the ploughing matches. In fact, he turned in one day after lunchtime, which was unprecedented, and shocked everyone with the news that he had in fact got married to Mona that morning but that he was back now so let's get on with the work.

I would like to pay tribute to Jacko as a friend as well as to his many skills - primarily a good joiner but he could turn his hand to many trades when called on to do so - a builder in the true sense of the word. One of my earliest memories of Jacko was when he would bring his car to the yard, maybe to fix it or even to take part in a funeral cortege. It was a 1934 Riley Nine Monaco MAN 5.

In the village at that time one fast expanding business was Crosby Wholesalers in Station Road. It was founded after the war by Heywood Gelling - a brother of Len and Daisy and occupied a large wooden hut brought from the old airfield at Andreas.

The access was the lane between the Methodist Chapel and the Methodist Hall adjacent to it and all the goods had to be man handled in and out that way. A lot of the goods would be collected from the old railway station on their arrival from Douglas by train, by Juan Kelly in a pre war Standard Atlas van painted green.

These goods would be stored in a big shed at the station which was accessed by a big white gate next to the thorn hedge which bordered the memorial playing fields. As the wholesalers expanded, more Andreas huts were added to form the warehouse up until the late 60's when the first steel framed building was built and a new access formed off the Peel road. Heywood Gelling was a good business man and steadily built up his business, soon buying new vans to replace the old Standard and cope with the expansion. Mr Gelling not only entrusted all his building work to Kissack Bros but he also garaged his vans at our yard as well. I remember George Quayle and Clair Gelling bringing various vehicles back in the evenings, always smart and clean in their livery of a shade of red ochre over drab grey and always nicely sign written. I think their c.c Model Bradford van followed the old Standard, then a Morris J, a couple of Morris J2 vans probably brings us up to the 1960 era when they got a new Bedford CA - 2371 MN.

The new entrance to Crosby Wholesalers is just about opposite what was the Crosby Police House - the first semi-detached in Woodlea Villas and home to various constables over the years. The first 'copper' I remember was Albert Edmond who lived there with his wife Brenda and daughters Ruth and Sandra. Albert was always very smart in his uniform and very keen to keep law and order - sadly lacking today - and I think his biggest challenge was to keep rick on the 'big boys' of the village with their motor bikes.

Some names that spring to mind are Robin and Jerry (Ganger) Smith who were brothers with BSA 350 or 500cc bikes I think; Gordon Corlett also with a BSA ; Ernie Leece (Junior) with a BSA Bantam NMN 949; Mike Kelly - 500 Triumph Trophy and his brother Juan, I think had a 350 BSA.

These lads, between them dug out with shovels a banked dirt track in the old playing field at the bottom of Station Road, and as a small boy I was thrilled to watch them race round and round until Albert would come down and tell them to stop their noise! This sparked an interest in motorbikes in me which I still hold to this day.

Just across the road from the old playing field is the entrance to the Highway Board Depot and quarry where all those years ago, the fleet of steam rollers would be parked overnight - as many as four or five would be there, some still hot from the days work - I think one found its way round the quarry with some older lads at the helm (I can't name them!) until Albert arrived on his Matchless police bike! I seem to remember him in his shirt sleeves chasing youths and I don't think he caught them but they knew the score and 'laid low' for a while. High jinks indeed but harmless enough by today's standards of violence and vandalism. In fact the word vandalism was almost unheard of in Crosby and only once can I recall broken windows. These were smashed by 'naughty boys' at the old Eyreton Cottages at the top of Eyreton hill which were empty except for being used for the storage of potatoes since Alfie Fayle and his family had moved out. If I recall, Albert was hot on the scent and soon brought the culprits to book!

Alfie was a character with a fine singing voice, working at several farms in the parish by day but dressed up smartly on his evening excursions to Douglas, always with a fresh button hole and Trilby hat. Passengers on the last bus home were often treated to a fine medley of songs as Alfie practised for the Guild or some Eisteddfod or other.

Along the road towards Douglas at Glenvine there was another little shop where Marown T.V. is now. This was Mrs Lewin's shop and when out for a walk with mother we would call there maybe for an ice cream. She lived next door I think where Jack Lewin used to issue licences for motor cars and dogs.

Next to another row of cottages nearby on the Crosby side was Clarkes the builders yard which was taken over by Tom Creer and Percy Kelly who ran a very successful firm there till the yard was eventually sold to Richard Evans and they moved into the original Marown Engineering building nearby. Richard Evans still occupies these premises along with what is now a dwelling house but which was originally the petrol station built for Bert Roach. I well remember this being built in record time with a big gang of bricklayers working on it and if I'm not mistaken when it opened, I think they sold Fina petrol for a while, the first time I had noticed this brand.

On fine days mother couldn't get us in the house as we would be joined each day by friends to play football, tickle trout in the stream, maybe build a gang hut or dirt track racing on our bikes - we were never bored as the yard and surrounding area was a magical place to grow up. Sometimes on wet days or possibly 'sick' days we would be in the house with mum and in those early 50's days before 1955 when we got T.V., I recall mum listening to the BBC radio. Such programmes as 'Mrs Dale's Diary', 'the Archers', 'Workers Playtime' and for us 'Listen with Mother' - a nice lady's voice would say "It's quarter to two and Julia Lang is here to tell you a story - are you sitting comfortably (to which we would answer yes!) - then I'll begin…."

One sad incident that sticks in my mind was the loss at sea of the ship 'Flying Enterprise', the reports of which were broadcast on every news bulletin and we had to be quiet while mum listened avidly, I remember, with tears in her eyes. I think this was because her own father Alf (Bingy) Cowley was a ship's engineer and served in both World Wars in the Merchant Navy. I know he was torpedoed on at least one occasion in World War 2 and by then he was no longer a young man. Mum would tell us that he was a real character in his time and though I'm sure this is true as many people have confirmed it, sadly he died when I was four years old. I remember him holding my hand whilst sitting up in his bed where he died at home in the Old School House at Garwick Corner. He is buried at Maughold and one day, I think we were going there to put flowers on his grave, we were travelling down the winding road from the Hibernia Cross Roads when confronted with an oncoming 'pop' wagon, mum had to put the old Morris Major in the roadside ditch! I think the wagon was one of Qualtroughs Bedford's but I can't remember any bad language or such like and I think the driver must have helped us back on to the road as people did in those days!.

The old 'Major' came to an end about 1953 and I remember being very upset about it! There was nothing really wrong with it but dad scrapped it because he needed the engine for the Morris Tonner wagon which was vital for the business. It lay engineless on the yard for a while and we played in it pretending to drive around. The final insult to it, which upset me even more, was when the bodywork was unceremoniously removed and hay racks welded to it, it became a mobile feed rack at Ballavitchel Farm.

I think it was around this time that my Uncle Henry ceased trading in his garage business at the yard and returned to work as salesman for the Quayle family at the Peel Road garage in Douglas. He went to sell Renault cars and David Brown tractors and George Gelling who had been his apprentice and just back from National Service, went with him. Henry, although a somewhat loveable character, left a legacy of partly dismantled vehicles and it has to be said, a number of unpaid bills! I think these were eventually settled by dad and his father Harry. They all seemed to stay friendly however and Henry continued to be a welcome visitor at our house for many years after. Maybe a case of brotherly love, maybe blood being thicker than water, I don't know which, but I can say that I liked him a lot and I was always glad to see him.

Henry's daughter Wendy was often round the yard to play with us as along with 'Pally' we were all born in the same year(as in fact were quite a few others in the village) there was never a shortage of playmates. Wendy, in fact, was my first little sweetheart!

It is probably apparent by now that my early life was influenced by motor vehicles and indeed all things mechanical. There were various makes of vehicles partly dismantled around the place as spares were very rare for certain models. I can recall the remains of Marques such as M.G., Terraplane, Invicta, Humber, Auburn, Armstrong Siddeley, Lanchester, Citroen and Ford as well as Riley and Morris which seemed to be very popular at the time.

I don't know why it was but certain makes out numbered others in the Crosby area. As with the Jowett Bradord Vans, Morris Commercial T type ton trucks were very popular. As mentioned our own lorry a 1932 version with rear wheel braking only - nothing on the front wheels at all! With an engine adapted for it to replace the original it was fitted with a hand operated screw tipper. Father bought it in the 1930's and I think it was damaged by fire, so he rebuilt it and fitted the tipper. It was used in the war time as an emergency fire tender for the Home Guard and was very well known by everyone around the village. It was used in numerous Douglas carnivals in a humorous capacity and was a most versatile vehicle being used for just about everything. Its registration number was MN 7234 and it was just one of eight or nine similar wagons round about us at that time and I can recall Tom Gelling had a black and brown one MN 9... - Ernie Leece (a brother of Fred, Bert and Sydney and Edith Lightfoot) and his son Harold ran one in the nursery business, also painted green like our own and registration number DMN. My uncle Henry had one also - MAN 931, painted green and it had bigger front mudguards than the others. A Mr Giovanelli did a fruit and veg. round with his. I think it was red and blue but I can't remember the number. There was a van version owned by Alfie Kennaugh but ours was the only one I can recall that was fitted with a tipper and as well as being the oldest it was the only one with just the rear wheel brakes, all the others had four wheel braking. This little lorry was used every day for close to 30 years and one job in particular stays in my mind.

Henry about 1932

MAN 931

Derry and Wendy

14

The Bungalow and TV!

I think it was in the winter of 1957 - 58 when dad secured the contract to demolish the 'Bungalow' Hotel on Snaefell for the M.E.R. I think work at the time was fairly thin on the ground and when the advert came in the paper for tenders for the work, my mum was instructed to make an offer for the sum of £27.10.0d to be paid to the M.E.R. and the site to be left clean and tidy for the following June and the T.T races. Some weeks later I remember great excitement on the news that the bid had been successful - but "hang on a minute" said father "it says here £37.10.0d!" "Yes I know" admitted mother " I stuck another £10 on just to make sure!"

Money was very tight at the time and after some chuntering and muttering at the shock of this huge overspend, father eventually came down off the ceiling and I think, in his own way, he was very pleased! Not before, however, I had learned some new sayings such as 'money growing on trees' and 'do you think I'm a bloomin' millionaire?'

Work was soon started on the demolition but just prior to this we paid a visit there one Sunday to 'inspect the premises'. The whole building was timber framed, lined with tongue and groove boarding and clad outside with galvanised sheeting of the 'Trafford Tile' profile. As I remember it was in generally very good condition and very pleasant inside with a long sunny room facing south on the Tholt-y-Will road side. It had a very long bar counter running almost the whole length of the room with a very wide mahogany top. There were various rooms, some of which were presumably for overnight accommodation and one of them on the right hand side of the front doors was stacked with surplus T.T. programmes, Castrol and Shell books and various other associated memorabilia - what would collectors give for it now I wonder?

Soon afterwards, work started and I used to go up there sometimes with father when school permitted. We would see Jacko and Dougie Ardern working in all weathers with hand tools only and lots of coats on! It soon became apparent that the little Morris wagon wouldn't be able to cope with all the long lengths of timber and indeed the sheer quantity of material to be carted home to Crosby each night.

Bungalow Hotel, Snaefell Mountain, I-O-M.

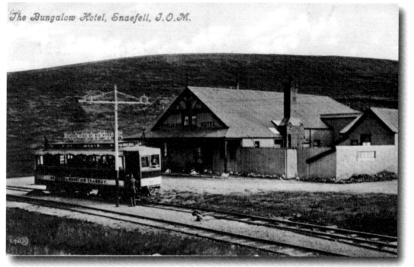

The Bungalow Hotel

Help was at hand when father borrowed or hired and ex Army Ford V8 W.O.T. model from a neighbouring farmer Terrence Corrish who farmed at Ballaclucas, Crosby Top Road. I can recall one trip up the mountain in the old Ford, when on rounding Windy Corner, dad told me to 'duck down' as there was no glass in the windows of either door and the wind howled through the cab! It was much faster than the Morris and being longer wheelbase it carried about three times as much. Bearing in mind that they would both be grossly overloaded by modern standards, to move such a quantity of stuff on two small trucks in the relatively short time available was quite an achievement.

Many days were spent up there in the snow and with no road closures then with a lot more snow to contend with it meant that travelling was a lot more difficult. Jacko has told me since that they never seemed to get stuck as the old Morris especially was very good to travel in snow but there was a concession occasionally when they would set off early for home at 3.00pm rather than 4.00pm if things looked bad! Tough men indeed as with no heater to clear the windows and certainly no 4 x 4 and the chance of help being almost nil if they broke down, they seemed to take it all in their stride and spent most of the winter up there.

When the timber and corrugated sheets started arriving back at the yard the wagons would be unloaded ready for the next day and there were big stacks of corrugated sheets and timber of all sizes, mostly 'contaminated' with nails of varying lengths and bent over for safety and transportation.

As young lads of about 8 and 9 years old, Howard and I would have a job every Saturday morning de-nailing timber and then straightening all the nails and sorting them into boxes. In those days building materials were scarce and expensive so everything was re-cycled including the nails. These would be thrown in a bucket prior to being straightened and we would sit on a stool with a big 1cwt weight or similar in front of us and armed with a claw hammer each we would set about them, nail after nail. It certainly was good practice for using a hammer and after initially hitting a few thumbs we got quite good at it.

Customers came from far and wide to buy the cleaned timber and sheets and for many years afterward the maroon painted sheets could be spotted on the roofs of lean-to sheds and such like all over the island. A lot of bigger section timber was cut or converted to different sizes as required on the big circular saw with the rope winch in our sawmill. The sawmill was originally powered by water with a 32ft diameter overshot wheel operating through friction wheels and no doubt being dual purpose to grind corn as well. I have always been told that this was the very first power driven sawmill in the Island and I don't know whether this is true or not. I remember as quite young lads watching dad set and sharpen the huge circular blades ready to cut big trees into planks. (These days they just seem to go for firewood.) The biggest of these blades was about 5ft diameter I think and although the power was by now converted to electric, the winch was (and still is) hand operated. It had a big steel handle which was wide enough for two young boys side by side or one man on his own. We would begin to wind and kept watching father in case anything went wrong or he needed to knock in a wedge to prevent jamming. When the cut started, father would pull the peak of his hat down to protect his eyes and he would be showered in sweet smelling sawdust. There was no 'top guard' as some of the trees were just too big to permit the use of one and underneath the bench the huge blade would be spinning totally unguarded. Scary stuff indeed but it certainly taught us to keep clear and be aware of danger.

The big water wheel was apparently removed during the war years but the mill race was shortened so that the water now turned a much smaller wheel connected to a dynamo or generator for electricity and this was installed in a hut made of corrugated sheets by internees from Knockaloe camp at Patrick. I don't think it was very successful and in any case 'mains' electric came instead and was used to power a big motor on the sawmill. The mill dam is still there and many hours of fun were to be had over the years either fishing there or playing on home made rafts that would often sink or capsize. Many wet and happy children would arrive home for tea in the Crosby area after an impromptu swimming lesson.

I think it was around 1955 when we got a new 'Ultra' television from Messrs Fox and Lane of Douglas. In these days either Mr Fox or Mr Lane gave their full personal attention to each and every sale they made and this often meant that they would be still at our house quite late on into the evenings on many occasions trying to get a decent picture. In fact, so poor was the reception that they became almost family. Several models were tried out and I recall names such as K.B and Ferguson as well as the Ultra which was eventually chosen at £59.10.0d This was a tremendous amount of money to find when taken into account that a tradesman at that time would earn about £7.10.0d per week. Compare that to the cheap electrical goods of today in relation to earnings.

We were however proud to say that it could receive BBC and ITV on a 14" screen although the screen seemed to be covered in 'snow' or flickering lines for most of the time. Having cost so much, it was treated with great reverence and switched on only at certain times carefully chosen from the 'Radio Times'. Childrens hour would be on from five o'clock and programmes such as 'Cisco Kid', 'Hopalong Cassidy', 'Range Rider' and 'Roy Rogers' were some of my favourites. In the evenings I recall 'The Army Game', 'What's My Line' and 'Double Your Money', as well as 'Wagon Train'.

Prior to our ownership of a T.V. we were lucky enough to have access to two other sets some years earlier. Dads brother Ralph and Auntie Doris lived in St Catherines Drive in Douglas and had a tiny 9" Bush set with a magnifying screen clipped on to the front of it. It was all very well if you sat directly in front of it but if you sat at an angle to it the picture became severely distorted. 'Muffin the Mule' and 'Andy Pandy' could be very tall or very wide depending on where you were sitting.

The other set I remember was a Murphy 12" Console model belonging to another auntie - Florence, my mum's middle sister who lived at the Old School House at Garwick Corner. This 'telly' must have cost a lot of money with a lovely wooden cabinet which had a pair of doors to cover the screen when not in use. I distinctly remember watching the coronation on this t.v. in 1953 with Florence, her mother (my grannie Cowley) and her dog Pete who was a big English Setter with a very dribbly mouth - ugh!

Behind his house in St Catherine's Drive, uncle Ralph had an allotment and along with his friend Alan Bell, who also worked for the 'Mona's Herald', they would borrow our old Morris Tonner to cart some dung for fertilizer on their produce.

These trips would usually be from Dallavitchel to Douglas with two or three loads of the wonderful stuff, all loaded by hand with the use of a grip. The wagon would then be returned to the yard with a rather strong 'bouquet' which lingered for some days! On one occasion I remember uncle Ralph telling father that a policeman had commented on the total lack of tread on one of the front tyres and father's reply was that the ones with the tread were on the back so that there would be plenty of grip in the mud and anyway the front tyre may well have been bald but it had done well and there was no canvas showing.

John 'Smell' - Douglas Carnival - Steam Sawmills

Whilst I am on the subject of borrowing vehicles, it reminds me of the time when Johnny Gelling loaned his Morris Bullnose to a man in the village. The man's name was John Clague and he lived in Woodlea Villas. I think I vaguely remember him working for Johnny and 'T.W.' but he later worked at 'Litts' the knackers yard at East Baldwin and this is where he gained the title 'John Smell'. Johnny was always generous and good hearted and when asked for the loan of his car, without hesitation, permission was given for a trip to Peel on the following Sunday morning. John Smell set off with his wife and all appeared to be well - however by the time Monday evening came around there was still no sign of the Bullnose being returned.

Douglas Carnival
The Bullnose - First prize

Douglas Carnival 1955 - MN7234

18

By now, in need of his car, Johnny was forced to pay a visit to John Smell's house to enquire about its absence. On hearing the reply Johnny was flabbergasted to learn that "we were coming back on Sunday afternoon when the damn thing ran out of petrol at the 'Highlander' and we had to walk over half a mile to get home and the wife was 'buggered' - she wasn't too pleased with you I can tell you!" Johnny's reaction to this was one of total amazement when John Smell added "Yes - I thought there would have been more juice in it than that - oh and by the way, when the wife got out she was that mad that she slammed the door and bust the window!" On this note I think John Smell closed his door and returned to eat his tea, leaving Johnny to ponder about just who had done who a favour and how he was going to retrieve his car!

In the summer holidays we always looked forward to the Douglas Carnival as there would be several entries from the Crosby Area. Without doubt the main inspiration came from the Gelling family and with a big squad of willing helpers numerous prizes were won over the years in the 'Most Humorous and Original' category. My earliest memory of the event was probably an entry by them featuring this same Bullnose Morris MN 4337. It was I think entitled 'Ballamidden Choir Outin' with everyone dressed in 1926 period costume and two king sized wooden barrels tied on to the front wings with the word 'Mild' on one and 'Bitter' on the other - I think they won! It may have been in the same carnival or perhaps a year later, when our old Morris Tonner made an appearance in an entry with Len Gelling and his family, with something to do with the 'Pools' and treble chance gambling.

These are my two earliest memories but I have many more in subsequent years. The first time I actually remember being in the procession was in the back of the first Landrover diesel which was driven by George Gelling and used to tow a large float. These floats were usually built on top of one of the Douglas Steam Sawmills 'bomb trolleys' - war surplus four wheeled trailers converted to carry the timber along the quayside from the timber boats in the harbour at Douglas. One of these trolleys would be decked over and I recall the use of two big green painted doors being used each year. These doors were from the old 'charabanc' garage which had stood behind the 'Bungalow' on the mountain, another bit of useful recycling.

Around the side of the deck, a roll of chicken wire would be tacked on and this would be laced with bracken and hydrangea flowers to form a valance with a most pleasing 'fresh' smell. The mention of Douglas Steam Sawmills brings back lots of memories and going there as a very small boy was always fascinating for me. A man in a brown dust coat, flat hat and with horn rimmed spectacles always made me laugh, his name was Freddie Holmes and he worked in what was called the 'Paint Shop', where as well as paints, all manner of other hardware was kept. There would be nails, glass, putty etc. as well as some black rope like stuff called 'tow' which smelled of tar and was used for caulking sewer pipes. There were no computers then and when a purchase was recorded a ticket was written out and a signature was required. Freddie said to me one day that if I could sign my name he would give me a shiny new 'Steam Sawmills' pencil - quite a challenge before school age and I don't know what my scrawl looked like but I remember coming home with a big oval shaped, orange coloured timber pencil.

I was fascinated also by the old steam engine which drove all the machinery. It was housed in the engine house now used to bag all the shavings and seemed to be almost silent running with just a hiss or two of steam whilst inside the mill it was a complete contrast with so much noise it was impossible to hear anyone's voice. Over a period of some 50 years since these early days, I have always found the 'Sawmills' to be a very pleasant place to do business. I have seen many changes of staff over the years and remember many of their names, such as Frank Skinner the foreman, Willie Garrett, Ronnie Parkinson and Willie Walker the sawyers and machinists, Sid Cowin and Jack Scarffe the wagon drivers, Alec Corrin with his hearing aid - always had a joke to tell and Charlie Herbert in the cement house. Sid Cowin drove a new Bedford S type, XMN, Jack Scarffe drove a Morris or Austin FG

Charlie Herbert   Ronnie Parkinson   Norman Quayle   Alec Corrin

Douglas Steam Sawmill

Model 8317 MN, one of two of these models in the early sixties but I can't remember the number of the other one. The company also ran and ex army Austin Champ and behind this they towed the chassis of a cut down Bedford OB coach with a flat deck to carry cement along the Prom to the Summerland site being developed at the time. I remember Charlie Herbert sitting on the old coach in all weathers totally exposed to the elements as there was no longer any roof and being towed along quite slowly while he fought with the steering. The Douglas Steam Sawmills is a very old established company and I am proud to say that our family firm, Kissack Brothers of Crosby, was one of the very first customers on their books.

Braddan School - Winter Hill disaster

As I mentioned earlier, Howard and I left the Collegiate School and started at Braddan Primary School in 1956. It was the beginning of a very happy time for me, I was in Miss Lace's class and sat next to a boy called Malcolm Magee, we had playtimes morning, lunchtime and afternoons and best of all - no homework. Miss Lace, or 'Fanny' Lace as we called her behind her back, sported a wonderful set of facial hair - moustache and sparse beard, much to the amusement of her pupils. She was probably nearing retirement age then but to me she seemed much older, with her hair tied back in a bun and always dressed in a wrap round type pinafore smock. She was very strict and I think just about everyone of us, at some time or other, felt the sting on the back of our hands from the two rulers she used to chastise us. She was a very good teacher in the old style and as well as making sure everyone knew what she was talking about, which is what real teaching is all about, she was very kind as well. I remember at the end of each term she would give us all a packet of 'Murray Mints' each and that would be about 35 - 40 of us, paid for with her own money. In those days 'Isle of Man Dairies' would bring crates of milk to the schools (not the Collegiate) with little bottles called (I think) gills and Miss Lace would use her thumb to depress the tinfoil tops so we could get them off easily. Later on, I think there was a little plastic device which could be used instead of the thumb, it had a half spherical shape on one side which was pressed into the top of the bottle - (another piece of useless information).

We would be served a nice hot dinner each day which was great for me after those years in the Collegiate where we had the same thing every day - sandwiches and 'Ribena'. I can honestly say that if I never taste 'Ribena' again it will be too soon, even if Miss Reid did use hot water on colder days!

I remember a jolly lady, Mrs MacEvoy who served the meals alongside the hall where we would sit at long tables which were put up and dismantled again later by the senior boys from Mr Quayle's class. I think one of the other ladies

Braddan & Marown British Legion Party, Braddan Church hall, 1957

was a Mrs Cowin and she was the mother of a boy called Arthur who died from leukaemia. I didn't really know what leukaemia was but I remember everyone being very sad and upset at the time and feeling sorry for Arthur's sister Brenda.

The big canisters of food were delivered by 'Happy Days Motors' in an old Commer van and deposited in the girls' porch ready for the dinner ladies attention. The porches flanked Mr Quayle's room, the girls on the Douglas side and the boys on the Strang side and when the window would be open on the girls side there would be some very appetising aromas around midday when the food arrived. The boys' porch and cloakroom also housed the big old fashioned coke fired central heating boiler. It had safety railings around it with a gate at the end to give access to the heavy iron door where the coke was shovelled in and the 'clinkers' pulled out. It was considered an honour to stoke the boiler and usually one of the senior boys would be sent out of Mr Quayle's

class twice a day to do the necessary raking out with a long handled scraper and then to 'stoke up' with fresh coke. I doubt very much if today's 'little darlings' would be allowed to do such manual work and they certainly wouldn't like the sulphur fumes which were inevitably inhaled when the furnace door was opened!

With a mention of the boys' porch a memory of a funny story springs to mind. One day when we were playing a ball game called 'against the wall' outside the porch door, a boy who lived in the Strang Road at Union Mills, by the name of Sheridan threw the ball at someone who ducked and the ball went through the open door, straight on through Mr Quayle's window and hit the attendance officer Mr Lord on the back of the head! He was standing by Mr Quayle's desk when the glass smashed and the ball hit him and he dropped to the floor in a heap. I'm not sure if the ball felled him or the shock but once he'd had the bits of glass removed from the back of his bald head and Sheridan had had the stick, he drove away in his Morris 10! Mr Lord was a frequent visitor to Braddan School as were the school nurses checking for 'nits' and the P.T. teacher Miss Griffiths. The nurse would usually be Nurse Quirk, I think she was from Raby Farm at Glen Maye and she drove a Health Services Ford Popular. Miss Griffiths drove a Hillman Minx and had a very severe haircut - just like a man!.

Another visitor to the school would be the groundsman with his David Brown tractor and gang mowers to cut the grass on the playing field. I remember a brand new diesel model 25D tractor and the driver was a Mr Kinnish from Laxey. He was succeeded by another Laxey man Bill Kneale who also drove their Morris 1 ton LC model truck, that was painted green and numbered UMN something.

The school field was a great place to play and at the top end there was a row of apple trees with small red, sweet apples that we weren't supposed to touch! It was also the venue of many an 'epic' football match with Mr Quayle as referee in his old gardening boots! There would be the two teams but each would have about 20 players all running around after the ball and rarely making contact with it. It was great fun as the play went from end to end like a swarm of bees and if the ball didn't end up in the main road or even Mr Moore's farm on the other side of it, occasionally it went through the goal posts.

Mr and Mrs Moore (Spud as he was known) had a nice little farm right opposite the school and we would go there for apples at about 1d or 2d each, oh and by the way, Spud Moore owned a green Jowett Bradford 'Utilabrake' (a van with side windows) for his vegetable round. This little farm was demolished when building firm Mill Baldwin developed the land with 'posh' houses and the charm of the area was lost forever.

My four years at Braddan School were without doubt, the best and happiest school days I ever had with excellent teachers (especially Tommy Quayle the headmaster) and very happy and seemingly content pupils who all did well with their 11+ exams. As I mentioned before, there was no homework, as Mr Quayle believed in real teaching and that meant that he would go to great lengths to ensure that everyone in the class understood his teaching no matter how slow at learning they were. The lessons were learned in the classroom whilst he was there to explain the problems rather than a baffled child scratching its head late into the evening at home. There was total discipline at Braddan and I think that almost everyone, at one time or another, had a slap or felt the edge of the cane, but having said that it must have been necessary and once administered things quickly returned to normal with no lasting effects or malice borne.

The Munich air crash happened in the late '50's and I recall being kept up to date on the radio bulletins by the boy who sat next to me at the time. His name was Edwin Caine and I remember us both being quite sad some days after the event when Duncan Edwards eventually lost his fight for survival.

Around the same time was the terrible air crash at Winter Hill near Bolton when so many local garage proprietors and motor trade people lost their lives.

In many ways the two disasters were similar - both happened in the snow and both saw a huge loss of life but in both, miraculously, there were some survivors. One of those killed was Mr Tonkin from Ramsey Motors and his daughter Elizabeth was in our class. I vividly remember her leaving the classroom in tears with her mother when the news reached us. Everyone was shocked and mention was made of my Uncle Henry who was thought to be amongst those who were missing. There were no boarding cards in those days and it wasn't until later that evening, after anxiously awaiting news of him, that we were very relieved when he walked into our house wondering what all the fuss was about! It turned out that for once in his life, being late had saved his life, and as well as being very relieved and tearful, my grandparents were annoyed with him for his lack of communication! It turned out that on missing the flight he had met a customer and gone to fix his combine harvester.

Our first car - motorbikes and Hondas!

Another victim who was not so lucky and lost his life was a man from Ballaugh Garage called John Bridson. This shocked us because we had just met him a few months earlier when we bought our first motor car MN 6523. The car was a 1929 Morris 'Square Nose' Cowley, two seater tourer with a 'Dickie' seat in the boot and it was derelict on Mr Bridson's land opposite his garage at Ballaugh bridge. We had spotted the old Morris some weeks earlier and after much persuasion we eventually got father to stop for some petrol so we could enquire about it. I don't know what Mr Bridson would think as two small boys approached him with an offer of 'thirty bob' for the old 'Square Nose' but luckily, instead of laughing at us he took the time to talk and explained that he would like to see the 'back of it' but that he didn't own it. It actually belonged to the famous Manx author Mona Douglas and she had abandoned it there one day when it broke down, much to the annoyance of

MN 6523. Our first car!

Mr Bridson, as she hadn't returned to collect it. Since then it had had the radiator 'pinched' for scrap as was often the case in those days when they were made of solid brass and copper. When we got home my mum rang up Miss Douglas and a deal was done for thirty bob (£1.50) and tow it away. Howard and I were very excited, when a few days later, dad asked George Gelling to come with us and one evening we went to Ballaugh in the old 'Tonner' and towed the car home suspended on chains beneath the back of its tipping body.

The search began for a radiator and this led us to Peel quayside where Hughie Dow the lifeboat mechanic had a garage. At the back of this garage, near to Quirk's coal yard, there we found another 'Square Nose' Morris Cowley,

but this time it was a black four door saloon, a year 'newer' than our cabriolet which meant that the radiator was chrome plated over the brass, but never mind, it would have to do as it was the only one available and we needed other parts of it as well including the front axle. A deal was done and it was towed home to Crosby, its Reg No was MN 7161 and although it was very shabby and 'past its best' it provided all the parts we needed before it was dumped over the tip. In hindsight I suppose it could have been saved but in those days it wasn't worth keeping and it went the same way as many fine old classic cars when all the usable bits had been stripped off them.

Around this time most of the old cars and unwanted 'artefacts' would be used for landfill to reclaim swampy ground and two such places were Crosby Quarry in Station Road and opposite the Highlander Pub. The land opposite the Highlander was very wet and swampy and the car park today holds many secrets beneath its tarmac surface. It was well known round the village that there was no 'clear title' to this piece of land as it was known that the owner had emigrated many years previously to America or somewhere similar, so in a tidy and orderly fashion a lot of people used it as a tip. This was not appreciated by the then landlord of the pub however, as car parks were not at the top of his priority list! His name was Donald Irquhart and I well remember him running or hobbling across the main road in his carpet slippers shaking his fist only to be informed that neither he nor the brewery owned the land! Once levelled off it became a fine and nowadays necessary car park.

In the 1950's Marown A.F.C. was well established and their pitch was a field behind the Crosby Hotel, now built on with the old persons complex. The changing room was an old Maudeslay coach which was positioned behind Tom Gelling's workshops and it was not until 1954/5 when the Marown Memorial playing fields in Station Road were opened that it was disposed off to a farmer for a hen house. The 'playing fields' were built on land donated by Harley Cunningham (of Ellerslie Farm and Holiday Camp dynasty) and the work was all done by volunteers including the Gelling families, our family -

Martini

Beauty

the Kissacks, local farmers and many more to achieve a lasting 'treasure' for the local community. There was, as well as the football pitch, two fine tarmac tennis courts, a children's area, goldfish ponds, a cricket pitch and a little while later, the public toilets or 'Taj Mahal' as it was known locally.

Mention of the tennis courts brings to mind my first venture into motor bikes. At our yard, Howard and I discovered one day, a 'Cymota' which was a small engine made to clip on to the front forks of a bicycle. We weren't long bolting it onto a small bicycle and trying to get it started up. The drive was by friction roller onto the front tyre and as well as being quite heavy and unbalanced it proved to be very hard to start. We pedalled it round for ages changing numerous plugs and cleaning the points till we were blue in the face, eventually getting it started only to find that it was so poor that it would hardly pull your hat off! It was no good on hills so it was decided that the only place for it was the tennis courts as we were too young to go on the main roads. It was loaded onto a wheelbarrow and we took turns to push it all the way down to the playing fields because we knew if Albert Edmond had caught us, even pushing it on it's own wheels, then we would be nicked!

We had a few happy hours on it but I think that the return trip, uphill, with the wheelbarrow, finally saw its demise!

This first attempt had whetted our appetite for bikes and the old Cymota was replaced by a 'Power Pac' which fitted onto the back wheel of the bicycle, this was very fast and a much superior engine but its power made the bike quite difficult for a small boy to ride! Howard had purchased it from Juan Kelly and we had great fun with it until one day he fell off it at the tennis courts and hurt himself quite badly, vowing to get a proper motor bike instead! I think he sold it for 27/6d to a boy called Ashley Shepherd from Onchan and we moved on to a BSA Bantam.

I think it was just prior to this time that our mum introduced us to horse riding at the Tromode Stables run by Jennifer Latham. I think it would be fair to say that Howard never really took to is as much as I did and although I never really mastered the art of jumping, I thoroughly enjoyed riding on the Douglas beach and trekking as well as the Sunday morning hourly lesson in the paddock opposite Mr Jones's farm. I met lots of people there who I still see today, such names as Pam and Barbara Kelso, Steve Carter, Caroline Cretney and Michael Doddrell spring to mind as well as Jackie Lee (now McCubbin)and Beverley Kneale (now Parsons) who were Jennifer's main helpers. One memorable occasion was a 'Mock Hunt' on New Years Day I think 1958 which started at Ballashamrock at Port Soderick and covered the Santon area - South Hampton and Knock Froy etc. before hacking back to Tromode on the roads which held much less traffic than nowadays. The horses were good fun but there was no engines in them and we moved on to cars and motorbikes! Looking back, I think I would have liked to have continued further with my riding as I have always had a love for horses but that was not to be until forty years later when I bought Ballakissack Farm.

Petrol rationing - Woolworths fire

Something that happened round about this time was the Suez Canal crisis in the Middle East and we learned about Sir Anthony Eden, the Prime Minister being in conflict with President Nasser and of course the rationing of petrol and oil here in the island. At that time dad was a stockist of 'Esso Blue' paraffin oil which was widely used for domestic heating in paraffin stoves such as 'Aladdins' and Valour', in the days before bottled gas. It wasn't however intended for use in motor vehicles. As with red diesel today it was duty free and a bit illegal when used in the wrong circumstances. It was also very low octane and its sustained use could 'soot up' an engine and cause burnt valves however, if mixed about 50 - 50 with petrol, it was passable on certain vehicles. Some would run better than others and some were quite hard to start if too much was added but I have to say that quite a few vehicles in the Crosby area were kept on the road throughout the 'crisis' even if they did have a faint aroma like a 'Fergie' on T.V.O. (tractor vapourising oil).

When, as mentioned earlier, the old Morris Major was scrapped and its engine went into the lorry, its replacement was a 1939 Morris 10 series M and its Number was KMN 270. I never really liked this car although I believe it was much easier for mum to drive and more economical to run. It had a 'modern' synchromesh gear box and O.H.V. engine. By this time both Howard and myself were quite proficient at mechanical jobs such as changing wheels when necessary and I well remember changing the nearside front wheel on this car and replacing all the nuts but I must have been distracted or simply forgotten to tighten them sufficiently and when seeing the hubcap had been replaced the jack removed, mum set off for Douglas with Howard in the front seat. Well - good progress was apparently made until Quarter Bridge when, on cresting the 'hump' the steering 'felt a bit funny' and the car was overtaken by a wheel. Being more than able and having driven old bangers all her life, mum very skilfully brought the old car to a stop opposite to where the fire station is now on the remaining three wheels and one brake drum. Obviously in those days the roads were not so busy and speeds were a little slower but she was a very good driver and this is a tribute to her. As I've said Howard was in the car with her and he made short work of retrieving the wheel, still with its hubcap and nuts inside - and replacing it, tighter this time, before they continued on their way to Douglas. After this episode we always sought the strength of a 'grown up' to put the final tighten up on the wheel nuts as a nine year old boy was not yet strong enough.

Many happy trips were made in this old car and it was not unusual to see it loaded up with six or seven kids from roundabout Crosby heading for either Douglas or Peel beach for the day, in the midst of what seemed to be much nicer summers than we have today or maybe it was just that everyday seemed a sunny day as a small boy. I'm not sure which, but they were wonderful school holidays spent splashing about in the sea and enjoying ice cream usually made by Wards or Felices. Another treat for us would sometimes be a nice meal in Wilsons Silver Service Restaurant in Victoria Street which was roughly opposite to the Shakespeare Hotel and near to Bill Kennaughs sports shop. I remember the waitresses smartly dressed in starched white aprons over black dresses with white 'coronets' or caps on their hair and that we had to be on our best behaviour or we wouldn't get the next part of the adventure which would be the matinee in the Regal Cinema to see 'Pinocchio' or something similar. If we were going to Nobles baths (which were next door to the Regal cinema) it would be to learn to swim, possibly with the help of a Mr Brady, who wore a very old fashioned black swimming costume which looked rather like the one worn by Captain Webb of matchbox fame. I think he was a retired police man from Manchester and I have to say that, no matter how hard he tried to teach me, he remained a much better swimmer that I could ever hope to be. I must have swallowed so much water and disinfectant that I wouldn't be surprised if they had to top up the level of the water after I went home! He did have a measured success though, as I can do a few strokes before I sink and as promised all those years ago, my dad bought me a 'Timex' watch with an unbreakable metal face and strap, for my swimming a full length of the baths. I seem to remember that the unbreakable strap broke soon after and the watch itself never really worked properly - probably in sympathy with my prowess at the noble art of swimming!

While I am talking about Douglas, one thing in particular stays vivid in my mind. I was in Woolworths store with my mother when the big fire started, I think it was in 1952 so I would be four years old. I distinctly remember a big tarpaulin hanging from the ceiling, presumably to hide the builders and associated works taking place and it started to burn at the bottom right hand corner but no one seemed to be taking any notice. We were upstairs at the time and mum was shouting 'Fire Fire' as she grabbed hold of me, dashed down the staircase which had a mahogany handrail and a big newell post at the bottom, and out into Strand Street. For some time afterwards I had nightmares about burning canvas but they did leave me as I grew up. The place was completely gutted and I think someone died in the fire when the wooden floors gave way, so we were very lucky not to be trapped and lived to tell the tale.

Another early memory of this era was of a spell in Nobles hospital with a hernia. I was in the old children's ward which was separate from the main hospital and later became the Path lab, down by the ambulance garage and mortuary and accessed by the drive on 'Hospital Corner'. I remember being very sore and upset and told the nurses that my mum was coming with the 'Major' to take me home. This of course caused much hilarity when it was explained that mother was not 'involved' with an army officer and the 'Major' was our car! I think one nurse was called Cannell and they were all very nice to me even when I climbed on top of the wooden locker next to my cot in a bid to escape. I used to watch the ambulances coming in and out and well remember two Austin K8 'Welfarer' models and the old Morris Commercial which was much longer, all three painted in the drab grey/green colour in immaculate condition with their nickel plated warning bells (no awful sirens then) and their drivers' in full uniform with peaked caps. The children's ward had a covered terrace or verandah on the side that faced the main hospital and I remember being wheeled out in the sunshine for a while. I also recall a nice coal fire in the ward for heating which would be unthinkable nowadays but which certainly made a nice atmosphere. The surgeon's name was Mr Vernon and he must have done a good job on me as I've had no trouble with the problem since

Some good memories of the 1950's and indeed since then, came from learning to 'work' as such. I was always interested in dad's work round the yard and in those days that could mean anything from blacksmith work with the forge in the smithy to general engineering, welding, joinery and making a coffin.

Alongside the normal kids games of football, dirt tracking on pushbikes and tickling trout in our river, Kissack's yard was a wonderful place to grow up and I spent countless hours helping dad and the other men such as John Kelly (joiner), Bert Leece (joiner and signwriter) and of course 'Jacko' Gelling. I learned a lot from all of them and others besides, about how to go about jobs in general and the method of working safely with the utmost respect for sharp tools and machines. At this young age of 9 or 10, I learned to enjoy making and repairing things and indeed making something out of nothing. I have vivid memories of helping to make farm trailers, wooden wheelbarrows and 'cheese rakes' for Harold Richmond at Wards Ice Cream factory. Also as mentioned jobs such as de-nailing timber, softening putty, creosoting timber and chopping sticks for firewood.

The Austin Sevens

With the mention of welding comes the story of the three wheeler soap box trolley or 'Reliant' as we called them. This invention was dreamed up by my father and possibly a dozen or maybe more were made in our smithy. They were made from a bicycle frame and front forks, a car steering wheel, an old bedstead, three pram wheels and a pram axle. Also needed were lots of welding rods and hacksaw blades! So many in fact, that dad began charging 5/- for the rods and 'bring your own hacksaw blades' was the order of the day. These quite unusual trolleys attracted quite a big following and probably would be bought today but sadly I know of none that have survived. As well as the local kids, several of our friends from Douglas had them as well, in varying shapes and sizes normally depending on the size of the pram wheels. Their names that spring to mind - Andy Sykes, Trevor Cretney, Philip Watterson and George Kerruish from the St Catherine's Drive area of Douglas and they would come out to Crosby, with their supply of hacksaw blades and the 5/- and return to Douglas on the steam train with their new three wheel 'Reliant' trolley - a Saturday well spent!.

I remember my mum feeding all and sundry and providing a level of hospitality rarely seen today, while father would fashion these creations out of the goodness of his heart and weld them all together ready for testing, which required a big strong lad to push while the proud owner sat on and steered, while shouting 'Push, push' to get more speed.

My brother Howard and myself had both learned to ride 'two wheeler' bicycles at the early age of about four years old. We were started off on the big front lawn of my grandparents house 'Rose Villa' which is next door to the cottage 'West Lynne' our home at the time, by father running along behind us holding on to the saddle and then casting us adrift! Needless to say you learned very quickly either to fall off after ever decreasing circles or to get the hang of it. The grass helped for a soft landing which was just as well in the

The three wheeler 'Reliant" trolleys

days when training wheels or 'stabilizers' were unheard of. My best bike was a brand new one from Gilbert Hardings in Duke Street and I remember going with mother to the shop which was between Todhunter and Elliots and the Manx Co-op. The bike was a new Hudson with blue frame, white mudguards, 'North Road' handlebars with 'pull up' brakes and 24" wheels. What a beauty - we were served by Mr David Harding for the princely sum of £14. 10s. 6d and he promised to put the bike on the next train to Crosby. Sadly David Harding lost his life along with his brother Billy in the Winter Hill disaster some months later. I was probably around eight or nine at the time and we had great fun building 'dirt track' bikes out of spare parts retrieved from the tip. One such bike and a great favourite of mine was basically a 'Rudge Whitworth' that I

made up out of various bits including cow horn handlebars and a 'gripster' back tyre that I paid 4/- for at Kings Cycle Shop on Prospect Hill. At Eyreton Castle, just up the road, we enjoyed what was probably one of the best 'dirt tracks' in the Isle of Man. It had been 'hacked' out of the jungle of trees some years earlier by the 'big boys' of the village and had various corners and features named after places on the T.T. course. A big mound of earth at the start was called 'Bray Hill' and a great course followed through.

A dense forest to 'Ramsey Corner' then back to the start and many happy but tired youngsters would emerge from the 'Castle' with red faces, often cuts and bruises, but most of all everyone smelled strongly of garlic as the forest floor was covered with it, giving irrefutable evidence as to where we had been all evening!

It was toward the end of the 1950's, probably '58 or '59 when we became interested in Austin Seven cars and one day on a visit to the south of the island we spotted an Austin Ruby saloon, with some accident damage, laid on the forecourt at the Shore Garage at Port St Mary. On further enquiry, we discovered that the owner was a Mrs Ryland from Leeds who, whilst on holiday on the island, had suffered a collision and bent the front axle. She had returned to Leeds by this time, so mum was persuaded to write her a letter offering the princely sum of £5 for the little black saloon - AWR 322. When the offer was accepted we were very excited and it was decided that Howard would be the new owner partly because he had some money saved up and also, he was the oldest! As ever, father was great on these occasions and he decided that the best way to bring our latest acquisition home would be to use our boat trailer under the front of it 'like an ambulance'. Once again, with the help of George Gelling, the little Austin was towed home articulated on the boat trailer behind our Morris 10. I remember the event well and our route home from Shore Garage was via Colby Level, Ballawhetstone, Ballasalla and St Marks - and not a policeman in sight to hamper our progress but I wonder in hindsight what they would have said had they encountered our unusual

Howard's Austin 'Ruby' Saloon - AWR322

'convoy'! I seem to remember Howard removed the front axle and dad, with the help of some heat and a sledgehammer straightened it up as good as new. It was refitted with great haste and great joy was experienced when, after a few swings of the starting handle it started up first time! Many, many laps round the yard were completed as we practiced our driving skills, often, I'm sure, to the annoyance of the neighbours but they all seemed to take it in good spirit. The big problem was petrol - or the lack of it and various methods of procurement were employed. Possibly the best and certainly the most honest, was to use a two gallon 'Pratts' can and cycle the half mile to Glen Vine petrol station. Being only nine or ten years old had its pitfalls, as trying to ride a bicycle while holding a full can of petrol could be quite hazardous and I remember at least once coming a real cropper on the hard road when the can jammed between the handlebars and the top of the forks and chucked me off! Not only that but at the 'pumps' petrol cost 3s 9½d a gallon which was quite a lot of money even by today's prices. Ways of raising the money were always a challenge and could vary from gathering empty 'pop' bottles and claiming the returnable deposit (3d for small and 4d for large) at Daisy Hill's shop, cashing in full cards of 'Brooke Bond Dividend' stamps from packets of tea for 5/-, maybe chopping sticks for a few bob or even gathering rats tails to be taken down to Maurice Kneen the station master who handed out the 2d bounty on them!

All these efforts were well and good but on occasions, when no money was forthcoming, we would resort to siphoning some 'juice' out of one of dad's vehicles. The preferred method was to strip out a piece of the red rubber tubing from around the upholstered draught excluder fitted to the door openings of old vehicles, then a handy can or jug would be sought and armed with the necessary 'kit' we would proceed to 'suck' the petrol out of the most accessible vehicle on the yard. The favourite for this was the old Morris 'Tonner' as it had a gravity fed system with the tank high up on the scuttle and was relatively easy to 'suck' without getting too much petrol in the mouth. I do remember one day being distracted whilst pinching a small amount and for some reason left the scene leaving the tube running, for goodness knows how long, but successfully draining every drop out of the wagon! Needless to say father was very annoyed and I think a 'good hiding' was received followed by the confiscation of all the rubber tubes that he could find.

Soon after Howard's purchase of his 'Ruby' it became apparent that I too 'needed' a car (doesn't every 10 year old?) and the next move was a visit to Union Mills Garage to visit Mr Slater. At this time Union Mills Garage was a real 'time warp' as Mr Slater the proprietor had retired some years earlier and simply 'closed the doors' with everything still inside including all the antiquated garage equipment and his own little Austin Seven 'Box' Saloon which was parked in one corner with some accident damage almost the same as Howard's Ruby had sustained. Indeed the front axle was bent on the left side along with the same front mudguard but other than that and the smell of stale petrol there was very little wrong with it. A deal was done for £5.0s.0d and Mr Slater, an elderly and well spoken man informed me that the car would need a new accumulator. Well, not wishing to show my ignorance, I waited 'til we got home before I enquired from dad ' what's an accumulator' and was informed with good humour that it was in fact the battery! With great excitement the damaged front wing was removed and straightened out ready to be refitted but, when it came to the bent front axle, unlike on Howard's Ruby, it was too badly bent

and a replacement was needed. It was a 1931 model, quite rare apparently, because of it's 6'3" wheelbase and its registration was CMN 372. The hunt was on for a front axle and it wasn't long before a suitable donor vehicle was located at St Judes crossroads near Sulby Bridge. A small croft to the north east corner of the crossroads was occupied at that time by a man called Philip Corlett and he sold us the remains of a 'Top Hat' Saloon without its engine but otherwise complete for about two pounds. It was of around 1929 vintage but the axles were the same and it was dismantled for spare parts, the front axle being hastily fitted to my 'new' car. I find it hard to express here the sheer excitement and achievement experienced by a ten year old boy when the Austin started up instantly, after many years lying idle, with a tank full of stale petrol which really has to be smelled to be believed. Many happy hours were spent learning to drive and maintain those little cars and we taught many of our school mates to drive as well on Saturdays and school holidays. Indeed we had 'moved' from push bikes and 3 wheeler trollies to motor vehicles, soon adding quite a few more Austin Sevens of varying types and models of different vintage. I think we probably owned most types with the exception of a van or special models such as the 'Nippy', 'Ulster' or 'Swallow', which we were also well aware of as we had read

My first Austin 7

John Seed   Howard Phil Tasker   Derry   Mn5246

Howard   Neil Richmond   Philip Richmond   Derry

every available book on the marque! It is interesting to note that when you are keen on something in life it is very easy to learn everything about it and I think it would be fair to say, that at the time, aged about 10 or 11, Howard and I knew every nut and bolt and most of the data on every model of Austin Seven! We became quite well known on the Island for spare parts and I still see some of our 'customers' to this day, forty odd years later. Some of the poorer examples that we bought for parts and persuaded dad to bring home for us would either be scrapped or passed on to friends, one being a 1934 four seat tourer model that was bought from a Sulby man, Billy Graham and passed over to a good friend and school mate Willie Layfield who lived in Onchan. I think he still owns it to this day, along with a 1934 saloon that he bought himself from a man in Ballasalla. Willie also bought a 1931 model from us for restoration that we got from a man at Laurel Bank and this car was without doubt the fastest and best engined that we ever owned! Unfortunately the rear bodywork was very bad and we eventually made it into a truck and had great fun with it including an appearance in the Douglas Carnival.

The two oldest and possibly the most interesting of these little cars were both circa 1926 - one a 'Top Hat' saloon RMN 19 came from Billy Graham at the Clenagh Road in Sulby and with the help of two long planks of wood, it was pushed over the top of his midden on to the back of the Morris Tonner for it's trip home to Crosby. The other one, a four seat 'Chummy' was discovered at the Slieu Whallian home of our coal man Mosey Pitts. Mosey or Moses as his real name was, drove a Fordson 4D model coal lorry for J.R. Bradleys of Queens Street in Douglas, RMN 912. (Bradleys had a similar lorry, painted green with the name L.H. Fargher still on the doors, which was driven by Stanley Callow from St Johns). The Austin 'Chummy' was almost unrecognisable, having had a 'home made' hard top fitted which was fashioned out of the roof of a later model and 'butchered' to fit through necessity brought about by the acute shortage of cars in the post WW2 years. The registration was MN 5246 and after many years as a hen house it was cleaned out and placed on a better chassis and axles, still as a saloon to begin with, but later on its 'Heath Robinson' roof was removed. As there was no engine or gearbox at this stage it was decided to scrap the old 'Ruby' and use it as a 'donor' vehicle. This being done, with some modifications to permit the four speed gearbox of the later unit, it was a great success and many happy days were enjoyed with it including trips to Douglas Carnival. It was eventually sold to a very good friend of ours, Keith Kennaugh from Silverburn Farm at Ballamodha and some cine film exist of him at the wheel.

The sale of the 'Chummy' really marked the end of the Austin Seven era for us as it was the 'last of the line', my own car CMN 372 being sold the year previous to this in 1963. I sold it for £6.0s.0d. to Nigel Kermode and he used it on the roads for some time with a new Reg No 321 MAN. However it was laid up sometime later for some reason and the Highway Board re-issued the coveted number - much to Nigel's annoyance. He still has the car to this day, stored in his garage at Greeba along with numerous other 'artefacts' all awaiting restoration.....someday!

Real motorbikes & a drive on the road

As I mentioned previously, Ernie Leece or 'young Ernie' as he was known to distinguish between him and his uncle, had owned a BSA Bantam some years earlier and being one of the bigger boys in the village he was kind of a hero to us impressionable young lads. In fact, if something was 'good enough' for Ernie, it was certainly trendy and good enough for us! I think the 'Bantam' had been his first motorbike so naturally Howard and myself wanted one each, so the search was on.

It was the start of our 'graduation' to real bikes from the old cycle motors, when a somewhat bad tempered and easily excitable man called Henry Midghall brought a dismantled example of the BSA Marque to our yard and insisted on £5 for it. After some deliberation we deduced that some of the parts were missing, including the clutch but Henry promised to bring that the next day. We gave him £3.10s.0d and told him, much to his annoyance, that he could have the other 30bob when he brought the parts as promised. Well, he stormed off in his van (a new Ford 15cwt Thames) and we waited, and we waited but after a few weeks it became obvious that, either he didn't need his money or that he just didn't have the parts. This question was answered one day when he rang up some time later playing 'hell' with my mother in an almost hysterical voice demanding his thirty bob! On hearing this, mother explained to him that the bike was no use without the clutch but this only seemed to make him worse and when she suggested that he should calm down a little he uttered some unprintable expletives and hung up! I seem to remember that he called round some days later and although it was against our wishes, mum paid him the remaining £1.10s.0d on the promise that he would bring the clutch 'tomorrow'. We had to wait a couple of years to resolve this little dispute but as they say 'What goes round comes round' and a much more 'humble' Henry arrived one day with a sob story about a collapsed wheel on his trailer and being from an obsolete model, the only one he knew of on the Island was on an axle on our scrap butt right behind where dad was standing at the time! Well! Obviously the tables had turned a bit and not only were we in a strong bargaining position but we had both grown taller than we were two years ago when he had not only promised to bring the clutch but to give us a 'thick ear' each as well! Not to put too fine a point on it, it was eventually decided after some 'discussion' that, as there was still no sign of the missing clutch, the status quo should remain and that Henry should leave the yard without the wheel he so desperately wanted!

We eventually sent away for the missing clutch parts and a points cam by mail order and with everything now 'complete' we attempted to start the machine's engine. Well to this day, I think we pushed it further than we ever did ride it, before George Gelling spotted that it had no condenser in the ignition. It seemed as though we had push started it for weeks and although it would fire and run after a fashion, it was like a breath of fresh air and a huge sense of achievement when, after a condenser was fitted, it burst into life and roared off in a cloud of blue two stroke smoke! All we needed now was another Bantam - for me - and I think it was Ollie Gelling who told me about one for sale at Willaston. I must have been twelve by this time because I remember walking to the house from St Ninians High School which wasn't very far - in fact it was nowhere near as far as it is from Willaston to Crosby. My intention was just to have a look at it and if I was to buy it I would ask Dad to pick it up for me in the van. I must have got carried away with the excitement, as when I saw it was NMN 949 which had belonged to Ernie - my hero - I just had to buy it! A deal was done for £2 as it had been sorely neglected over the years and I paid the man and began the long push home to Crosby through Tromode, up the hill and along the Strang and Mount Rule Top Road, eventually down Eyreton Road whilst keeping my eye open for the copper at that time - Eddie Prescott. It was a distance of about four miles and I remember being knackered but very happy with my purchase, when after my tea we cleaned the points and it started up and ran well with little encouragement except petrol and a good push.

Meanwhile, things were still happening with cars back at the yard and the latest project was the total rebuild of Jacko's old Riley 9 - MAN 5 now owned by Ernie Leece. By this time the Monaco style bodywork was in a bad state so Ernie stripped it all away to leave the chassis and started to build a sports car onto it. Many hours were spent fashioning the new body and with some help from my dad and the front wings and bonnet from a burnt out Ford 100E Anglia that Ernie acquired from the Port St Mary District Nurse's car, a very pleasing and attractive vehicle was produced. It was formed with conduit electrical tubing all welded together and panelled in with new galvanised steel sheeting. Rather like the first Riley Special made by George Gelling many years previously, the 'Ernley' was an open tourer without doors! It was a real 'eye catcher' with black 'Rexine' or vinyl upholstery, expertly tailored by Ernie to complement the bench seating and two tone paint job in crème and damson red. At that time he was manager at the Midget Racing Cars at Onchan Stadium for his employers the Peel Engineering Company and after work had finished in the long summer evenings, the Ernley Special could be seen touring up and down Douglas Promenade, literally crammed full of young ladies, such was the fun that surrounded him - a true 'John Travolta' character of the 1960's.

A collection of strange sounding horns from old vehicles such as Klaxon and A.R. were hidden under the bonnet and caused many a laugh when sounded at appropriate moments, and along with the various expertly painted cartoons and caricatures that adorned the bodywork, it all added to the general aura of fun that surrounded Ernie and his car. He was a very talented painter and signwriter and could make an instant likeness with paint brushes or pencil, of such characters as Andy Capp and Florrie or Sylvester and Tweetie Pie, Mickey Mouse, etc. I may stand corrected when I say 'was' because as far as I know he may well paint and draw to this day along with his other talents of music etc. of which he is well accomplished. The name Ernie Leece, along with that of John Molyneux (father of multiple T.T. winner David) is remembered by many for his great 3rd place in the Sidecar T.T. which was achieved on a 'homemade' outfit - of course - in the early 1970's.

Truly bitten by the motor bike 'bug' it was inevitable that we would look for better bikes and a natural progression seemed to be the 197c.c. Villiers engine powered bikes of that time. The main snag was that a lot of these bikes had 'lost' their engines to the very popular Karting movement of that time and it proved to be quite difficult to locate a bike at all, let alone find one for around £5 which was all our limited budget would allow! Howard eventually found a Francis Barnett in a hedge at Lambfell Farm at Cronk-y-Voddy and managed to buy it for £5 albeit minus the clutch and clutch cases. This was soon sorted out and he had years of fun out of it, especially after we fitted a slightly longer pair of front forks and wheel from an old Excelsior which improved handling quite considerably. In those days, as mentioned earlier on, our bread was delivered by C.A. Kermode of Onchan and by now the roundsman was a young man from Laxey called Chris Quayle who told me that he had a 197c.c, DOT that he no longer used. Naturally I used my loaf and was delighted to be able to buy the bike OMN 492 for the usual £5. We certainly kept dad (and even mum on occasions) very busy bringing motor bikes and parts home at nights and weekends as many more followed as and when available, to meet the demand created by our mates such as John Kissack, Phil Tasker, Mike Staley and Barry Trimble! Needless to say we were still too young to go on the public roads with motors vehicles - officially that is! It was always a great challenge however to drive a car or ride a bike faster and further than just round the yard or the adjoining Ballaharry field. Perhaps I'm letting the cat out of the bag now but I think that after some forty years have passed, the police might turn a blind eye to some of our escapades of the early 1960's when we would have a 'little go on the road'! I have to admit that one of our main reasons for entering the Douglas Carnival with the old Austin Sevens and other vintage vehicles was so that we could drive them along the Promenade and even on a couple of occasions - a bit further.

I had a very close encounter with the Police at the age of twelve whilst driving my Austin into Douglas to begin the procession with the Marown Youth Club entry which was entitled the 'Larkins' after the T.V. series starring Peggy Mount and David Kossof. Everything was going well as I sat on top of some extra cushions to make me look bigger and along with the bowler hat and false moustache, I thought I looked very 'grown up' and competent - that is until I rounded Braddan Bridge and looked ahead to Quarter Bridge. To my horror, an Austin J4 van belonging to Terrence Corrish of Ballaclucas had crashed through the wall of Port-e-Chee meadow just opposite to the pub! I remember a sudden urgency to use the toilet and probably uttered a few choice expletives but decided to bluff it out if the policeman stopped me. Well it must

have been my lucky day because after his initial stop signal with raised hand and just as I was about to manufacture a few 'buttons' he changed his mind and waved me through with a wide eyed expression on his face and although I can't lip read I think he said something like 'What the ….s this?'. Anyway I didn't look back or stop to find out and when I got down to the quayside assembly point I got out and distanced myself from the car 'just in case'. Phew, truly a close encounter of the worst kind with no tax, no insurance, dodgy tyres and brakes, not to mention that I was twelve years old on a public road - how would that have read in the paper?

Howard was much taller than me at that time and got away with a few more trips in carnival guise and although Dad didn't actually give us permission he turned a blind eye and told us to 'be careful' advising me however that until I grew a bit more not to chance it again. We did however venture out on the short stretch of public road at the top of Eyreton Hill on a few occasions. While one of our mates kept watch we would emerge from the end of Bluebell Lane onto Eyreton Road and go as fast as we could up to the then derelict cottages and onto the stoney track leading up to the 'Triangle' and ultimately Eairy Vane Farm. I remember a few adventurous trips up this road which was quite a stiff pull for these little cars when overloaded with goodness knows how many of our mates, most of whom I still see to this day. These would probably be Phil Tasker, John Kissack, Willie Layfield, Norman Pallister, Mike Staley, 'Marzy' Marsden, Michael Challenor and maybe Raymond Corkhill (who I taught to shoot a rabbit and gut it as well as how to drive!) also Robert and Juan Cannell would sometimes be with us but the names and faces would change from week to week such was the wide circle of friends who 'knocked about' in those days. One such friend at the time was David Yewdall and it was perhaps ironic that he should be with us on a trip to the ruins of Eairy Vane farm as some years prior to our visit, he, his brother and sister and parents were the last family to live there albeit without mains water or electricity at this very remote but beautiful place. It must be around two miles from Crosby and David then aged about five along with his brother Ken and sister Rose would walk to Marown School and back each day, surely unheard of today but they all grew up much stronger people because of it. David lived up at Ellerslie by this time and as well as travelling to school on the train together we would go out shooting rabbits and pigeons sometimes in the summer evenings. It would be quite dark sometimes by the time we had walked round the best places at Ellerslie and one night I desperately needed to 'water the horse' in the twilight and near to some trees by St Runius Old Church I completely failed to see an electric fence in front of me at the crucial moment! Well needless to say, the shock of electricity to such a sensitive place haunts me to this very day but it was much to the amusement of David and I can still see him almost doubled up while laughing at my misfortune.

Ballakermeen

This era of the early sixties was brilliant for me at nights and weekends but whilst this was happening, the days were a different story. By now I had moved on from the very happy and indeed excellent Braddan Primary school to 'Balla' or Ballakermeen Secondary School. In fact 'Secondary' was just about how I would describe it as it was a rough and rude awakening for a country lad such as myself. I had never heard language like it in my life and the sheer aggression and viciousness shown by some of the 'low life' bullies, that were mainly from the lower Douglas area, had to be seen to be believed. Don't get me wrong on this, I'm no angel, but I would never start a fight for the sake of it as these thugs would often do, sometimes for no other reason than their victim was a bit smaller or weaker than they were and was an easy target for fists and boots. I soon learned to be canny and keep out of trouble whenever threatened and being quite strong seemed to help a bit, only lashing out in self defence. It was not a happy school for me and I found that it wasn't only some of the pupils who were bullies but some of the teachers as well. In fact, after joining the school with great enthusiasm and being told on my first day that I was to be in form 1S (which was the top form) my joy quickly faded as I found that not one of the teachers assigned to me was a patch on Mr Quayle or any of his staff at Braddan school. A few of them ponced around in black gowns and appeared to love themselves as they clipped the new boys round the ear if they so much as strayed from the obligatory right hand side of the corridor, or worse still, started to run whilst indoors! It was a totally impersonal place and after coming in from a happy and friendly school like I was accustomed to where Mr Quayle made it his business to know everyone in his charge by their first name, I was no longer Derek or Derry but - Boy! (usually shouted not spoken). Lessons I had previously enjoyed and even looked forward to became alien to me as one after another these self styled 'professors' droned on like the sound of a Lancaster bomber and totally baffled me with useless lessons such as Latin and chemistry. The famous Bertie Reid (a brother of my first teacher at the Collegiate) took us for maths and I say 'took' rather than 'taught' because, although he was a very nice man and indeed a brilliant mathematician himself, when it came to teaching me he was totally useless. He 'performed' numerous calculations all over the blackboard but often seemed to be pursuing the answer to a problem that was eluding himself and rarely communicated with the rank and file who had often by this time started to misbehave and fire catapults at each other.

Some of the 'swats' and mathematically orientated boys seemed to be able to follow him but as far as I was concerned he was talking a foreign language - or maybe just bollocks! He talked about algebra for hours - a new name to me, that conjured up images of a zoological animal and I can quite honestly say that for all the use algebra has been to me since leaving school some forty years ago, he should have saved his breath! We had French lessons with Mrs (Fanny) Taggart which I didn't mind too much and she wasn't a bad sort at all, doing her best with the 'basics' some of which rubbed off on me as

I can understand a lot of French words even if I can't actually speak them! We had music with our form master who was also deputy head and known as Mr (Hitler) Holroyd, a nice man who tried to teach us the recorder, he lived at Ballagarey, Marown and drove a Morris Minor TMN 744, black in colour with the divided windscreen and 803cc engine. He was deputy to a Mr Boulton, a tall man with ginger hair who was always dressed in the black robe and sometimes even the 'mortar board' hat too as he strode around the school with an air of dignity. I never remember him speaking to me or indeed me to him in the two years I was there - such was the unfriendly nature of the place compared to my beloved Braddan where I had been so happy and received the best education of my life so far. Instead of the good old 'knock about' football matches I had been used to with Eddie Convery as captain of one team and me as the captain of the other, when Eddie's team always won and Mr Quayle was referee, I was informed that from now on we were to have 'games periods' instead. Yes, they even managed to spoil that as well with warm up exercises and ball control and rules and regulations that presumably were supposed to turn us into 'Stanley Matthews' or at the very least semi-professionals! This was all very well for the 'star' boys who were assembled into a team but as for the rest of us 'hackers' it probably meant standing in the cold for half an hour in the middle of winter while Mr Gregory coached his pets and forgot about the rest of us lemons!

I don't know to this day what the point of it was, maybe it was to be a centre of excellence but I still think it would have been better to involve everybody in a good old 'footy' match and keep our interest and enthusiasm alive because at a rough estimate I would think that about 75% of us would never be Stanley Matthews or Bobby Charlton.

I suppose that looking back on things the only lesson I really enjoyed was woodwork with Mr Jack Sayle who I got on well with and of course because I was interested, I did well at it usually being top or second in the class. I have mentioned that I was fairly good at English having had very intense teaching of

it at the Collegiate School from the age of our, but even in this subject I found my interest fading under Ken Corkill who to me was another sarcastic 'cloaked crusader' who had a very high opinion of himself and no doubt had a high knowledge of his subject but failed miserably in passing it on to me. I distinctly remember the approach to my first Christmas break and looking forward to the holiday, when he announced that we were to spend our time during the break to write an essay! Not only that the subject was to be on the ridiculous theme of 'The Coming Year 1960', he said it would stimulate our imagination and I think he was probably right because I imagined many times over in that holiday, that he helped to spoil, that I was some kind of clairvoyant that could gaze into the future and also do some unspeakable things to him! I think in hindsight that the general decline was brought on by my increasing lack of interest which was undoubtedly generated by these almost bland, uninteresting people who all seemed to have leather elbows and a very quick arm action when wielding a cane but sadly very little teaching ability. Their main pastime seemed to be sarcasm and with this type of bullying they would single out some poor unfortunate soul and bring him to the front of the class to belittle him for no other reason than that he was a bit slow on the uptake. This was a world away from the real teaching of Tommy Quayle who would spend extra time with the slower learners instead of bolstering his ego on the 'clever' kids as these graduate types seemed to do.

One notable exception to this trait came in our history teacher Mr Bob Forster who really was a good man at his job as he kept me interested enough to gain second from top of the class for the terms that he took me and I did enjoy his lessons. I was glad many years later to be able to thank him for his efforts when he attended a school reunion that a good friend of mine Peter Kelly persuaded me to attend some forty years on. Sadly Mr Forster, who later became principal at the Q.E. 2 School in Peel, died some time after this so I was apparently 'just in time' to thank him.

My verdict on Ballakermeen was then and is now, that it was really 'secondary' in the true sense of the word and for me the best part of it was going home in the evening on the train. I suppose that after my interest in some of the seemingly pointless lessons had waned I would switch off and think about the yard back home in Crosby and the Austin Sevens and the motor bikes and the old Winchester .22 that I used on the rabbits - until it was time to go home at four p.m. The first stage of this daily journey was by Road Services double decker. One of the well kept and maintained fleet of Leyland PD1 or PD2 buses would take us on the short journey from 'Balla' to the Douglas Railway Station where there would be a mad stampede through the station building and along the platform usually barging the ticket inspector to one side as he made a futile effort to inspect our 'contracts' while shouting 'slow down' or 'walk don't run' He wasted his breath every day! In fact he was very lucky not to be trampled underfoot on a few occasions as the double doors of the old red station building would burst open with the sheer weight of the stampede which comprised Peel, St Johns, Foxdale, Greeba and Crosby kids in full flight such was the delight of going home!

The old steam railway was just about 'on its knees' by this time and if my memory is right, I think they stopped using the trains for the school run after my second year around 1962. I was very interested in the buses and trains, as I still am, and used to memorise the registrations of the buses and their fleet numbers. Often on the Peel to Douglas route would be the lower numbers such as seven, eight, nine etc and I must have been an 'anorak' of the day when I noted that No 7 was GMN 777, No 8 was GMN 778 and so on..... 'Oh really '- I hear you say, but wait there's more - No 8 was the only one of the fleet with a chrome plated radiator cowl! - very interesting!

When it comes to the old steam trains, there is a sadness in me because one of the engines that took us to school, No 3 the Pender which was in truth probably three parts knackered at the time, later had the great injustice of being cut in half and 'sectioned' as a moving exhibit in the Manchester Rail Museum. I think most of the sixteen engines at that time were out of action and very badly worn because the Peel train always seemed to have Pender or G.H. Wood No 10, which unlike Pender is still running today.

I suppose my daydreams in class were normal enough because in view of how lucky I was with all my interests and money making schemes back home, it was almost inevitable that as the lessons became more boring, the more I yearned for the practical things of life as against the academic path that I was compelled to follow. Just before I move on from the Ballakermeen era, I should mention that I also learned the dreadful habit of smoking whilst I was there as well!

Some mischief - Youth Club

Meanwhile, in the evenings our garage at Kissacks Yard was a meeting place for lots of our mates who all shared our mechanical interests, as well as, perhaps an occasional 'foray' into one of the neighbouring gardens for some apples when in season of course! On one of these apple pinching trips we were 'accompanied' by one of the Douglas kids, 'Marzy' Marsden, and he left a trail of half eaten apples behind him because he was either fussy about their taste or maybe just stupid! Anyway, no more was thought about it at the time because we weren't aware of his lack of stealth, that is until Albert Edmond, the copper, appeared from over the hedge bordering Charlie Clark's garden and heading towards us. He had apparently been summoned by Charlie to investigate the loss of his prize apples which had been destined for some show or other and thanks to Marzy, Albert had little trouble tracing the culprits and making a full report in his book resulting in a lecture about stealing and an official caution! I think this was the only occasion out of maybe dozens of such escapades when we were actually 'nicked' but there were a few 'close shaves' that I can recall but still can't mention because Albert may still have an open book!

At the age of eleven or twelve we were obviously not old enough to 'attend' the Crosby Hotel but we were eager to learn the 'grown up things' of life and

Crosby Youth Club circa 1961: Johnny Gelling 'in the chair - Tricia Tarrant puts forward her point of view

as I said, we had already picked up the awful habit of smoking so it seemed a natural progression to try the local Okells bitter at the pub. A seemingly undamaged, new but rejected enamel jug of about 1 gallon capacity was discovered one day in the rubbish heap at Crosby Wholesalers - well this was perfect for a visit to the back door of the pub where we would have it filled as a 'carry out' and bring it back to the garage to share between us with a few fags and a 'natter' - what a good idea!

That wasn't quite how it turned out when we arrived at the black painted back door complete with thumb latch as it was then, to be greeted by Bob Grimshaw (Senior) who enquired as to our needs. As Phil Tasker's dad Joe was

the only one of our parents who was a regular at the Crosby, it was decided that Phil should have the 'honour' of asking for the jug to be filled with best bitter for his dad. This duly requested, Bob disappeared into the pub again with a wry smile on his face and, waiting intently, maybe three or four of us, all huddled around Phil, we were suddenly aware of a roar of laughter from inside, closely followed by an even bigger roar and the reappearance of Bob Senior with the jug, leaking profusely from the bottom rim joint all over his boots as he handed it over and said 'twelve bob please' 12/- or 60p today. The money was handed over as we tried to plug the leak with fingers and thumbs and the reason for the laughter inside the pub became evident as he added 'by the way yer father says he'll enjoy that ale when he comes home tonight, he's sitting at the bar!' Red faces all round I think! The remains of the bitter were passed around between us and I remember it being quite good when we eventually brought what was left of it back to our garage and the warmth of the old sawdust burning stove. We laughed about it and of course the reason why the 'perfect' jug had been discarded in the first place was now quite obvious with a trail of beer all the way back - what a waste! I think Phil's dad took it in good humour when he got home luckily and so not much was lost in the incident perhaps some credibility on our behalf and of course a fair amount of the beer that had, despite our efforts to save it, leaked away on the ground.

The Crosby Youth Club was in full swing at this time, very ably run for the most part, by the Gelling family, as mentioned earlier on, by Johnny who was the leader and assisted by his sisters Voirrey and Joice, along with various others when necessary. It really was a very happy and well run organisation with most of the village teenagers of the time being joined by the young people from surrounding farms and even from as far out as Peel and St Johns and Greeba, and even one or two from Douglas as well, eager to crowd into the little Methodist Hall in Station Road (now called Old Church Road) where lots of organised games and self entertainment such as rehearsals for various concerts took place on a one night a week basis where the next one couldn't come round soon enough. Such was the enthusiasm generated by this family, who have done much for the village over the years and helped to keep kids busy, amused and most of all - out of mischief and off the streets in the evening, which sadly, seems lacking today in some of the bigger towns and more heavily populated areas of the Island.

I particularly enjoyed the concerts we took part in and have memories of packed halls of spectators after such events as the Marown Ploughing Match where Johnny would be compere with his beloved piano accordion along with Joice on the piano and maybe the Youth Club 'Group' called the 'Nignogs'. This comprised a wash board, a tea chest with a brush handle held on top to tension a piece of string which was plucked by hand, if my memory is right, by Dennis Gelling, and Ernie Leece on his guitar with maybe someone else as well but I can't now recall who, possibly David North but I am not sure. The younger ones at the time, including myself, would take part in comedy sketches or maybe sing a song or two which really was good fun after the lines had been learned and was usually well rewarded with a 'Church Hall' type sandwich supper of the soft unsaleable tomatoes (probably donated by some kind soul) followed by a piece of fruit cake and copious amounts of hot tea, poured from a huge double handled tea pot non stop into the closely positioned cups which I'm sure demanded not only considerable strength but a fair degree of accuracy as well for a minimum of spillage. With these memorable concerts still in my memory it always gives me great pleasure to attend the Young Farmers Concerts of today, which really are superb and a great way of bringing the young people together in a very happy and productive way. I see the Young Farmers movement as a good wholesome breath of fresh air and surely one of the last bastions of true decency and Manxness to survive today in a world gradually declining in standards.

Anyway, I must now get down off my soap box and carry on with the memories - back to the early 1960's.

Bikes & St. Ninians

I was by now very interested in motorbikes and was greatly drawn to competition such as trials and scrambles. In fact I must have been greatly influenced by people such as Tommy Quine, who was a hill shepherd and used to visit our yard on a lovely AJS trials bike in the late 1950's. He would be dressed in a long coat or a 'Barbour' suit with a black beret trapped onto his head with a pair of goggles. This is probably the first 'proper' competition bike that I remember and I was impressed by the shining black paintwork coach lined in gold around the AJS insignia and the chrome plated exhaust which was upswept at the rear end at the silencer. I remember also that the font part of the pipe had a bluey, purple tint to it and this was remarked upon by Tommy or Dad as being caused by hot running possibly because the timing was a little retarded, whatever that meant! Another regular visitor to the yard, albeit because of work commitment, was Ray Kissack who was incidentally no relation to us but was a good friend and grocer by trade who, at that time, managed a shop in Christian Street in Peel that my dad owned. Ray had a brand new 197cc Greeves trials bike YMN 572 and he used to park it in our Smithy and take the Bradford Van to Peel every day for the shop deliveries that were then commonplace before the emergence of the 'Supermarket' system of today with no personal service being available anymore. When he moved on, after the sale of this shop, he landed the job of travelling salesman or rep' for Brooke Bond tea and as such he still came to the yard on the Greeves everyday to collect his nice new Brooke Bond van which was garaged in one of our lock-ups. Sadly Ray died young leaving his widow Jennifer and two daughters Chris and Annelie and I know Jenny won't mind if I tell you that Howard and I had an occasional ride round the yard on the Greeves in Ray's absence, always returning it to exactly where he had parked it!

The 'Trials Bug' was certainly beginning to bite as when Stuart Clague from nearby Ballawilleykilley Farm would come round on his new 250cc

Greeves, he would tell us all about it and mention such prestigious events as the Conway Shield and Wallace Shield full day events. I made up my mind at that time to work my way up to a 'decent' bike such as a Greeves and began the campaign to earn and save as much as I could to buy one for myself.

I was however, much as I disliked it, still obliged to go to school every day and by now I had moved on to St Ninians or Douglas High School as it was known. Once again the 'grey men' with the leather elbows on their jackets failed to capture much of my interest or imagination and one sarcastic bully called 'Jakey Hogg' really stands out in my memory to this day. In my opinion this man should not really have been in charge of us at all and nowadays he would certainly have been charged with common assault for the way he clipped our ears and slapped us around the head for what seemed trivial 'crimes' such as forgetting one's homework. He certainly seemed to have a chip on his shoulder and I don't recall his ever being in a good mood - not with me at any rate.

One man I had respect for was my form master Harry Underwood who genuinely did his best to teach in the old fashioned way of explaining instead of what seemed to be the 'norm' at that time of first baffling everyone and then going on to either sarcasm or shouting. Indeed, sometimes, - both! As in the case of Hogg who I have to admit actually used to frighten me and as a result of this the only thing I learned from him was how to keep out of his way and be crafty.

Although he never taught me, I remember one of the P.T. teachers of the time being Brian King who had a brand new 'Cotton' 250 trials bike which I much admired. I still see Brian around sometimes and he hardly seems to have changed, always with a ready smile he was one of the decent masters who served under the head - Frank Luckman. I think that the only other master who travelled by motorcycle at that time was John Timpson who had a nicely kept 250c.c BSA C12.

I had opted to take metalwork in the third year instead of woodwork and this entailed a walk down to Ballakermeen for the teaching of Sid Tyrer. Sid was a decent chap and he had been a plumber in an 'earlier life' with a lot of experience of what life was like in the real world as against the sheltered well paid teachers who in reality had never left school and consequently had never had to look for work. He was a small man with his fingers stained in nicotine and he spoke to me without sarcasm which was most welcome, teaching lathe work, beating copper, folding tinplate, forging hot steel and soldering as well as the theory side of workshop engineering. He held my interest well and I enjoyed the lessons and his style of teaching and ultimately achieving good exam results in the subject. I mentioned the nicotine on his fingers which in fact was quite a common sight in those days among heavy smokers at least, and that is what quite a large number of pupils at that time were becoming. When dodging down the many back lanes on our walk between the two schools it was a matter of course to light up a 'fag' and smoke it, whether it was enjoyable or not, because that seemed to be the trendy thing to do. It was a rather 'clandestine' operation as smoking was strictly forbidden, so if a teacher or even a nosey 'grown-up' spotted us it meant the cane for certain! Unlike these days where the youngsters seem to openly defy authority and smoke when and where they choose. I unfortunately became hooked on the infernal things and smoked until my mid twenties when at last, thankfully, I saw the light and packed them up for good.

For the most part therefore I found the weekdays long and boring at school with few if any high spots even worth remembering and I must admit to a certain amount of daydreaming in class. This soon showed up in my G.C.E. exams and my results were apparently 'only average' and certainly not good enough to pursue a career in teaching or banking or such like. These were two of the options for future life that were offered to school leavers, along with an engineering apprenticeship in one of the factories in the Island or, perhaps, a career in the armed forces. Not much of a choice really and I think that the school failed miserably with a very narrow minded outlook dealing mainly with future employment rather than any information on the possibility of self employment, about which of course these teachers knew absolutely nothing, having never left school themselves! In their sheltered employment with a cosy salary and lots of holidays I wonder if they ever dreamt of breaking free and trying to make a living in the very competitive outside world - I suppose not!

I think school leaving age is a very uncertain time in an adolescent's life and it certainly wasn't helped in my case by the options and suggestions offered by the Douglas High School for Boys, except for one possibility, which was a full time pre-apprenticeship course at Hanover Street College of further Education in Lord Street, Douglas.

Ballavitchel - Ronague Mountain

It was the summer of 1964, I was sixteen and had passed my motor bike test on a 197cc Francis Barnett and had also passed my car test in an Austin A40 with the help of a Mr Sheard who had a driving school in Union Mills at that time. The pre-apprenticeship course did not start 'til September so I went to work at Ballavitchel Farm with my 'Uncle' Jack Callister who needed help with the hay making as Robbie Gelling, his 'right hand man' was seriously ill. It seemed like a good idea at the time and the money would come in handy to buy a Greeves trials bike I had spotted in a garage in Peel. I went to see Jack and his wife Isabel and it was agreed that they would pay me the hourly rate for a casual labourer which was 4/- an hour and I was to start straight away because it was a nice sunny day but I wasn't to bother coming up if there was any sign of rain. I enjoyed the summer and can remember very few days when the weather was bad but maybe as they say, we only think of the fine days with the passage of time. There were two David Brown Cropmaster tractors there, one was PMN 658 and the other was HMN something but the numbers slip my mind. They were used in turn for the various jobs to save changing implements over as little as possible, one having the finger mower on and the other with the hay turner on and so on, but with me doing most of, if not all the work as Jack complained of a bad hip! I'm sure that they must have been watching my every move from the farmhouse window because Jack would mysteriously appear at the very moment that I stopped, for whatever reason, whether it was mechanical failure or just for a call of nature! - he would be there to push the job along. He was very good at man management and very astute and he seemed to have an uncanny sixth sense for breakdowns, arriving at the right moment with spare shear bolts for instance, when one would break in the Albion baler. On more than one occasion he brought Robbie out of his sickbed to assist and that was something that I didn't like to see because he really looked ill and clearly he shouldn't have been troubled but sadly on Jack's list of priorities the haymaking came above Robbie's health.

It was to be Jack's last year in Ballavitchel as he wanted to sell up and retire so a lot of the hay was being sold 'off the field' and taken away on wagons belonging to the 'Farmers Club' as it was then known. These wagons were nearly new Austin FF Model flat decks fitted with telehoist bag loaders and I was lucky enough to drive them on a few occasions in the fields when permitted to do so by one of the drivers who I think were Dougie Corkish (now a post man) and Charlie Kennish who later drove tankers for Manx Petroleums. I think the Austins were numbered 5573 MN and 5574 but I'm not too sure about that. I had agreed that, rather than be paid weekly, I would leave my earnings 'in the pot' so I would have a nice amount saved by the end of the summer and despite warnings that Jack, and Isabel especially, were 'quite mean' I somewhat naively decided that this was the best course of action. What a foolish decision this turned out to be as after a long hot summer's work when I really did my best for these people, they actually cheated me. I clearly remember the last load of bales that I had loaded single handed and feeling a sense of satisfaction at having managed for the most part entirely on my own. Carting in and stacking in the barn some 30 acres of bales with the remainder being sold off the fields was no mean feat as far as I was concerned but Jack and Isabel obviously thought along different lines. On that last day I finished clearing the field opposite 'Highcroft' in Ballavitchel Road and was just about to emerge from the gate with the David Brown and trailer with about forty bales on board (because that was as high as I could stack it without help) when Jack did one of his magical 'appearing tricks'. He had actually free wheeled down the road from the farm on my old Francis Barnett, presumably to save paying me for possibly another half hours work! He produced an envelope from his pocket and thanked me for my endeavours but what he said next left me totally flabbergasted to say the least! He couldn't look me in the eye as he went on to say that Isabel had been checking up on the hourly rate and the four shillings previously mentioned was for a 21year old, so we've given you the three and fourpence which is right for a 16 year old! Well, I was gobsmacked and I think quite upset as well, having genuinely done my best for these people but I took it on the chin and without further comment I rode home on my bike. Of course knowing a lot more about life now, I certainly wouldn't stand for it but that was in the days when youth respected grown ups and one didn't cheek ones elders even though it was a very shabby trick and indeed crooked to say the very least. Sadly, it got even shabbier as far as Robbie was concerned, because at the farm sale which turned out to be a 'very good' one, Jack had promised the proceeds of the Bradford Van RMN 261 to him as a reward for many years of loyal service to him and Isabel. This may seem to the reader to be a rather nice gesture and maybe, on the face of it that is how it would appear but no - the sale, as I've said was a good one with brisk bidding and good prices and when it came to the sale of the old Bradford it was no exception and it fetched far more than Jack had anticipated. I'm not sure that 'shabby' is quite the right word for it but the gist of it is that Jack told

Robbie that he had only expected the van to fetch about £35 and as it had fetched £75 he would split the proceeds with him! It was a bad do all round as Robbie died soon afterwards. Meanness is a dreadful thing and remains one of my 'pet hates' to this day. Two others are arrogance and snobbery but read on.

On a much brighter note I was fortunate, through a friend of some years earlier and the 'Reliant' 3 wheeler trolleys, in being able to buy from him a 1929 Ford Model AF Cabriolet 7315MN. This old Ford was a real eye catcher with its soft top and dickey seat and I can't remember how much I paid for it but at the time it was fully roadworthy and in quite good condition. It belonged to Ken Bawden, he was having trouble with it and as it was quite unreliable and heavy on petrol it must have been a bargain, for me that is - not him! After some sorting out of the coil, condenser and points we got it going well and it was indeed 'quite reliable', so on the strength of this I decided to trace its ancestry and Isle of Man history at least, as its registration number was from only recently in about 1963. Someone told us of a similar model that was owned by a Mrs Williams at Niarbyl Café and Gift Shop down on the beach at Dalby, so we went to see her and she told us that her car had also been a Model AF Cabriolet but it had been sold for scrap to a Mr Keith Kennaugh of Silverburn Farm at the bottom of Ballamodha Straight. Keith was a jovial character whose interest in mechanicals and vehicles was probably on a par to our own and we became good friends with him, soon learning that Mrs Williams' car and our own were indeed one and the same! It emerged that the old lady had in fact requested that it be scrapped but Keith just couldn't bring himself to commit what would have been no more than vandalism, so he painted it a different colour and re-registered it instead. He had really liked the car and he was sorry that he had parted with it, proving this to be true a couple of years later when he bought it back from us.

This chance meeting with Keith opened up a whole new circle of friends and activities for us as he obviously knew all the farm lads in the south of the island and through him we got to meet quite a few of them and became friends.

At the time, dad had bought an Austin LDO Van that someone had used to bring his furniture over to the island then disposed of it. Its number was TOM 504 (later 985 BMN) and with Howard driving it we would set off for Ronague every Sunday morning loaded up with our motor bikes and usually John Kissack and Phil Tasker with theirs as well. We would meet up with our new mates and race around the mountainside on all manner of bikes dating right back to a 1929 TT Sunbeam belonging to Francis Garrett from Ballafodda, that he paid the princely sum of 2/- (10p) for! I often wonder how much it would be worth today! There were all types and models including home made specials such as Johnny Masson's Norton engined Panther, a real 'beast' of a machine with a 500cc ES2 engine complete with full racing exhaust and open megaphone. Geoff Comish from Ballastroke had a rigid framed 350cc BSA ZB Model Gold Star, which was a very quick bike but it came to a very sticky end some time after when he sold it to 'Big' Frank Maddrell from Port St Mary. The track we used at the time involved part of an overgrown lane which provided some shelter for a 'natter' and a smoke after each session on the bikes and this was a great part of the meeting of old and new friends each Sunday morning, where for the price of a gallon of petrol, a lot of good fun and yarns were enjoyed by all those present. The rest of the course was through fields and over low hedges between gorse bushes forming a rough oval which was basically up the side of the hill, along the top then back down again. It was on the down hill part that most of the crashes happened and I think I can lay claim to the first of these, when attempting to leap over a hedge, something went wrong, I came off my Greeves and broke my left collar bone and Ritchie Faragher took me in his Austin A30, first to his mother's house for a cup of tea, then to Dr Jackson in Castletown and finally to Nobles' Hospital.

One notable crash at the same spot was when 'Big' Frank Maddrell destroyed the old BSA. To us spectating at the time it was one of the funniest crashes ever although I don't think that was quite the way that Frank remembers it! Someone had replaced the front forks at some time and made a poor job of welding a new stem to the bottom yoke with what we would now call 'chicken shit weld', which stuck where it landed, basically with no real strength or penetration where it was needed. Well, this gave way at a crucial moment on the downhill section of the course as Frank 'touched down' after cresting the hedge at breakneck speed, which was probably approaching about 25 - 30mph and to cut a long story short, the old BSA stopped dead in its tracks but Frank and the handlebars, forks and front wheel didn't!! He was doing an exaggerated run, seemingly in slow motion with his feet hardly touching the ground but with his hands getting lower and lower until he eventually ploughed his chin into the ground and broke his teeth while still holding the handlebars with forks and wheel still attached. The result was another trip to hospital with Frank bloodstained and badly concussed.

These were good days indeed and in those times of little or no money we spent many hours visiting each others garages or workshops in the evenings for a good old fashioned natter, where yarns were told and lots of humour and laughter was the order of the day. Spare parts and indeed whole bikes would change hands along with the tall stories and these social evenings would inevitably end up with a cup of tea at the house we were visiting at the time. I remember one evening whilst visiting Ballacricket at Ronague to see Johnny Masson, someone said that chickens could be hypnotised with the help of a stick of chalk and maybe we should try it out. Basically what happens is that the chicken has her beak held to the ground and a straight chalk line is drawn for about 4 - 5 feet from immediately in front of her eyes and leading away into the darkness. She is then released and will stagger all over the place as if drunk. Well we certainly proved this to be true but Johnny told us later that his granddad was most annoyed as we had put a number of birds 'off the lay' for a few days. If he had found out why this had happened we would certainly have had a right old telling off but to my knowledge he never did and just to make sure, we kept away for a while 'til the heat died down.

At Ballastroke, also at Ronague, there was a big wooden hut where Geoff and David Comish performed their feats of engineering and this would be followed by first a testing session round the back field with what ever bike was being worked on, then a few stories and then the cuppa which was a vital part of the evening. Geoff rebuilt a nice BSA 350 Gold Star Scrambler he had bought from Gary Preston and he ventured into 'proper' competition with it, enjoying a fair degree of success although it was no match for the modern bikes of the time like the Greeves Challenger or BSA Victor. He eventually dismantled it and I bought the frame which I still have today, embodied in my 500cc trials sidecar outfit.

I still see lots of these friends to this day and I recall names of the 'regulars' at Ronague Mountain in 1963 some forty years ago! Names such as Alan 'Bo' Johnson (Greeves), Eric Kissack (Ariel), Phil Taubman, Gordon 'Hoss' Clague and Nigel Warren all on Greeves, Peter Maddrell (D.M.W.), Howard Kissack (Matchless), Phil Tasker (Tandon), John Kissack (D.O.T.), Geof Comish (BSA) and David Comish (BSA)

Johnny Masson (Norton Panther) Keith Kennaugh (Norton 500T) Francis Garnett (Sunbeam) also many regular spectators such as Teddy Garnett, Joe Faragher, Jack Kennaugh, David Shimmin, Dennis Quayle and 'Specs' Condon would be there.

Tough times - Emigration?

The Ronague mountain memories bring me up to 1964 and 1965 when I started in real competition by joining the off road motorcycle clubs as I came to the age of 16 and could ride on the road. There are many more memories of my earlier life that keep 'popping' up to the surface but obviously it would take far too much paper to record them all and not wishing to put everyone to sleep altogether I am being selective. Some may say mercifully!

To go back to the mid fifties I have lot of memories of my father being wet through on winter days from working in the rain and bad weather, as at that time, there was a general scarcity of work and a poor outlook for the building trade with many good tradesmen and labourers leaving the Island to look for work in England, some never returned and emigrated to Australia and Canada. This would be around 1956 I think, when our family very nearly emigrated to Toronto in Canada and this story could have turned out very differently or never been written at all. Things must have been quite bad and I can remember a man called Jock McGarver in tears as he shook dad's hand in gratitude for giving him a job or a few days work. This stays in my mind mainly because he used to come to work on a bicycle with the very same 'Cymota' engine bolted to the front forks as we had on our first machine.

Promotional films were being shown in St Georges Hall in Hill Street, Douglas, urging people to emigrate to the Commonwealth Countries but mainly Australia and Canada, where a much better standard of living and full employment were promised, all for a special cheap fare of £10. I really enjoyed these films, which in hindsight I suppose only showed the good side of things but seemed so bright and colourful after a Manx winter day at the Collegiate School. Things looked all set to happen, we were going to Toronto and Dad was fixed up with work in his cousin Art Kimberley's business in lumber and saw milling there. Apparently Art had no male relatives or descendants and he

Grandfather Harry Kissack

wanted to retire, so it all seemed to be settled….that is until my grandfather Harry took a very bad stroke, losing his speech and movement on his left side and becoming bed ridden for the next two years until his death. The result of this was that we stayed in Crosby, Isle of Man instead of the promised world adventure to Canada. Maybe this was fate, call it what you will, but I think I was glad really as I've always been a 'home bird' and I love the Island.

Father made the best of it, as always, and being well able to turn his hand to anything, he was never really short of work although I suspect that often, the remuneration would be quite small or even non-existent occasionally, when a customer couldn't or even in some cases, wouldn't pay. He did have good customers however and they must have kept us going, along with the undertaking side of the business which although a 'dying' trade was always steady.

This mention of undertaking sparks a memory from 1963 when in very deep snow, Higher Foxdale was 'cut off' for about a week and an elderly man called Thomas Whitton passed on, not knowing what complications he was about to cause with his untimely death! His widow Mollie (nee Callister) was one of the 'old style' district nurses and she had him well laid out in the downstairs front room of the little terraced house on the side of South Barrule, dressed in his best striped pyjamas and covered with newspapers to keep the dust off him. In those days it was common practice for the funeral to leave the person's home on their last journey, rather than from a Chapel of Rest as it is today. I think the roads were just about passable when dad went up to sort out the funeral arrangements and of course to measure Thomas for his 'tailor made' elm coffin, to be hand made in our joiners shop. Well, after this visit the snow got worse and set in for one of the worst winters of the 1960's and although the arrangements were in place and the coffin ready and waiting it was quite clear that we were at the mercy of the weather. After some days of waiting for the snow to stop, during which time we had great fun, having been sent home from school 'til further notice, dad decided to make an attempt at getting the coffin up to Foxdale in a rather innovative and unique way. Although no motor vehicle had been able to negotiate the climb, he decided to bring a sledge along with the coffin on the back of the old Morris Tonner and to see how far we could get! The old original Morris MN 7234 had been replaced by this time by an almost identical model from the Ramsey Hydro which was numbered MAN 251, so this was simply painted the same colour, the registration changed over along with the tipper and life carried on as before. This old vehicle was 'simply magic' at travelling in the snow and for the one and only time I remember, it needed snow chains on the large rear wheels as father expertly drove it all the way up through lower Foxdale and right up under the Old Railway Bridge before we were eventually stopped in our tracks by a huge drift a hundred yards before Brookfield Terrace. It was now time to unload the sledge and with the coffin covered over with a small piece of tarpaulin and tied securely, Howard, Phil Tasker and I set off like a team of huskies pulling the sledge behind us for the next half a mile or so up the hill. The cottage is opposite Barrule Farm and we crowded into the room and placed the coffin on the little pair of hardwood trestles while Mollie gathered the pages of the newspaper which were covering the corpse and said she wouldn't waste them as they would come in handy for lighting the fire later on. It was at this stage that Phil went a whiter shade of pale and hurriedly sat down in a feint, this being the first time that he had seen a dead person, albeit one dressed in striped pyjamas and covered over with the 'Monas Herald'!

What an experience and education for young lads - priceless to say the very least. Well by the day of the funeral, the Highway Board had managed to clear a single track road so we were able to get the Humber hearse belonging to Corkills Garage of Onchan (MMN 391) through to Foxdale churchyard for the service and interment. The graves were dug in those days by a Foxdale character called Jacky Clarke of Brookfield Terrace and as the coffin bearers prepared to lower the late Thomas to his last resting place, it became apparent that the Vicar was very much the 'worse for wear' as he repeatedly lost his place whilst reading the committal from the book and it was at this point that father took over and recited the remaining words and prayers entirely from

The Morris Tonner

memory while he held the Vicar's arm and steadied him in case he should slip and follow the coffin into the hole! This was much to the amusement of the assembled congregation which seemed to consist of most of the senior citizens of the area and for some reason, a number of workers from the nearby 'Manx Flux and Mica' brickworks in Mines Road. They all wore hard hats and with the logo of their firm printed on their Donkey jackets, while they whispered to each other 'Who was he' or 'Who's getting buried' - it made quite a comical gathering indeed.

Real trials and Competition

In September 1964, having finished the summer at Ballavitchel, I bought my first Greeves trials bike XMN 673 from Ray Gale in Peel and began practising on it with Stephen Swainston, my friend at the time, who also had a Greeves. His father was a manager in Dowty's (or Iloman Engineering) and Steve had already competed in one or two trials and was able to give me a few handy hints on bike preparation as well as making a few practice sections of the required standard for us to try our skill - or lack of it as it turned out. Steve's bike was immaculately turned out with many parts cadmium plated or anodised courtesy of Dowtys, as well as being sprayed a nice shade of drab grey, which just by coincidence was the factory colour for many of its components. My own bike was reasonably smart but being only 197cc and three speed gearbox, was sadly lacking in performance. The engine unit was from a road bike and was all I could afford at the time to slot into the Greeves rolling chassis and although I did eventually upgrade it with another barrel and piston and a four speed gearbox, I was never really happy with it.

I made my trials debut on this bike at the 1964 Boxing Day trial, which was probably a bad decision as it was a timed full day event and by far the toughest event in the calendar being both observed and timed! The main award presented by the Peveril M.C.C. was the Wallace Shield and it was justly won by the great Roger Kelly who was the undoubted master of these timed events, which had a notoriously high retirement rate with around thirty starters and perhaps about six finishers only! It was the forerunner of today's enduro competitions but in those days the bikes were much less reliable and a lot heavier than they are today, so a full eight hour trial at an average speed of 20mph including observed sections on the old two ply Dunlop and Avon tyres, was no mean feat by any standard of rider. Anyway, I was persuaded by Steve to have a go, so I entered at the Salisbury Garage in Fort Street and got a copy of the route, along with a 1" to 1mile ordnance map of the island.

Dennis Craine was the garage manager then as well as being in charge of the entries and he gladly took my entry fee and advised me to buy the map. I would have to know where I was going as there would be absolutely no route marking and that I would get lost would be a certainty if I didn't do the necessary research and exploration beforehand. There was only a few days left before the event and I didn't even have any proper motor cycle clothing, let alone the very necessary leather boots so I borrowed five pounds from my mum and went back to Dennis' to buy a 'Barbour' jacket which was a must at that time of the year with lots of snow still lying on the high ground, and of course, the inevitable wind and rain of a Manx winter, making the jacket a priority. With no money left for either boots or Barbour trousers I thought I would be alright wearing jeans and Wellingtons….another bad decision but not the one that eventually caused my retirement which in hindsight was almost inevitable. Over the next couple of days I desperately tried to learn the route but it was difficult because the tracks were named on the card such as 'Honey Hill', 'Gorse Tipps' etc but many of them, although marked on the map were not named on it as such so it would be very easy to get lost as Dennis had warned. Still determined to ride the event, no matter how ill prepared for it I really was, I set off for E.B. Christian's Bridge Garage in the rain at 8am and was absolutely soaked and frozen when I got there! What an initiation, all the 'old timers' were there with spare inner tubes, cables taped alongside the originals, and all looking very relaxed while they did a few last minute adjustments such as tyre pressures etc. Well!! Relaxed is a word that I certainly wasn't! My sphincter muscle was making buttons and my nervous state certainly wasn't helped when the starter of the day Mr Norman Christian waved me away on my start time, but not before warning me that I really shouldn't be riding in wellies! The first few tracks such as Trollaby Lane and the Rhyne to Nab were easy but then came the ride up from Crosby, over Eairy Vane to Brandywell, an infamous track called Cronk Breck! As any one who has ridden it will confirm, it is hardly a track at all after the last gate onto the

The start of the Gill Shield Trial at E. B. Christian's Bridge Garage, easter Monday 1966

mountainside above Eairy Vane and is more akin to a sheep path as it winds its way north through the heather and bogs. It is very easy to lose the way in the mist and rain on this path but it wasn't the weather that stopped me, it was the 'notorious' Cronk Breck bog near to the Brandywell end of the moor side and just before the hardcore track starts again. I seemed to be surrounded by floundering riders at one stage as I desperately tried to extract my bike which had all but disappeared except for the back wheel, mudguard and registration plate. My situation seemed hopeless and looking around me I realised that very soon I would probably be left on my own as one by one the more experienced riders were freeing themselves and riding off into the mist. I had to think quickly so I left my machine and went to offer my help to the next competitor who had almost got free of the very deep mud without my help and was none too pleased that he had to return the favour and come to help me! We struggled and heaved and together we finally extracted my bike and muttering something under his breath about sex and illegitimacy he dashed away to his own bike (a Francis Barnett) and disappeared into the mist! By this time, now quite exhausted, soaked through from the waist down and with both wellies full of mud and water, I decided never the less to try and continue, but on close inspection of the bike discovered that the complete back brake assembly of pedal and brake rod had been torn away and was wrapped up in the spokes of the back wheel. Well that was the end of competition for the day but I put it all down to experience and vowed to do better next time. Later on that day I went along to the finish at the Crescent Hotel and found everyone to be very welcoming and friendly as people in the motor cycling world are generally - a great bunch of people and I have made many friends through a lifetime of off road sport in the years following that 'Baptism of Fire'! The man with the Francis Barnett even laughed about it although I had probably cost him some precious minutes of the very tight schedule which demanded an all day average speed of 20mph. This certainly wasn't easy when punctures and mechanical failure were taken into account,

not to mention the physical exhaustion of the novice rider, the total absence of route marking and the many gates which seemed to be tied shut with enough wire and string to fence a small field. The man's name was Malcom Quiggin and even today when I meet him we have a laugh about it some forty odd years later. It turned out that he himself had not been riding for very long and he introduced me to his 'gang' of fellow novice riders who were mostly from the cycling world. Names that spring to mind are Dave Wood, Niels Skillicorn, Peter (Jasper) Cain and Brian Roche but I met many more new friends that evening at the 'Crescent' which, under the patronage of Jack Quirk with his wife Bee and family Louise (later of Manx Radio), Mike and Peter, really was a great headquarters for the Peveril M.C.C. I remember being introduced to Stanley Wardell who was I think the President and a former chairman of the club and I was quite shocked to hear some days later that he had taken ill and died that very night. I hasten to add that I don't think his sad demise had anything to do with his meeting me!

From then on Wednesday nights were 'Club Night' and not to be missed at any cost and in those days the gatherings were well attended in that front bar with a nice fire always in the grate and the fine full size snooker table always in great demand. I used to go along there with my mate Stephen Swainston and have a couple of pints which was all we could afford unless we got lucky and were treated by maybe Ken Harding or Dennis Craine as they vied for the possible sale of a bike from their respective businesses. These were of course Gilbert Harding Ltd and the Salisbury Garage Ltd and many a deal was done over a drink in the Crescent on a Wednesday night. One of my mates Bert Cowley (who later became a Police Inspector in Hong Kong) bought an old C15 BSA 250 - 2439 MN that had once belonged to George Peake and had certainly seen better days but had had a glowing pedigree in the front bar of the Crescent when its many virtues were extolled by Dennis Craine!

I myself bought a bike from Dennis but not I hasten to add, in the pub! It was to be my solo trials bike for a few years to come and I think he did me a good deal at £90 for the ex Geoff Cannell Greeves 24TE Model with Parkinson Square barrel, 6866 MN. By this time I was attending the College of Further Education at the Old Hanover Street School in Lord Street, Douglas on a pre-apprenticeship course for the period Sept '64 til June '65 and it turned out to be a very happy year for me. It was indeed a breath of fresh air to be treated properly by the teachers or lecturers under the principal Mr Ken Roberts who was a real gentleman. Other good people there included Kath Corkill who taught or tried to teach English grammar to us and indeed did a grand job with many of us passing in the subject with high grades in the G.C.E. exam which followed. Also, we were shown various trades such as electrical installation, engineering, motor vehicle maintenance etc. as well as practical science and physics with maths, by people who made it interesting for us and consequently I think I learned a lot more in one year there than I did in the previous five years at the high school.

We had a lot of fun in the motor vehicle workshop where a retired motor engineer and insurance assessor called Fred Cotton did his best to show us the basics with the collection of old pre-war engines which had been stripped and reassembled so many times that the nuts and bolts had been rounded off with ill fitting spanners in the hands of ham fisted students! Many parts were missing, making it almost impossible to be serious when re-building an engine with only three of the four pistons available and no gaskets to be seen. There was also a brand new unregistered Triumph Herald Coupe that had been donated to the College free of charge by the Triumph factory courtesy of the local agents W.H. Shimmin of the Crescent Garage on Douglas Promenade but I think this vehicle was for the more advanced apprentices. The car was parked over the pit and it was here that we all hid one day to baffle Fred. He was a heavy smoker, as holes burnt in his trousers were evidence from his dropping fag ends whilst he was driving his car! Bearing in mind that he was probably in his late sixties and maybe even 'losing it' a bit we thought it would be rather a good prank to take advantage of one of his 'senior' moments by disappearing when he left the room for one of his many smoke breaks. With some of us down the pit and the rest hiding in the Herald the sight of an empty room seemed to fool Fred and he went out again shaking his head in disbelief to see if he could find us. In the meantime we all reappeared and sat on the chairs and benches as if nothing had happened so when Fred returned he looked totally baffled but he never cracked on or said a word about it!

The year at Hanover Street College came and went with many happy memories and new friends and acquaintances along the way. One of my mates at the time was (and still is) Andy Sykes who had also bought a Greeves 250 and wanted to start trialling so I was pleased to bring him along with me to his first trial. It was at the Kirk Michael venue at Ballakilleyclieu at the bottom of Barregarrow Hill and we travelled in one of my dad's 'Minor' vans, VMN 272, with the front wheels of both bikes hanging out of the back of the van and with the doors tied together behind them. I remember that we both finished a fairly tough event and that I won the Novice award - my first- and it was a Peveril Club tie that I still have to this day.

By this time I had been voted on to the Peveril Club Committee with the somewhat illustrious title of 'Club Captain' no less! It was explained to me that part of my job would be to show the 'newcomers' the ropes and organise 'ride outs' to learn the many tracks and rights of way - a somewhat tall order as I hardly knew anything myself. I think that the committee at that time was a very healthy mix of some older members as well as experienced competitors and newcomers like myself. The meetings were held in the Dalton Street home of the Chairman Ralph Lowey and his lovely wife Bernice who spoilt us all with lots of homemade scones and sandwiches and cups of tea while we deliberated on important issues such as who would put up the folding wooden toilet cubicles at Ballacallin for the next scramble.

With the mention of scrambles (MotoX today) it reminds me that the main event of the Club and the 'big' money earner for the year was the 'Grand National Scramble' at Douglas Head Old Golf Course. This event had a great pedigree

reaching back to the early post war years and was originally held at a very wild wet and usually windy venue at Windy Corner on the T.T. course. I remember well, a quite heated discussion about the 'refreshment' tent at the event and it was an eye opener to me as a 16 year old. Apparently it cost the club a staggering £20 for booze for the 'old guard' - senior officials and timekeepers etc and this was thought to be grossly unfair to the rank and file of the Club as they were not admitted to the tent at all for even a cup of tea. I think it was pointed out that if we failed to keep the timekeepers 'sweet' then they were entitled to charge for their services but the general feeling of the meeting was that it would be cheaper to give them one bottle of whiskey at a cost of £3.10s.6d and put an end to the scandal. The tent itself was a large brown coloured, two pole job which was kindly lent each year by Gilbert Harding later to be 'inherited' by Goo Owen when he took over their business and renamed it Tiger Tim Ltd at Peveril Square in Douglas.

In the meantime all the necessary equipment for the event was kept at E.B. Christian's White Hoe Stores and it had to be transported up to the 'Head'

over the space of about three weeks prior to the Tuesday evening of T.T. week event. At this time Goo Owen was the Clerk of the Course and he certainly ran the event well, rallying the 'troops' for the many work parties necessary for this big national event and bribing them with the promise of a free pint at the end of the evening. He used to borrow a Bedford T.K lorry from 'Ski Cojeen' and we would load up stakes and miles of ropes and lay them all round the course ready to be erected by teams using post 'bumpers' and man power only. These 'bumpers' were made by Mike Nicholson who worked at the Pulrose Power Station and really were quite heavy but with practice and with the right technique, the two operators could knock in a post with about three bangs. It was a huge task with double roping around much of the mile long course and literally hundreds of posts and miles of rope to be erected. As is the case nowadays, there were a few members who were 'unavailable' for the work parties but always seemed to be able to turn up on the night to watch the event, some having a genuine reason but others being nothing short of 'work shy'. The event itself was always brilliant with all the stars of the day over from the U.K. as well as the local 'aces', and locals and holiday makers who were admitted through no less than six gates opened up through the wire stock fencing and manned by civil servants.

I myself eventually became Clerk of the Course, after Goo Owen, for two years (1972 and 1973 I think) and by this time the event had attracted sponsorship from Players No 6 cigarettes, so being a smoker at the time I asked their 'rep' for a carton of their product to share with my helpers. Well he was a tight fisted individual and took some cajoling from myself, Terry Gilmour and Jimmy Kennish until we eventually managed to get most of a carton and on receipt of the same wasted no time in telling him that we thought No 6 fags were shite anyway!

To go back to my year at Hanover Street College of Further Education, as I have said it was a very happy time for me and I will always be grateful to the lecturers there at the time. When I left there in the summer of 1965, I was

Derry and Phil at Ballacottier Mines on the 500cc D. H. Special BSA - 500KMN

successful in a job application as an apprentice engineer at the new Iloman Engineering factory at School Road, in Onchan and along with Andy Sykes, Roy Garnett, Roy Noble, John Alderson, Michael Corkill and possibly a couple more names that slip my mind, we became the new influx of 'highly privileged' apprentices - at least that's what the works manager said!

First job

The works manager was a man called Wilf Simm and he told me that the company held a good future for the right people and that we would be moved around the various operations in the factory to assess our aptitude for the differing skills that were necessary. These included lathes, grinders, cadmium plating, automatic machines, the inspection department and of course the drawing office in which I was really interested and looking forward to my turn there. I was placed with a good man called Norman Rhodes on a line of three ancient No 7 Ward lathes which were the biggest machines in the place and used for machining huge castings on their first operation such as boring out, internal tapping of threads and facing in readiness to be passed on to the next process. Two of the three lathes were operated by identical twin brothers Stan and Harold Lee who had worked for 'Dowtys' since the war time and were highly skilled at their job. They were dressed alike in bib and brace overalls and sleeveless pullover over a shirt with the sleeves always rolled up, the same horn rimmed spectacles and polished black boots. They were very nice middle aged men from whom I learned a lot, I think they were originally from Lancashire and some years later I met Stan who told me that, sadly, Harold had died but that he himself had worked on at the factory until his retirement, loyalty indeed.

Well I'm afraid to say that my loyalty to the place never really materialised and I found it a very claustrophobic sort of atmosphere in which to work. I didn't like being 'shut in' every day and treated rather like a battery hen with a 'clock number' - 157 and although I did try hard to settle down and despite learning quite a lot, after a period of about fourteen months I had had enough. To be perfectly honest I don't think that the management were 'playing the game' with me because all the other lads seemed to have been moved around as promised from one department to another and they seemed to be happy enough with their jobs whereas I had moved only once, albeit not to another department but to another line of lathes nearby which was just as ancient but were called Herbert 2D's. I remember saying to one of the foremen at the time who was called Charlie Crowe that I felt like a bit of a 'Herbert' myself and if this was what the firm meant as a great future then I couldn't wait 'til I finished my time and that I would be 'off' as soon as I was 21 years old. This must have struck a nerve because within a few minutes I was summoned to see Wilf Simm and given a severe pep talk or bollocking for daring to speak my mind and told in no uncertain terms that they weren't 'spending money' to train me for me to then 'bugger off' as soon as I was 21! I replied that this wasn't the case at all as I was by now setting up three of these lathes for their lady operators for about £9 per week wages and that the time served engineer next to me was looking after six of the same for close to £30 a week, so I didn't think I owed them anything! After muttering a few expletives that sounded like 'ruddy clever dick' or something similar he told me to go back to work and watch my step!

I decided there and then that it was time indeed for me, in the words of Mr Simm who had a lot more experience and company loyalty, to 'bugger off' and work somewhere else. This was a big step, to throw up one's job, as I had always been taught not to be a quitter and to see things through, so how was I going to tell my Dad?? Fate often takes a hand in life, or so I believe anyway, and that night I met my friend Niels Skillicorn at the club night at the Crescent and told him of my situation and after a couple of pints it seemed only natural that I should become an apprentice joiner instead with the highly respected

Onchan builders J.T. Skillicorn Ltd. Niels told me that they were very busy and that he would speak to the 'boss' who was at that time his uncle - Bob Skillicorn. It was arranged that I would have an interview at their Royal Avenue workshops in the former Cinema building and although Mr Skillicorn tried to persuade me to be an apprentice mason rather than a joiner he eventually extended his hand and said 'start on Monday'. This made it very easy to hand in my notice at the factory and I had great pleasure in doing so! Mr Simm seemed to be wearing a slightly different hat and he was quite polite as he asked me why I wanted to leave this wonderful firm to go in the building trade for much less money and what didn't I like about Iloman Engineering Company? I explained that I didn't like being 'shut in' every day, that I wanted to work out doors as well, and most of all I didn't like him! At this he went very red in the face, pointed at the door and said there was no more to be said and that I would be sorry! I left feeling somewhat nervous as I remember, but determined to prove him wrong as I'd burnt my boats by telling him to more or less shove his job!

I told my dad when I got home and to my dismay he laughed and said he wondered how long I would stay as he could see that I wasn't happy there. He did say however that although he was very pleased about my going to Skillicorn's, I would be well advised to stick to it this time as he thought I was very lucky to get a second apprenticeship at the late age of 18 and certainly wouldn't get another chance as I would be too old. Niels Skillicorn had become a good friend through the bikes and the Peveril Club and I soon got to know his elder brother Bob and remain good friends with them both some forty odd years later. In fact the Skillicorn family were to play a big part in my future life although I was unaware of it all those years ago.

My first road accident - sidecar trials

In the winter of 1965 I took part in my first 'Treasure Hunt' organised for the Peveril Club by Ken Harding, I think, and it was to start at the 'Crescent' on the Wednesday evening club night. I went along in my mum's Morris 1000 Traveller 7299 MN with my mate Stephen Swainston, armed with a torch and a 1" to the mile ordnance map of the island. We were informed by Ken at the 'briefing' that all the clues would be found at the various bridges around the middle part of the island and that we would finish back at the Crescent - in case we should lose our way. It was a very wet October evening and the country roads were covered for the most part with leaves and other debris so a certain amount of caution was called for to say the least. By any stretch of the imagination, a Morris Traveller could never be compared to a rally car and certainly not in the handling stakes, especially when fitted with a set of Michelin 'X' radial tyres! So if we look in hindsight and plus the fact that I was 17 and probably carried away a bit with the occasion, what happened next was probably inevitable. All started off well and we got the first few clues which led to Sir George's Bridge and thence to East Baldwin via Ballaoates, toward the Paper Mill Bridge - read on because this is where we came unstuck! We were going well along past 'Litts', round the bend by the water trough at Poyll Breck and down the slope under the trees toward the bridge when the back end of this ill handling car began to 'hang out' to the left on the steeply cambered road surface. Probably going too fast for the leaf strewn and flooded road surface, I realised that, although I was 'opposite locking' and had the slide fairly well under control, there was just not enough road left for me to straighten up completely before we would surely strike the end of the bridge wall and end in disaster. That's exactly what happened! We struck the wall right between the two headlights, doing no damage at all to the wall but completely smashing up my mum's car! It was well before the days of seat belts and we both suffered severely bruised knees on the solid metal dash board and glove pockets as well as some facial cuts from the broken windscreen as we were thrown forward with the impact. Pushing hard on the steering wheel, I managed to push it through the screen somehow but not before it bruised my chest quite badly and I could hardly breathe, but miraculously we weren't too badly hurt and to our surprise the car had ended up neatly parked to the left of the bridge, in what was then the track leading to the old Paper Mill. Even after this terrific impact, which moved the engine and gearbox back sufficiently to bend the back axle like a banana, I distinctly remember that both the headlights were still working and I switched them off before staggering from the wreck!. Luck would have it that Niels and Nick Corkill were following us in Niels' mum's Mini 590 MAN and they stopped, picked us up and took us to hospital and then they continued in the rally! We were duly checked over in 'Out Patients' and discharged so I then had to break the news to my dad and mum that I had 'bent' the car a bit! And request a lift home - a lesson in eating humble pie and apologising indeed. It took some explaining over the 'phone as to what 'bent' actually meant and when I explained that it was in fact immobilised and needed a suspended tow, dad and Howard began to get the gist of what had happened. They set off from home in the old Morris Tonner, on what was to be one of it's last 'breakdown' trips and by this time the rain had turned to snow. By the time they had slung the Traveller on chains suspended under the back of the tipper body and lifted it up for the journey home, they were, to say the least, not too pleased with me and completely soaked. I have to say that I received more than my fair share of ribbing and I was cursed on more than one occasion during the following months as a whole new front section was fitted to the car at nights and weekends. One result of that night which bothers me to this very day is the painful state of my knees as they have never been right since their meeting with the steel fascia panel of the Morris Minor and I often wonder what lasting effect, if any, my friend Steve Swainston has suffered over the years from his injuries which were similar to my own. He and his family moved away to Cheltenham in Gloucestershire some time later in the sixties and I haven't heard of him since then. Steve bought the very first new Greeves 'Anglian' trials bike (at the end of 1965 or early 1966) to be brought to the island numbered 695 DMN, a lovely machine which was soon to be followed by a number of similar bikes for the other competitors of the day who could afford them. I was not one of them as I had taken a significant pay cut from £10 per week at Dowty's to £1-19-6d per week in my new job. Such was the differential in engineering and building trade wages. Being very happy in my new job I wasn't too bothered about the money, so when in March 1966 the Peveril Club decided to run a trial at Cornelly Mines for Novices, Veterans and sidecars I was very pleased to be loaned one of these lovely new Greeves 'Anglians' by another good mate Peter Blackburn.

The date 3rd March 1966 holds a lasting memory of great significance in my motor cycling life, as not only did I manage to win the Novice class on the Greeves (149 EMN) but also I had a hand in the construction of one of the sidecars. My financial means at that time had a lot to do with my future pathway through the biking world. It became obvious to me after my ride on the Anglian that my old bike was grossly inferior and not being able to afford a new one, I quite fancied a go at the sidecars which were very cheap to build and seemed like a lot of fun as well.

Howard owned an old Matchless 350 that he had ridden in a few scrambles and it was decided that we would build a sidecar onto it, using the bottom frames of an old school desk for the chassis, some old conduit electrical tubing and an inverted pram for the body work all panelled in with the aluminium sheeting from an old Austin van! I think the wheel was from an old bin cart and used with no suspension but I have to say that the finished article was quite an achievement for us. We made the whole thing entirely without plans or drawings of any kind, in the space of a few hours from Friday night through to Saturday midnight and we had great fun testing it around the yard in the dark until dad shouted at us and told us to get to bed at once or he would put a match to it!

I remember that the day of the event was a lovely sunny one with quite a few spectators showing up to see the 'chairs' of which there were three altogether shared between four crews. The contest was won by the instigator of the sidecar movement in the island Roger Quayle passengered by George Kewley on an ancient A.J.S. 500 which had a 'pukka' but very dated factory built sidecar, with a coach built body (possibly by Watsonian) and a huge 21" side car wheel. It was probably the heaviest of the three but being a '500' they coped well on it. Second were Keith Shimmin and Malcolm Cleator on a 350 A.J.S. with a nicer factory built sidecar (maybe by Swallow) numbered 9952 MN which had belonged to Peter Babb but never trialled by him. Third was our Howard on our own homemade 'Kissack Special', passengered by Phil Tasker and to my certain knowledge they had never ridden it together before setting out in the trial! Its number was 431 EMN and it was registered as the first 'H & D Special' at the Highway Board in Douglas. Fourth were Goo (Gwillin) Owen and George Kewley (yes he was 1st and 4th on the same day!) riding Roger Quayle's bike to make up the numbers and I don't think they had ever ridden it before but George certainly got his money's worth that day. A lot was learned about sidecars and many adjustments were made before the next event, including my solemn vow that I too would build one and turn out at the next trial.

As luck would have it Ken Harding told me that he was clearing out his garage at Market Street and if we would like to come down there were quite a few bargains to be had! Ken was always a kind of 'mentor' to me and put a few opportunities my way and this was to be no exception as we left 'Back Strand Street' with a fair number of spare parts and obsolete but useable old four stroke bikes with little or no difference to our wallets! Probably spending about £10 in total we had a crashed BSA B31, a 600 Panther, a couple of AJS road bikes and various others that I can't recall - what a haul! One of the AJS 350's was a runner so I decided to put a 'chair' onto it and this was again achieved in record time but this time incorporating a 'Flexitor' suspension unit. Cousin

Norman Pallister was to be passenger and he did the first few trials with me until Phil Tasker became 'available' after a disagreement with Howard! I soon became hooked on the sport and Phil continued to be my passenger for the next thirty years which I think may be an all time record in sidecar sport of any kind, especially when in all that time we never had so much as a cross word! This 'outfit' was registered 468 GMN and I later passed the log book on to Charlie Moore and Norman Pallister for their newly acquired Ariel some years on and that became an 'H & D Special' too. We went on to build somewhere in the region of six 'H & D Special' for ourselves and other people and friends and I still use the log book for 500 KMN that was built around a BSA 350 BB32 in 1968. This bike was bought new by Gordon Millward as VMN 362 and in its early days it was 'drowned' in the pond at Cornelly Mines resulting in a bent conrod. Later on it passed to Jack Quayle and to Peter Corrin who eventually sold it to Roger Quayle. Roger knew I was looking for a replacement for the old AJS (which by this time had a Norton 16H engine) and a deal was done at his garage in Alberta Drive, Onchan for the sum of £20.00.

This 350 'Beezer' just suited me, and Phil and myself experienced almost instant success with it by winning the next trial at the 'Arragon' in Santon. Over the next six years we had numerous wins with it including two Centre championships (1971 and 1974) and a fine 3rd place in the 1973 Manx Two Day Trial and for sentimental reasons I still own it today.

Yorkshire

Meanwhile back to 1967 which was a great time for me, my job was great and I really took to it, my social life was real fun and the music of the time was (and remains so for me) the 'best ever' being the 'Flower Power Era'. It was in September that year when I first ventured into West Yorkshire on an unscheduled holiday which sticks in my mind as being one of the most memorable of my life.

It came about quite by chance one Friday evening as I sat with my mates of the time having a pint in the Peveril Hotel near the Sea Terminal. I seem to remember one of the crew men who knew Keith Shimmin, coming into the bar for a pint and saying that he was going to 'clock' on for the midnight sailing to Liverpool. Well - one thing led to another and after someone said they had always wanted to go to Somerset, Keith, adventurous as ever, said 'Why don't we?' Bearing in mind that it was probably about 10pm by that time, there wasn't much time left for planning a trip anywhere but that's what happened next. We rushed home and grabbed a quick suitcase each and told our Mums not to expect us back for a while (a 'while' being an open ended period of time!) and to please advise our employers that we would be away for a few days. When we arrived at the boat it was pretty full up and we were parked at the very top of the spiral ramp and so we were allowed to sleep in the car all the way across which was great but certainly wouldn't be allowed these days. So started a brilliant week's holiday, not in Somerset, but in West Yorkshire instead! We made our way up through Huddersfield, over Nont Sarahs to Brighouse and wound up in Otley (not a Motorway in sight in 1967) to visit an old mate of Keith's called Pete Edmondson. A real 'wheeler dealer' character was Pete, come to think of it he still is and remains a good friend to this day. He took the four of us (who had been able to go on the trip at such short notice) namely Keith, Howard, Phil and myself, in for the night in his bungalow. He explained that his wife had just left him for someone else and that he had his young son Derek and even younger daughter Julie, possibly five and three years old respectively. Pete is a big hearted man and welcomed us to his home and although it was obviously a tough time for him, he simply laughed off his troubles and moved the kids into his room to make way for us. He said years later, that our visit had lightened his mood and helped him to get through the 'worst'. Well I can certainly say that the mood was very 'light' as we went on to visit almost every hostelry in the area. Pete had his own business in the main street in Otley selling new and used motor bikes, mainly trials bikes I remember, but also doing good business in sales and repairs of the wonderful little Honda 50 'step throughs'. Being a dealer meant that if there was a 'wage in it' he would buy and sell literally anything and certainly whilst we were there it was a real eye opener for us! For example, we were only there for a matter of minutes before he had us kitted out in a new white shirt each at a bargain price of 5 bob (25p). The man who lived next door was cutting his grass with one of the brand new 'Flymo' lawnmowers that had recently 'fallen off a lorry' and he was the local policeman called Bobby John. He told me that the Flymo was a great invention and that Pete had been able to get him one 'at the right price'!

Most evenings we would travel up to the Timble Inn high up on the moors between Otley and Blubberhouses and we were pleasantly surprised by the 'elastic' opening times as we had never seen pints pulled 'after hours'. Albeit from under the towel which was placed over the pumps at the official closing time. To cut a long story short, one night ended up as seven nights because we were enjoying ourselves so much and making many new friends along the way. We met most of the top trials and scrambles riders in the area at the time thanks to Pete who organised their company for us throughout the week. We visited 'Post Hill' for a scrambles meeting, Croft for a car race meeting and Halifax speedway for an exciting evening watching the 'stars of the day' Eric and Nigel Boocock. There seemed no end to Pete's energy and he could walk in anywhere as he was so well known .....or so we thought. In actual fact, Pete was such a character that he told us afterwards the he just 'laughed' his way through. A typical example was the night that we visited Halifax Speedway, we paid to get in and went to a seemingly deserted vantage point at the first corner where the 'action' was sure to be and waited for the first race to start. Even now I seem to remember that Pete was standing well back from the barrier and sure enough when the first race began we were in the 'thick of it', in fact the story of the 'town mouse and the country mouse' springs to mind as the memory of us being showered in cinders vividly reappears in my mind. But what a thrill!! We had never seen anything like it and I still love it to this very day. The sheer excitement of the bikes hurtling towards us and peeling off at the last moment without shutting off the throttle but throwing the bikes down on their side and sliding around the corner stays with me even now.

So what if we were showered in cinders and Pete was laughing his head off? What a night out and it got better as behind the main grandstand there was quite a 'posh' club and bar for 'members only' as it said above the door. Well we marched up to the door, at the conclusion of the meeting, behind Pete and he waved his hand to the doorman with a greeting something like 'Good evening John' - 'Just a minute' said 'John' as he looked at four 'country mice' - covered in cinders and following closely in the shadow of this flamboyant character who seemed to know his name - 'Are you a member sir?' to which Peter retorted 'Am I a member? Am I a f......ing member?' followed instantly by hearty laughter and a pat on the back of a somewhat surprised but seemingly delighted 'John', we all walked in behind him. Some minutes later I remember saying to our hero that it was a good job that he was a member here because it seemed fairly exclusive and his reply was that this was the first time he had been here as well - 'So make the most of it before we are asked to leave!'.

We had a wonderful week in Otley with Peter and his new girlfriend Kath, whom he later married and had two more sons with and now lives in Birmingham and through him we met many people who we are still friends or at the very least, still in touch with, all these years later. A few names that spring to mind are Malcolm

Kath and Pete with us at Harefield Hall

and Gerald Rathmell, Paul England, Dave Carr, John 'Killer' Kendrew, Terry Wright, Peter 'Torsten' Jarman and Hedley Cockshott.

In fact one memorable occasion was the 'signing up' of a very young Malcolm Rathmell to the Greeves Factory team when Pete organised Bill Brooker to come up to Yorkshire and see his protégé. Celebrations took place afterwards with a visit to 'Harefield Hall' at Pately Bridge and I remember Malcolm driving his girlfriend's red Triumph Spitfire up to Pately despite the fact that he was only sixteen at the time and as such under age to hold a driving licence!

Those were happy days indeed, with so much fun and the wonderful music of the 'flower power' era ringing in our ears to add to the magic as well but like any other good time it's all over too quickly and it's back to work, with I may add, empty pockets.

From engineer to joiner

By this time I was about a year into my apprenticeship and really enjoying it, I had learned a lot from the numerous good tradesmen and labourers and Mike Corris the new digger driver as he took over from Dickie Moore. This change of staff came about one day at the site of the new Ballachrink housing scheme where we were employed on the building of fifty two new dwellings and two shops. I remember a wet and cold winter on this large site where Reg Latham was the foreman and 'presided' over the site from his site office which was a small wood hut about the size of a hen house! Near to the general store now operated by Ernie Russell, an excavation was made to make a sewer connection and I think Dickie who was the digger driver at the time had a disagreement with Bob Skillicorn senior. This grew into a full blown row in the middle of the road which resulted in Dickie telling 'old' Bob to shove his job 'up his ass!'. To this Bob retaliated by telling Dickie that in that case he had better find somewhere else to live as if he no longer worked for the firm then he no longer lived in a Skillicorn house in Church Avenue either! Harsh words indeed in the heat of the moment but I seem to remember that when things cooled down a bit the next day, Dickie stayed in the house for a while but he did leave his job and went back to his former trade as butcher/slaughterman at the abbatoir in Lake Road. His job was taken by Mike Corris and I struck up a friendship with him and would give him lifts to and from the various sites with fuel etc. when necessary. Mike would let me operate the J.C.B. and showed me a lot of useful tips which have come in very handy over the years since then when operating my own machines.

At this time I was teamed up with Buster Kennish and John Looney (joiner and his apprentice) and a very good 'all rounder' joiner George Gregson. We were roofing the first six houses on a site adjacent to the shop. These six were for the use of Dowty 'key' workers at the nearby factory that I had just left and I wondered that maybe I hadn't got away from it at all! The roofs were of a very heavy construction unlike today where lightweight 'Hydro-Air' trusses would be used. Instead, we were building in the old way, with individual spars each cut from a pattern with hand saws, with a plum cut at the top and a 'bird mouth' at the wall plate. This alone was a laborious task in the middle of winter with soaking wet 3" x 2" timber and hand saws which demanded frequent sharpening and lots of 'elbow grease' to power them. The ridge boards were 'scarf' jointed and wedged and the huge 10" x 3" purlins were chamfered on the spar side with a sharp axe and dressed up with jack planes - all this in cold wet weather and not an electric socket in sight! Also in the middle of the roof of each house was a huge 'principal' truss made of tanalised timber by Quiggin & Co and these were something of a nightmare to haul up onto the wallplates with a team of about six men with ropes, such was the weight of them and not a crane in sight. My mate George Gregson, a man of about 45 at the time or possibly 50 yrs of age was a very able man and taught me a lot, including a very valuable piece of 'wisdom' that I still laugh about today. He had been 'through the mill' and had worked for many years at Blackpool Pleasure Beach and on the railways in Lancashire, his native land, before settling in Begoade Road with his wife Jessie. I had never before worked with a man who could manage to introduce as many swear words into a sentence and one such story that he often told me was something like "Nineteen thirty 'effing seven lad, watter coming outa 'effing lace holes of me 'effing boots! Not any more lad let get in outa 'effing rain!" This would often be said on the dark winter days of wind and rain. George had been to numerous driving schools in a bid for a licence which would ease his plight of the daily walk up and down the Whitebridge Hill and he explained to me that he had bought a little Morris 8 to learn in. He also explained that this was a replacement for his Volkswagen Beetle which had been written off by another of our joiners John Boyde whom I had not yet met as he was still off work with his injuries. Anyway, George went on to make me an offer of a cooked dinner each day in return for some driving lessons. The plan was that we would go to his house each lunchtime in my van, have some lunch and then he would drive us back in the Morris 8 for work in the afternoon. Great! I thought a welcome change from sandwiches in a draughty hut and it was, as George and Jessie made me most welcome with a lovely cooked meal each day. My first observation was that George, who swore at anything and everything all day at work, suddenly changed as he entered the little kitchen of No 2 Begoade Road! On the removal of his cap and the wiping of his boots he became the perfect gentleman and in the presence of Jessie, he never swore or even raised his voice in the slightest. This would be short lived however as, soon after kissing Jessie on the cheek and bidding her farewell he would replace his cap and when safely out of earshot he would say something appropriate such as "Brr, it's not so 'effing warm lad!"

So, on to the driving lessons. The first one was quite a terrifying experience for me and he went on to tell me that he had had five tests and that it had cost him a " 'effing b'stard fortune up to now!" I think to this day that the driving schools were either not up to the task or they were simply 'taking the mickey' and his money. To cut a long story short, the old Morris 8 took a dreadful hammering every day as we started with the basics and worked our way up. He had no idea whatever about the amount of revs necessary for the changing of gears. The kangaroo start was made an art form by George with his almost total lack of mechanical knowledge and I had to grab the hand brake on more than one occasion but slowly and steadily he got the gears in the right order and eventually got his act together and after about six months teaching he passed his test! He was over the moon and decided to give the little Morris a coat of paint which was a shame really because it was a tidy car finished in it's original factory grey and although a bit faded it certainly looked better than it was destined to in the very near future. Not having a garage of his own in which to perform the transformation, he asked old Mr Beale next door if he could have the use of his small garage to give the car a quick facelift, with a quart tin of black Valspar gloss and an old 3" brush that he had found! Well.

There was no mention of any sandpaper or undercoat or rubbing down or anything like that and with hardly enough room surrounding the car for a small child to squeeze past, he proceeded to apply the paint. All went well, he told me later, until the single 40w light bulb failed and as he had nearly finished he decided to carry on with just the headlights of the car switched on for illumination. Now for anyone who has ever tried this sort of thing, I'm sure that they will agree that the finish can end up rather less than perfect, as indeed was the case with George's Morris 8!! His overalls had more black paint on them than the body work of the car, as he had squeezed his way around it and the vertical panels such as the doors had huge treacle like festoons hanging from them where the unstirred gloss had sagged but in George's own words "There now lad, that looks 'effing better doesn't it?" I think he summed it up quite well.

After some months, the Morris was passed on to a new home and he bought another Volkswagen and I can honestly say that I was quite chuffed to have succeeded with him and his driving skills, where two or three driving schools had failed and I know in return that he and indeed Jessie too, were grateful for my contribution. For my part I will never forget the wonderful hospitality, kindness and friendship that they gave to me on those cold wet winter days.

It was around this time, one afternoon in winter on a very damp and misty day, George and I were fixing fascia board and soffit to the newly cut spar ends on that same 'six block' of houses when we heard an almighty 'bang' from around the area of the Whitebridge Hill. This was followed by almost total silence for some time and then came the bells and sirens of the emergency vehicles as they raced to the scene. It transpired that there had been a dreadful crash at the corner by Ballakilmartin and the entrance to Bibaloe Moar involving a big Mk10 Jaguar and an old 100E Ford van. When the story came out it appeared that the Jag was going at over 100mph down the hill driven by a man called Nikimarr who lived at the then Garwick Hotel (now a private house) and he was quite intoxicated. Later he was charged with causing death by dangerous driving and dealt with accordingly but the tragedy lay in the ruins of the Ford van. I was very upset when I learned of the story because the driver of the van was Tommy Kelly who was a good friend of Ernie Leece's and our family. A brilliant mechanic, Tom was a frequent visitor to our yard often using the facilities of our garage for the motor repairs that he did as 'foreigners' to supplement his wages from W.H. Shimmin & Co of Douglas Promenade where he was employed. It was in this role that he was working when travelling up the hill towards Shimmin's other garage, behind the Liverpool Arms to repair one of their fleet of coaches, when disaster struck. He was accompanied by his apprentice Bobby Douglas and knowing Tom the mood would be jovial and light hearted up to the moment when the car hit them full head on with little or no warning. It was a tragic loss of a very hard working, honest and jovial character who was, as I have said, a great mechanic of the 'old school' and a keen motor cycle racer with some degree of success in events such as the Southern '100'. I didn't know Bobby but the loss of his young life and that of Tommy took me a long time to come to terms with.

Around this time, back in the world of motor cycling, the regular scrambles course used by the Peveril Club was Ballacallin at Patrick, next to Gordon Farm House. In those days, as a young committee member, one of my jobs before each event, was to erect one of the wooden fold up toilet cubicles as a 'Ladies' loo. This was possibly the only 'luxury' provided in those days and it was felt by the committee that we should look into the possibility of providing a tea hut to provide some refreshments at events. Through the generosity of retired farmer Stanley Corlett, who had farmed at Glenville in Onchan for many years, and now lived in a bungalow in Hillberry Road, we were offered free of charge, an almost unused hen house that could be modified for the purpose. At that time, before the building of the Birchill Estate, Stanley's bungalow was the last dwelling on the right hand side of Hillberry Road next to what is now the Beehive Kindergarten, and along with

Niels Skillicorn and 'Waller' Kennish we had little trouble entering the field in 'Skillies' old 'O' type Bedford WMN 649. We parked alongside of the garden wall and with a mighty effort, lifted the small but well made shed onto the wagon, said our 'thankyous' and left, little knowing that soon that field would be covered with bungalows. We took the shed down to the workshop in the old cinema and modified it with a serving window and counter at the front and completed the job by raising the front of the roof so that the girls would be able to stand up inside in relative comfort. Having completed the new tea hut we re-loaded it on the wagon and took it out to Ballacallin where it became a great success and was a real asset to the club for many years to come. It was ably operated by Liz Cain and her friends Lorraine and Bev Blunden and I must admit to having a soft spot for Liz in those days, but I never quite got round to saying anything! From memory I think the old Bedford ran out of petrol on the return journey and our Howard had to bring us a gallon or two to enable us to get home. Running out of 'juice' was quite a common occurrence in those days as many of the older vehicles had either dodgy gauges or even in some cases none at all! These were the last days of the old Ballacallin course because the club was considering the possible purchase of land at Knock Froy at Santon.

Peveril Club and Knock Froy

It brought the end of an era at a good old course where many memorable events had taken place over the years including the Yorkshire versus the Isle of Man events which were fathered by ex works rider Frank Bentham who used his contacts in Yorkshire to bring some good teams over for the Morning Trial/Afternoon Scramble events and then of course the return bout which would take place in Yorkshire. There are so many memories of those days to recall here but one I think deserves a mention is the style laid on by Jack Sweetman as he drifted his D.O.T. in a perfect speedway slide around the front field in view of the majority of the spectators - a real showman!

By this time Goo Owen had formally proposed that we should buy Knock Froy and after some discussion at an E.G.M. at the Crescent Hotel, it was decided to go ahead and buy it from the owner Edwin Moore for around £9,000, I seem to remember. We were full of enthusiasm as we set about ways of raising the balance of the money and through our secretary John Dodsworth we latched on to a very good money spinner. John's brother Peter was involved in the Villiers Hotel and through him we secured a number of Saturday evening 'slots' where we would have a good live rock group such as the Phantoms and they would easily fill the ballroom at 4/- (20p) per head with their superb performance. Our biggest problem at these dances was overcrowding and we were warned by the police more than once, so we genuinely tried to limit the numbers with house full signs and the like but let me just say that when fund raising, it is very hard to turn money away and consequently there wasn't much room to dance - very sexy! On one occasion when it was my turn on the door, the police were adamant that if any more were admitted then they would close us down. This was all very well and we agreed to comply with their wishes, which we endeavoured to do, until confronted by a rather larger than life character called 'Taffy' Sayle. I say 'larger than life' but what I probably means is rotund as 'Taf' who was an

apprentice mason, got stuck in the oak double doors which entered the long bar and ballroom! To be truthful he wasn't 'stuck' in the true sense of the word but rather squashed by his mates trying to push him through from the outside and us trying our best to keep him out in compliance with the police. There was nothing personal in the confrontation as we all knew each other and certainly weren't enemies but the harder his mates pushed him and the more we resisted, he turned first red and then purple in the face as the oak door creaked and bent over his belly under the strain. Poor 'Taf' you may say and he very nearly succeeded in his bid when a rather drunk Phil Tasker who was supposed to be helping us, decided that he should be admitted and began to pull him in! Absolute mayhem ensued with half of our mates trying to stop Phil and reason with him but to no avail and 'Taf's' mates who were all big lads as well, equally determined to join the dance from their side! I shudder to think what might have happened if the police had not made a return visit and restored the status quo but to the best of my knowledge this was the only 'skirmish' I can remember during these happy and relatively trouble free dances.

We were certainly on to a good thing here which was definitely a 'closed shop situation' and a licence to print money with no other comparable venue available for young people in Douglas on a Saturday night. The only other club that got a 'look in' at the Villiers were Douglas Rugby Club who, through their connection with Peter Dodsworth, were able to fill the remaining 'slots' to raise money for their new clubhouse at Port-e-Chee Meadow.

So the purchase of Knock Froy went ahead and we moved all the rope and stakes from Ballacallin along with the little tea hut and prepared for the first event there. It was resolved that we build a block of toilets as a priority and I volunteered to engineer it! You may say never volunteer for anything but I have to say that I enjoyed most of it and with the help of my dad we drew a sketch plan of the toilets and septic tank and provision for a large Jurby Hut to be annexed to the scheme at a later date. Nick Corkill worked as an architectural technician and I asked him to transfer the plan onto proper planning paper so we could submit it to the planning committee, this achieved we were granted the necessary permission to go ahead. With the generous loan of Skillicorn's J.C.B. and the enthusiastic help of Mike Corris who, incidentally, has helped many clubs absolutely free of charge over the years, we did the necessary excavating for the footing, sewer trench and septic tank in record time. I then hauled the bricks from Peel brickworks on our old Commer and likewise, the necessary sand and gravel, all tipped on site with the old hand screw tipper which was a real energy sapper! We had working parties on Wednesday nights to concrete the base of the toilets and these were good fun as we would end up across the road at the old Alex Inn for a couple of pints afterwards. With this well on the way it was time for Stuey Clague, who is in my opinion one of the best bricklayers in the island, to brick up the double chamber septic tank and associated man holes in readiness for my old workmate Billy 'Boofah' Brew. Billy laid the sewer in the old 'ware' or vitreous enamel pipes and to the best of my knowledge, some 38 years later, it has never been touched, given any trouble or needed any attention. The toilets were then built, again in Peel brick, with Stuey on the 'trowel' and Norman Pallister mixing for him. I think it would be the following winter when we added the base for a Jurby hut some 55ft long by 18ft wide, if I remember rightly, and once the surrounding brickwork was up, the task of filling the base with hardcore began. Many tons of rubble were needed for this and bit by bit we managed to fill up to the necessary height and compact it ready for the membrane and concrete. A hut was eventually purchased for about £120 if my recollection of the time is correct, and Skillicorn's were paid for the dismantling at Jurby and re-erection on site. This took about a week I think with Maurice Rhodes, Peter Crellin and myself travelling down each day and bringing a load home at night. We used the new Ford wagon 376 KMN as scaffold to take it down and loaded the sections onto a small Bedford TK flatdeck which belonged I think to John Yates. Anyway, we soon had the large

weather board hut rebuilt and it stood till the 1980's when it was replaced with the present building on the same footing.

One funny occasion springs to mind about Ralph Lowey and myself and the people who lived in a nearby cottage when we joined up the water supply one day. I remember it was a lovely sunny day and Ralph and I started digging near the cottage to find the water supply which we were assured would be there! Well we dug for quite some time before we eventually found it but that didn't matter at all as we were hilariously entertained by eaves dropping on the conversation taking place in the kitchen next to us courtesy of an open window. The conversation between the two rather large and rotund women was indeed comical as is sometimes the case with mother and daughter and it went something like:-

"Yer a bit smelly Tish and I think we should get some washin done"

"Deeow" replied Tish "I can't be bothered". Then mother in a more stern voice - "You just listen to me yer lazy beggar and get yer knickers arf an put them in the wash"

"No" Tish retorted "I won't - you can't make me!"

"Damn it" said Mother " Yer stinkin, now just you do what am telling yer or yer'l be forrit when 'he' comes home cos al tell 'im!"

"Yer wouldn't dare" was the reply.

I have to say that we were laughing so much by this time that they must have heard us and the window was slammed shut with some force. Sadly, we never did find out the rest of the dialogue but 'Mother' must have won the day because sometime later there was a full washing line with a few pairs of huge old fashioned 'big' knickers or 'dung hampers' as they are sometimes known, proudly fluttering in the breeze.

Tim Sutherland   Stuey Clague   Ian Gale Dennis Christian   Alan Newton   Chris Kennaugh   Peter Blackburn   Geoff Cannell
The line up of new Montesas outside 'The Hawthorn' - 1970

Soon after this we got an electricity supply connected as well as the water and Knock Froy was 'up and running'. I seem to remember that 'Big Dennis' Christian acquired a full size snooker table from somewhere and it was stored for quite a while in the back of an old 'Cadbury Cakes' van that Jasper Cain had donated to the 'cause' but although a great idea the snooker table was never used.

It would be around this time that Ralph Lowey had a heart attack and stood down as chairman although he did make a remarkable recovery and became a very fit cyclist. He made a terrific contribution to the Peveril Club, spending most of his spare time at Knock Froy 'beavering' away at all manner of jobs that needed doing and probably wouldn't have got done without him. Ralph was a big hearted man in so many ways and indeed his generosity caused me to be ashamed of myself on one occasion.

I had been doing my best to acquire hardcore as I have said and spent many hours hauling and delivering load after load of it on the site when one day I discovered someone removing a load I had just previously tipped. Well I wasn't pleased to say the least, and the man (who shall be nameless) assured me that he had Ralph's full permission to take 'as much as he liked'. I suppose I was a hot headed young bugger in those days and when Ralph confirmed the man's story was true then I blew my top at him.

In hindsight (which is a wonderful thing) I wish to this day that I hadn't shouted so much and clearly upset this kind and generous man that had done so much good for the club. However, it was out in the heat of the moment as so many things are in those circumstances and it was Dennis Christian who had a few words of wisdom for me and a quiet word in my ear! He pointed out to me that I should show some respect for an older (than me) man in Ralph's position as not only was he the chairman of the Club but that I should think twice next time before I fell out with such a good man, especially over five tons of 'paltry' hardcore. He was of course right and after I had made a full and sincere apology to Ralph, I actually thanked Dennis for my 'bollocking' and his useful lesson in the 'university of life', because of this I am very pleased to say that, largely thanks to Dennis, I remained good friends with Ralph for some thirty or more years until his untimely death.

Dennis Christian lost his father in the aforementioned Winter Hill air crash and later lost his sister in a car crash at the Railway Bridge by the Arragon in Santon, but despite these tragic setbacks, he was always a somewhat mischievous man with a wicked smile, wonderful deep laugh and great sense of humour. He had a motorcycle garage in Derby Square, ably assisted by Richard Crossley and around 1969 - 70 he sold a lot of the new Montesa Cota trials bikes to the local trials fraternity. He was also responsible for the beginning of the schoolboy tuition on motorbikes and taught many of today's riders the basics. Each Saturday morning Dennis would arrive at Knock Froy in his green Mini Pickup loaded down with old bikes for the youngsters to learn on and great fun would follow for the next hour or so. Some had riding gear such as a helmet and gloves but most had to wait their turn and use an old helmet or two that Dennis would bring with him. Most, if not all, wore wellies, as in those days - 35 years ago there was no such thing as the tailor made childrens' riding gear and boots like today. No doubt it would be frowned on today for lack of safety but Dennis's enthusiasm conquered all that, he would sit a young lad on a bike and with the very minimum of instructions i.e. 'that's the clutch, that's the brake and that....makes it go faster', with this he would twist the boy's wrist on the throttle, pat him on the back and off he would go! Needless to say some fell off and some didn't but usually by lunchtime, every one could ride. Well after a fashion anyway! I had the dubious honour on many of these mornings, to help Dennis and I can honestly say it was a lot of fun, with little or no lasting injuries and even today some of those boys from all those years ago approach me and say 'Do you remember me?' Needless to say, I do remember some of them that have followed the motor cycling scene through the years but there are others who surprise me as their obvious joy shines through when they recall those happy days. Two names that spring to mind are Davy Craine (now Peveril Chariman) and 'Ronnie' Russell the M.G.P. star.

An apprentice in the sixties

With the previous mention of the old cinema in Royal Avenue in Onchan, this building brings back many happy memories for me. With all the seating removed and the floor levels altered, it made a wonderful workshop and store, being so airy and light inside (a bit cold in winter perhaps) with plenty of room for everything under one roof. Many features of the cinema were still intact such as the projection room with souvenirs lying around like the carbon rods that I think were used to provide the bright light necessary to show the films of the day. A huge electric motor and fan were positioned high up in the vast roof space for the extraction of smoke and one or two of the 'art deco' uplighters' or half round 'shell like' wall lights had survived the conversion and still worked. The place had superb facilities with proper 'ladies' and 'gents' toilets still in good condition. Up at the front of the building, near what had been the foyer there were 'proper' toilets for what was now the general office of the firm. This fronted onto Royal Avenue and made a sort of grand entrance to the building with a shop front in the middle of the façade and a smaller shop on the left hand side. The office was run by Harry Berry, ably assisted by Ann Inston who was a former pupil of Braddan School with me. Harry was quite a good architect and drew up many of the plans for the bungalows that the firm was building at the time around the Onchan area i.e. Snaefell Crescent and the new Birchill estate. I think he did this as a sideline as he was always kept busy in the office with the day to day running of things which would include the time sheets and wages of up to eighty staff at that time. Ann was a nice girl and good at her job, as well as brightening up the office when us young lads came in. She was later joined by Paddy Kennish who was a sister of my mate at the time 'Waller'Kennish and daughter of one of the only survivors of the awful Winter Hill air crash, Fred and Connie his wife. Another feature of the old cinema to survive the conversion was the stage and I remember when a very young John

Quirk, who had just joined the firm, asked why did we have the stage, I told him that it had been retained for our annual concert. This he readily believed and started to question me about who would take part in the show. Well, one thing led to another and with a sly wink here and there, most of the other men latched on and went along with the ruse, telling young Quirky that they were rehearsing their various party pieces for the big night! Freddie Farrar, the electrician was going to play his banjo and ukulele, Joe Brown the painter was going to sing a song, I was doing a recitation and so on. So it went on and young John was to be seen busy rehearsing a tap dance routine, at which I have to admit, he was very good, but needless to say the 'concert' never took place but it provided a lot of amusement and to this day John still does a mean tap dance routine!

There was a big area downstairs in the building where the vast array of necessary equipment was stored as in those days there was no such thing as 'plant hire' as today. This area and indeed the janitorial needs of the firm, was ably looked after by Benny Cowell who was reputedly the longest serving employee in the place who had been there some forty odd years. Benny was caretaker, tea maker, sweeper up etc and made the worst tea I have ever tasted! He used to boil the kettle on an old gas stove which had been left over from the days when that area was used by the Onchan Scouts and he would then brew the tea in a huge old tea pot adding the sugar and milk and stirring the whole lot up with an old stick! This was then offered to all on a take it or leave it basis and I seem to remember some of the older men actually enjoyed it! I didn't share their enthusiasm for this brown, stewed tasting, sweet and treacle like concoction and when Benny was absent one day, I threw the stick away and actually cleaned out the old teapot. Personally, I thought the tea tasted much better but when Benny returned he found another stick and the status quo was restored - ugh! There was lots of 'banter' in the 'Brew Hut' as it was known, often becoming a bit heated when Hughie Condra and Ernie Redpath would cross swords with their Laxey area politics and opposing views on life! Various delivery drivers would join us for 'brew' such as Sid Cowin and Jack Scarffe from Douglas Steam Saw Mills and drivers from N.R. Corlett and Ferguson and Harveys and occasionally Quiggin and Co.

Next to this stores area, the cement, air compressor and other plant such as concrete vibrator and extension ladders were stored leaving just enough room for the vehicles to be garaged overnight. These would include the two Bedford Wagons WMN 649, the older of the two which was driven at that time by Jimmy Craige which would go in first. That would be followed by 2494 MN, the green 'A' type driven by Terry Moffitt and then the remaining space would be occupied by one of the vans. When I joined the firm the vans were smartly painted in a 'drab' grey colour by Joe Brown and lettered by Barry Perkins the sign writer. My favourite was the Ford Thames 15cwt 3827 MN which would be driven on deliveries in the day time by Jimmy 'Locker' Hayes but taken home at night by Jimmy Craige as he dropped off the 'troops' around the Douglas area, usually with ten or twelve men in the back. The other van used for works transport was the ex Crosby Wholesalers Bedford C.A. van 2371 MN and this would be taken to and from Onchan each day by Bobby Ryan, a Scots man who was a labourer at that time. Both these vehicles would be considered by modern standards to be 'over loaded' each morning and evening as the numbers inside were known to reach as many as 18 on some occasions! In my opinion Bobby Ryan was never a great driver and he would often depress the clutch and rely on the brakes alone when descending hills. Indeed he nearly came unstuck one day at the bottom of the very steep Crellin's Hill in Douglas and arrived at Royal Avenue with a very pale and ashen face having suffered a burst brake pipe albeit at the halt sign at the foot of the hill and I shudder to think what could have happened had it been nearer the top with a van loaded with men on their way to work!

There was also the Ford Anglia Van 5921 MN used by Niels and a blue Anglia Estate 979 DMN used by 'young' Bob and the Riley Elf 751 FMN of 'Old Bob'. It is perhaps worth a mention that 'Old Bob' or 'Mr' Skillicorn (as he insisted on from the younger members of staff) used to drive at a great rate of knots and often scared the life out of anyone that he gave a lift to, out to a job or site. He would take great delight in surprising unwary men who had perhaps run over their allotted break time by a few minutes, by screeching to a halt in the little maroon Riley and dashing in to the brew hut to see who he could catch! And woe betide anyone who hadn't scarpered when they saw him coming. He would also swop over from the Elf to his other car which was a beige and cream Riley 4/72 numbered 1234 MN, probably around mid day when he knew the men would be on the look out for the Elf, real cat and mouse stuff! I thought he was a good boss, although he had a grumpy head on him sometimes and I had the greatest respect for him and the fairness he usually managed to achieve when his patience must have been sorely tested.

One great character who surely did try his patience was our beloved Percy Kneen. Percy had taken over Jimmy Craig's red Bedford 'O' type (when Jim's back cried 'enough' of the almost rigid suspension) and he christened it the 'Old Cherokee' after the Red Indian tribe. He was a very good driver of the 'old school' and found the 'crash' gear box and double-de-clutching to be no bother at all, in fact I think he thought the world of the old wagon and could often be heard talking to it! He had come to us for the winter as he drove coaches in the summer for W.H. Shimmin's on the promenade and my first thoughts of Percy would be at the Peveril Hotel job in the winter of 1966-67. I was there with Bobby Fick working on the basement conversion for the cellar bar and disco and also on the ground floor for the Bier Kellar. One day Percy arrived in the wagon with the big 60ft extension ladder tied on the top and he parked it outside the entrance near to the new roundabout with the palm trees on. Well in those days the roundabout was in a different position than today, being much closer to the corner which is now called 'Jeffersons', leaving possibly one lane of traffic access from Peveril Square onto the promenade. This was all well and good while normal size vehicles went by as they could easily pass under the ladder which was overhanging the front of the old wagon by probably as much as five or six feet. However it was a different matter when a double decker Corporation bus came along and being unable to pass by effectively stopped all the traffic and caused a huge queue all the way back up Lord Street and the Quayside. Up to now I have omitted to mention that Percy had perhaps a bit of a drink problem and had gone off with the key of the wagon in his pocket to seek a drink and a warm on this cold winter afternoon. Not too bad you may say? By this time the police were involved and had rung the workshop to resolve the situation and 'Old Bob' swung into action arriving at break neck speed and looking for 'KNEEN'!. Bobby Fick and myself were oblivious to the goings on outside and only when Bob 'Senior' came in to look for 'KNEEN' (as he almost screamed the man's name) were we aware of the situation. We untied the ladder and pulled it back to allow the bus to pass by and things calmed down a bit. Not so 'Old Bob' I have to say and the last words I heard him say as he left were something like "That's it! He's sacked when I catch him!"

I think Percy was in the Regent (now the Admirals Rest) and was unaware of the whole episode but arriving at work the following day however, some paces behind his long suffering wife who had come to plead with 'Mr' Skillicorn. The result of the tearful plea from Mrs Kneen (who had a large family to care for) was that after a 'mother and father of a bollocking' in front of the entire workforce, Percy was allowed to keep his job, but only just!

Episodes like this one and a big loss of money at the Peveril when the Hotel company went bust, took their toll on Bob and his health suffered badly because of it. In fact soon after this he decided to take things a bit easier and go on a cruise with his lovely wife Nora, but sadly and tragically for her, only a short way into the holiday, he died and was buried at sea. I remember shortly afterwards, a memorial service was held in St Peter's Church in Onchan and the place was absolutely packed to the rafters, with some outside as well such was the esteem in which he was held, a sad loss.

I was working at the old Howstrake holiday camp with Herbie Minnis and Ray Teare at the time and I remember being on the roof of the two storey chalet block (which housed a fine snooker and billiard saloon on the ground floor) when we saw the 'boat' leaving the bay at 9.00am on the day of his departure for the cruise. Whether or not Bob and Nora were on that sailing I don't know, they may have flown away to meet the cruise ship, but amid laughter and wry comments that day I was sent to put the kettle on because there would be no flying visit from the little Riley Elf for the next few weeks at least! Little did we know that we would never see him again.

I have many memories of the Ballachrink housing scheme and apart from the appalling weather, I have to say that they were mostly of a humorous nature.

The weather was bitterly cold that winter of 1966-1967 and I grew a beard to keep warm and I had to use my Greeves Trials bike to get to work when the snow made it impossible to use my Morris `1000' Van (324 FMN) but on the whole it was most enjoyable and I met some real characters. Reg Latham really taught me a lot and took me under his wing and this came about partly because of his reluctance to drive the van and asked me to chauffeur him around as he couldn't master the column change on the Bedford 2371 MN. This led to lots of handy tips and tricks of the trade that he shared with me and has stood me in good stead ever since when taking levels and 'setting out' houses and buildings in general. He was not infallible however, and one day while setting out a block of ten houses at the top of the site and on stopping for a break I was quite surprised to hear him muttering to himself that there were only nine houses! When questioned on the matter, he told me that 'we' had lost a house and despite my only having held the 'silly' end of the tape, he insisted that I was half to blame! It was quite a topic of fun for some days amongst the men and Reg got quite shirty about the many wry and witty comments that were to follow as we painstakingly re-positioned the whole block peg by peg! Ironically it was in one of the houses in this same terrace some months later that Reg got a big surprise that I think in hindsight, could have given him a heart attack!

The houses were nearing completion and as was the custom, we would have our lunch breaks or 'brew' in the nearest house that was reasonably weather tight and draught proof, until the decorators moved in and they moved us out and so on along the terrace. The men would sit around the room on whatever makeshift seat they could find, often an upturned bucket or paint tin or saw block, or maybe a bag of cement or similar would be pressed into service. Well to cut a long story short, some of the lads caught an old jackdaw with a broken wing and put it inside Reg's holdall bag with his old flask and sandwiches. So at ten o'clock when he blew the whistle for 'brew' we sat down and Reg sat on an empty paint tin topped with an off cut of floor board and placed his bag between his knees….. he drew back the zip and all hell broke loose as the terrified jackdaw leapt out flapping its wing in Reg's face as he yelled out some unprintable words and fell over backwards off his seat! It really was very funny at the time but looking back I suppose it could have ended in a very different way if Reg hadn't been so tough, as he was already well into his sixties!

While things were running smoothly Reg would claim any credit or pats on the back, but if there was a snag he would hastily employ the royal 'we' to spread the blame onto the nearest scapegoat that he could find. One such incident comes to mind with the memory of a joiner called Harold Jones who was possibly the first man on site that I ever remember wearing gloves. These days, of course, the wearing of gloves at work is commonplace, but in those far off days, forty odd years ago, no one wore them as it was considered 'soft' and anyway they weren't readily available. So Harold could be considered to be a bit of a rebel! He used to get up Reg's nose as he didn't readily agree with him or his methods which he considered to be completely out of date, such as the use of scaffold 'cripples' which were already banned in the UK from where he had just come! It was inevitable that he wouldn't reign long with his

attitude towards Reg and sure enough one day, as Reg and myself set off down the road in the van, Reg spotted him leaning on a wall and said to me "If 'gloves' is still leaning on that wall when we get back from the workshop, we will have to sack him!" Sure enough, on our return a little while later Harold or 'gloves' as Reg called him was still in situ. "Stop the van" said Reg, "and come and help me sack him!". Well, moral support is one thing but I kept well out of the way as Reg got within shouting distance yelling 'You're sacked! …… .That's it Jones, you're sacked!". This was taken on the chin by an irate Harold who retorted with some unprintable language but better still he started to chase Reggie at full speed across the site towards the refuge of the little site office threatening to pull his head off him! Safely inside, Reg locked the door till things calmed down a bit and emerged some time later after Harold had left the site! To be fair to Harold, I have to say, that on many of his points he was absolutely right (I'm not sure about the gloves though!) and I think he'd had enough of working outside in the bad weather anyway.

On the whole I would say that the site ran well, despite the occasional sacking or cock up which seem almost inevitable and unlike today, where nearly everyone is sub-contracted, a large percentage of the men were directly employed by J.T. Skillicorn Ltd. The late sixties did see the start of the subcontractor or 'lump' worker however and beside the plumbers and electrical contractors there were bricklayers and joiners working on 'lump sum' payment. The plumbing was undertaken by Alan Corlett and his men, ably led by a great character Alfie Cowell, who had two apprentices - Charles (Charlie) Lord and Vic Price. I also remember a Scotsman Andy Reid. The electrical contractor was Willie Craig from Royal Avenue in Onchan, who was island snooker champion on many occasions. I don't however recall the names of his men who worked on Ballachrink at the time. Billy Cain and Mike Creer were joinery contractors and they did some of the blocks of houses 'on the lump' along with Ian Carter who worked with them. I remember that they had an electric saw and an extension lead to a house across the road, 'what 'ingenuity!' I was in awe of them as the only machinery we had consisted of an ancient 'porta'saw' with a big J.A.P. engine on it. It was next to useless really as the fence was missing so the cuts had to be made 'freehand'and that of course depended on whether or not the engine would start in the first place! Needless to say it didn't get used much and was a great knuckle skinner when swinging the starting handle as it would spit back through the carburettor and reverse the direction of the handle very rapidly trapping the knuckles of the right hand as it did so! Billy and Mike were well organised and made rapid progress with their power tools compared to our effort with the handsaws! They later went on to become building contractors in their own right with a workshop in Laxey.

Another 'lump' gang of joiners was the partnership of Peter Crellin and Maurice Rhodes who also were well organised and worked well together.

Plastering contractors were Mills Brothers, Bernie (who later ran the Douglas Carnival for many years) and his brother Freddie, along with some notable characters, both plasterers and labourers alike, such as Danny 'the chin' Quayle, who, as his nickname suggests had a prominent chin! I remember Danny coming to work in an immaculate King William's College uniform that he had acquired at a jumble sale, complete with scarf and cap and I have to say, that he looked very smart and resembled a comedian of the day called Cardew Robinson ... that is for the first half hour! The thistle plaster and general dirt of the site soon changed all that but he got good 'mileage' out of that uniform despite some dirty looks from some older gentlemen who were, presumably, old boys of the College.

It is probably worth a mention that in those days 'proper' work clothes such as today's reflective gear and smart overalls were not so readily available or even affordable, so many men could be seen going to work dressed as firemen, army sergeants or bus driver's or what ever, depending on what was available from the likes of the 'Exchange and Mart' or in the case of Danny, the nearest jumble sale. If you did have enough money, Osborns in Fort Street was the place to go for the necessary Blue Bolenium bib and brace overalls that were required as the joiner's uniform and I have seen one or two apprentices sent home again as they were 'improperly dressed'. There was also Percy Crellin in John Street, Jimmy Lindsay at Quines Corner and of course Newsons on the Quay, who are still trading now and are still selling working clothing. The jumble sale however seems to be a thing of the past and no longer needed to clothe the worker or, as in many cases, needy families as well.

The brickwork on the site was started by the Goldsmith Brothers, Billy and Bobby, with their labourer Harold 'Jakes' Beattie, but as the site progressed Birch Brothers, who were a much larger gang, did the majority of the work. Roy Birch and his brother Tony led the gang, in a happy and organised way, with Roy's son Keith as the apprentice, labourers and expert hod carriers, George 'Jacko' Teare, John Marlow and Ronnie Hannah and brickie Eddie Lewthwaite.

Our own painter Joe Brown from Laxey carried out all the glazing to the 52 properties almost single handed with just some help from his teenage son Charlie in the evenings. In these days before double glazing had really established a foothold, 'Big' Joe cut all the glass at the cinema workshop and glazed a house at a time as they neared completion. It is of interest that Joe won the Parish Walk in 1963 with little or no practice, after someone said that a previous winner Stan Cleator had done really well, I think Stan was one of Joe's in-laws and not to be out done, Joe said it was no 'big deal' and that 'if Stan could do it then he could do it!' He was told to put his money where his mouth was and that's just what he did - what a man, and all on 40 'Park Drive' a day! Joe and Norah's son Charlie went on to serve his time with J.T. Skillicorn's as a joiner but was tragically killed on a motor cycle accident at Ballanorris Farm on the Southern 100 course whilst still very young.

I had lots of fun with Joe and on many winter days, if working together and in the Laxey area,we would go to his house at Gretch Veg for a spot of very welcome hot dinner and I have to say that this was when I first tried 'Batchelors Bigga' peas which I still like today - thank you Joe and Norah!

It has probably become obvious by now that I was a very well fed apprentice - and it's true - I was, thanks to the Gregsons, the Quirks and the Browns - thank you all!

The old cinema was a very busy workshop in those days producing some fine work at the hands of some of the best joiners I have ever seen. I don't think I could put these fine tradesmen into any order of merit as they would all be 'star' men, possibly with one or two with outstanding ability not only as 'all rounders' but brilliant machinists as well. Undoubtedly Harry Jackson was one such maestro! A brilliant all round joiner whether out on a roofing job, making a flight of stairs or setting machines to produce the finest finish possible. A typical example of his work would be the beautiful roulette tables manufactured in the workshop for the Crockfords Organisation who ran the Palace Casino at the time. I'm not sure how many of these tables were made, possibly a dozen or so and not for the Douglas Casino but for a cruise liner on which Crockfords had the gambling concession. They were a work of art made mostly of 'Iroko' with fancy pedestal type legs or base of a very heavy nature for stability and the top designed with an alcove or niche for the croupier to stand next to the wheel. They looked splendid when finished with fine French polish on the woodwork by Ralph Fielding, and an upholstered arm rest for the punters on three sides to compliment the green baize gaming surface, which were expertly tailored by Tommy Quine the upholsterer.

It was one of my jobs to collect Ralph and Tom each day as neither could drive and I remember calling for Tom at his upstairs workroom above the old Salisbury Garage in Fort Street. It was a gloomy place without much light but always seemed warm from the little fireplace next to which Tommy would be sitting awaiting my arrival. The place seemed to me to be in total disarray and chaos with half finished chairs everywhere and with lots of empty bottles lying around. These bottles apparently were a vital part of Tom's tool kit as he

needed a drink before he started! Despite this he turned out some fine work and was a real character.

Harry Jackson meanwhile is now around 80 years of age and has hardly changed in appearance in the forty odd years that I have known him, truly a very fit and able man and it is always nice to meet him in Onchan village.

Another good man I sometimes see around the village is Alan Stone. I worked with Alan on many occasions but have to say I never found it easy! I think he himself would agree that there was a bit of a clash of wills! I suppose we were both headstrong and I was probably a bit cheeky to him resulting in some 'differences of opinion', one of which scared me half to death!

We were given the job to replace the deck boarding on a brewery wagon, a Ford Thames 'Trader' model and after some disagreement on the method of working things got a bit 'heated' and after I expressed my full and frank opinion I started to run as Alan chased after me with his axe! I seem to remember running down Royal Avenue and thinking to myself that I could probably slow down a bit by now as the age difference and fitness would be telling on Alan by now and that he would be 'cooling off' a bit - not so! As I glanced over my shoulder he was right behind me with the axe held high and a look of rage on his face! I continued running as fast as I could and eventually he gave up the chase with the outcome that he didn't speak to me for a while and that I certainly never gave him any more cheek! Doug Quayle, one of the other top joiners and father of fellow apprentice Lyn, calmed the situation down a bit and helped me to finish off the wagon as it had to be returned to the brewery that night. I think the Registration was 7705 MN and I enjoyed driving it back to the garage behind the Falcon Cliff Hotel where the cooper worked repairing all the barrels at the time, before the days of the aluminium kegs.

I mentioned that Doug Quayle had calmed things down a bit and he had a nice mild mannered approach to things in general which certainly helped. I enjoyed working with Doug over a number of years and as with so many of these tradesmen, I learned a lot and not just about the job itself but about life as well. Doug was later to become general foreman at the new Stoney Road School site which was later named Ballaquayle Infants School. It was in the winter of 1970 I think and it seemingly rained every day. It turned the whole site into a quagmire making the necessary shuttering work for the base slab very difficult, as previously the site had been used over a number of years, as a tip and was quite unstable for propping and securing the shuttering. I think the bad weather and mud and the wearing of oil skins and wellies nearly every day made me stop and think 'Why am I doing this?' These thoughts would come to the fore everytime a lorry would arrive at the site and I could feel the warm air from the cosy cabs as the driver's alighted with their delivery notes and I, soaking wet, would take the docket from them and envy their job - the other man's grass is always greener! At that time the yellow fleet of Readymix wagons of Wright Aggregates ruled the roost in the world of concrete and their 'flagship' was the nearly new A.E.C. 'Marshall' six wheeler MAN 509 driven by Kenny Moore. Kenny was a very good driver who could manage to get in and out of anywhere without fuss and I never remember his being stuck in the difficult conditions. He had an unfortunate impediment of speech caused by a cleft palate or - 'hair-lip' and his constant companion in the cab was an old mongrel dog. On occasions when nature called, the dog would hop out of the wagon and have a sniff around, usually followed by a whistle from Kenny and a few words that sounded like 'Where's that ukken dawg gawne now!' Skillicorn's had by this time bought a new Ford D800 Tipper 193 PMN and I jumped at the opportunity to take my H.G.V. test on this fine new truck which was driven by John Quilliam. This lorry did many miles for the firm and I eventually bought it myself some twenty years later for my own business. I also bought MAN 509 the A.E.C. and owned that for a few years - coincidence maybe? A kind man, sadly Doug died young whilst still in his fifties, a sad loss.

Around this time in the summer of 1968 I spent a lot of time with my good mate Michael (Waller) Kennish and we spent most nights around Douglas at the many venues where in those days, things were really buzzing with holiday makers. These nights included the Douglas Head Hotel where Cecil Cowell was landlord and he had, as his chief 'Bouncer', my mate Mike Corris. This made for some good entertainment not only from the superb groups playing but from some of Cecil's antics as well, as night after night he seemed to cause chaos where none existed!

I can remember on more than one occasion, probably in the midst of the 'Scotch Wakes', when a slight skirmish or argument would be well under control thanks to Mike and his fellow 'doormen' - that is until Cecil would intervene and invariably get the wrong end of the stick! He would wade into the situation and usually attempt to throw out the wrong man oblivious to Mike's shouting 'No Cecil, you've got the wrong fella!' It was too late and Cecil could be seen chasing an innocent man across Douglas Head shouting abuse after him! It made a very funny scene as a breathless Cecil would return to the bar of the big concert room proclaiming something like 'that sorted him out, he won't be back!' While Mike would merely shake his head as it was useless to try and explain anything to Cecil!

'Waller' and myself spent many a happy hour having a bit of supper and a good old 'natter' with his dad and mum after a night out and Connie and Fred's hospitality was much appreciated as Fred would tell us of his dreadful experience of the 'Winter Hill' air crash many years previously when he was one of a handful of survivors. Fred later became a Douglas Councillor and did his term of office as the Mayor of the Town. Nice people.

In 1968 J.T. Skillicorn's won the contract to build the new offices for the Isle of Man Steam Packet Company at Peveril Square in Douglas, the workshop was buzzing with the joiners non-stop making all the door casings, windows, fitments and many sets of counters and cupboards. The apprentices would be sanding timber with the 'Stanley' hand held bench sanders of the time, using up quite a few belts in the process and occasionally (when unsupervised) racing the machines along the bench by simply letting them go when revving at full speed! This usually ended by the length of the flex or the plug being jerked out of the wall by the speeding out of control machine! Most irresponsible you may say and I have to agree but it was fun at the time. Along with Michael Corris and wagon driver Doug Gregg, I was one of the first on the site and we were greeted by a somewhat ghostly scene. The huge 'joiners' shop on the corner of the causeway where the 'Imperial Building' now stands, was only recently vacated by the 'Packet' men and they had left lots of 'slummy' behind. Slummy as we called it, or 'pickings' varied from scrap brass fittings and screws to lengths of timber such as mahogany and yang which they had not valued and simply left behind. Well I remember making quite a few trips along back Strand Street to George Osborne the scrap man with the brass and metals and we enjoyed a few pints of ale with the proceeds. When we started to demolish the place we discovered lots of the very old glass pop bottles (with the marble in the neck) hidden under the floor where they had been dumped over a period of many years and they included such names as 'Clinchs', 'Kellys Pop' and 'Mona Bouquet' if I can remember rightly. The roof of this old building was a strange shape and come to think of it resembled the new incinerator with a double curve to accommodate the rounded corner of the roadway. This though, I am sure had either evolved over the years or had simply been designed by necessity and still makes me wonder what excuse the modern day planners have for the 'apparition' they have spawned at the foot of the Richmond Hill!

The entire roof had been coated many times over the years with thick black tar or pitch, over tongue and groove boards onto substantial spars with the whole thing supported on 'backs' or purlins of about 12" x 4" some 35ft long. These were magnificent pieces of straight 'red' deal (pine) and one of the Steam Packet joiners called Bruce Maddrell rescued one and he used it to make the keel for a fine boat that he built. The tarred roof was cut into chunks with a chainsaw and burnt on site after being pulled down by the old J.C.B. 3C (556 FMN) and lengths of rope. No scaffold was used in the demolition and we just used ladders to gain access to the highest places which were probably 35ft or 40ft from the ground and simply cut a hole through where necessary, tied a knot and got out of the way as fast as possible while Mike did the rest with the digger! I wonder what would be said these days by the 'Health and Safety' man! As the site was cleared it became necessary to dig down to a lower level for the underground car park and old sea walls and remains of a pier were uncovered, as ton after ton of almost pure sea gravel and stone were removed. I remember the lorries of the time descending a makeshift ramp into the hole, to be filled in quick succession by Mike Corris who was in my opinion one of the best digger drivers' I have ever worked with. There was a 'Leyland Comet' tipper owned and driven by Louie Kneen which broke a halfshaft in the difficult confines and steep exit of the site and I seem to remember a Bedford 'J' type of either Kneens or J.G. Downward along with the two 'T.K' Bedfords 8020 MN (also of Downwards) one of which had a Leyland engine. Also helping out with an occasional load was our firms' own wagons, the old A type Bedford 2494 MN or the brand new Ford 376 KMN. The old 'O' type, or the 'Old Cherokee' was on site but just used for 'light duties' at that time. Some of our bonfires were quite spectacular and were much to the annoyance of the Pier Police at the time who called the Fire Brigade on more than one occasion only to be told that things were well under control as we had our own fire hose. I seem to recall one of these 'Pier Police' who was a bit above his station receiving a good soaking one day! Needless to say that he never found out who was responsible but he suspected one of our labourers called Norman Cringle and I couldn't possibly comment as Norman or 'Ginger' was a very good mate of mine!

As the job progressed, the site foreman arrived - none other than Reg Latham himself and we installed him in his hut, semi-detached to the Clerk of the Works - Frank Tidswell. More men were sent down including (from memory) Al Lewin, Billy Brew, Bob Fick, Pat Roberts and Ian Kelly. Concrete was made in the old 'batch' mixer with electric powered hopper or 'scoop' and in this way, the footings and basement were formed with Birch Bros subcontractors for the brickwork. Their gang included Tony, Keith and the late Roy Birch and Eddie Lewthwaite on the 'trowels', with Johnny Marlow and a great comedian George 'Jacko' Teare going non stop with their hods. The Peel or 'Glenfaba' Brickworks sent their lorries in the early morning and the clay bricks would be still quite warm from the kiln as they were tipped on site - 2,200 at a time. These loads would be quickly used up with the lads expected to lay at least a thousand bricks each per day. Needless to say that the 'crack' or banter on the site was great and the fun of it still makes me chuckle now, although at the time I must admit that on one occasion Eddie Lewthwaite and Jacko Teare had me a bit worried! They managed to convince me that they would call for me and take me out on a pub crawl where we would probably all be arrested for drunkenness and fighting and be barred for the next twelve months or so, from most of the pubs in Douglas. "But not to worry, because the fine wouldn't be very much" and they assured me, "your parents will eventually forgive you!" Well I was quite worried by this offer of hospitality and although not altogether sure that it was a 'wind up' I remember being most relieved when none of them called round for me that evening!

Reg, the foreman's hut was of 'weather board' or 'Shiplap' construction with corrugated sheets on the roof including one or two translucent or 'Filon' sheets for daylight. One of our tricks was to save up crusts and 'left overs' for when the 'phone rang so that at the moment Reg answered it, we would feed the seagulls on his roof - needless to say, the noise would be deafening in the hut as many gulls would fight for the scraps above! This racket would inevitably be followed by a tirade of bad language from a very angry and red faced Reggie as he dashed outside and tried to catch the culprits! They were good days indeed for an apprentice joiner and I loved my job although it was quite heavy work at that stage when we built all the form work or 'shuttering' from scratch to form the first floor. Unlike today, there was no tower crane, no 'acrow' props and worst of all, no power supply or power tools.

Even for the year 1968 this could not be classed as a 'modern' design as the construction was completely without steelwork as of today, save for the many thousands of individual steel reinforcing bars which had to be painstakingly laced together by hand 'twisters' to form the grillages for the beams and floors with not a single sheet of 'Weldmesh' in sight. A slow process for the 'steelfixer' as he was known, called Billy 'Boofah' Brew who was a very talented man of some sixty eight years of age and still going strong. He was one of the great characters of the time who could turn his hand to anything, with probably his great claim to fame being his ability to lay drains with the old clay pipes with amazing accuracy and speed as well. He told me that 'you have to be careful with machinery' and went on to show me that he had the third finger on his left hand missing - "That's nasty" I said "how did it happen?" "Machinery" was his reply "a wheelbarrow actually". And as ever with a smile on his face he went to explain that when working on the building of the Co-op in Lord Street/Duke Street, Douglas, he had a barrow full of concrete which bounced against a plank and the rebound of the tyre moved the 'machine' backwards so quickly that the left handle banged against the open end of a scaffold tube and in between both was Billy's finger which was sliced clean off! He had a wonderful sense of humour, drank like a fish and smoked as many as 60 'Kensitas' cigarettes every day. He continued working until he was seventy four, eventually calling it a day with the demise of Creer Bros, the builders of Demesne Road, with whom he did his last couple of years. A remarkable man indeed!

Another good friend and character on the site was Bobby Fick, an excellent all round joiner who always achieved a 'result' despite sometimes, seemingly working 'against all odds' in bad weather without equipment or electric. I remember cutting baulks of pitch pine and yellow pine measuring 8" x 8" and 10" x 10" with ordinary joiners handsaws for the propping of the shuttering of the concrete beams. These would be levelled up with wood wedges which enabled their removal after twenty one days when the concrete aired and were then available for re-use somewhere else, as in those days very little was wasted. Hand cutting of wet timber is not recommended if your saw is the slightest bit blunt or lacking in 'set', so needless to say we spent quite a few hours setting and re-sharpening which was a 'chore' but a great skill when mastered. Almost unheard of now with the advent of powertools and 'throw away' hand saws, it was just another part of a wonderful apprenticeship which has disappeared over the years. Some may say 'good riddance' but I still have my two saws which are 'Philadelphia Disston' and I like to keep them sharp although I too like to use power tools and being honest would certainly not like to return to those 'heavy' days.

I think I horrified the foreman old Reg by using a chainsaw to cut some sheets of ¾" shuttering ply one day, when we were fed up cutting sheet after sheet in the old fashioned way but he soon agreed when the job speeded up and we eventually got the first floor above the car park completely 'decked' in. Things started to 'move' a bit after this and a 'Hydrocon' mobile crane was brought on site to lift the concrete in. It belonged to 'Island Holdings Ltd' who were an early plant hire firm of the sixties, this being quite a new phenomenon as up until then, most of the bigger builders owned their own equipment. At the front of the building I had the honour of making the shuttering for the flight of steps leading up to the main entrance and I was quite chuffed to be entrusted with this job being a mere apprentice at the time. Reg said "get some shuttering made and if you're stuck you know where to find me." Such was the teaching in those days, the older tradesmen were eager to show you if you were interested but if not the alternative advice usually ended in ......off! I still feel some pride when I enter the building some thirty five years later and think of them as 'my steps'. Imperial Building was designed by T.H. Kennaugh the architect and he was assisted by an old friend of mine, Peter Kelly, who was in my class at school and now writes a very interesting nostalgia column in the Examiner each week. The building, as I have said was quite an old fashioned design without a steel 'skeleton' but it was certainly built to last and of the finest quality although I have heard that it may be due for demolition in the near future. Soon after the first floor was done and one very wet and misty afternoon, I disgraced myself and was very nearly sacked!

Reg Latham was on holiday and Bob Fick was acting foreman and for some reason Bob Skillicorn paid us early, around two o'clock I think instead of the usual four o'clock. Well it got to a point where we had done all we could for the day and we were sheltering in the new underground car park and looking across the road towards 'Tiger Tims' petrol station and the Peveril Hotel when someone said "I bet there's a nice fire going in the bar of the Peveril" - enough said! I remember Bobby Fick, 'Boofah' and myself looking at one another and Bobby licking his lips! Soon after that the three of us were indeed sitting by that fire with a pint of bitter each, drying on the outside and wetting our whistles which seemed a very good idea for about half an hour, until a breathless and soaking wet Al Lewin arrived to tell us that the 'Boss' had come back and wanted to know where everyone was! There was such a scatter out of the pub and we went back towards the site entrance as quick as possible to be met by a furious Bob Skillicorn. He laid into Bobby first and told him that he should have known better, to which Bobby agreed and apologised and then it was my turn, as quite rightly I was given the 'bollocking of my life', had my wages docked threepence an hour on the spot and told to report to him at eight o'clock the next morning. This I duly did and I remember feeling ashamed of myself because I knew that it was a hard time for the 'Boss' having just lost his uncle and having the whole weight of the business thrust upon him and his brother Niels, at this time he certainly didn't need to be bothered by something like this. The outcome was that I would be taken off the site and sent elsewhere and if I behaved myself I may get my threepence back! I apologised, moved on to work with another joiner called Wally Broad and so ended a very happy period of my apprenticeship but at least I still had my job.

The 'Tech' at Hanover Street - characters at work

One day and one evening a week I attended the technical college in the old Hanover Street School as I had done when I worked at Dowtys. The difference now was that I was with most of the apprentice joiners in the island and that included some real characters who I am still friends with today. My good mate John Quirk would take me with him at lunch time to his house and make us a good hot meal, usually chips or something equally tasty. I really appreciated his hospitality and got to know his parents Win and Tom, and his twin sister Susan. 'Quirky' was a good joiner and chip maker but I don't recall us ever doing the washing up afterwards! We had lots of fun at the 'tech' including practical lessons during the day with Harold Flavell in which some of the talent (or lack of it) was displayed by these budding young joiners. Needless to say, some were good and some were not so good and needed some 'help'. This is where one of Kelly Bros apprentices, Dave Christian and myself would endeavour to 'assist' those who were struggling, maybe by cutting off a tenon or possibly taking off a few more shavings than necessary when they weren't looking! Being an old building the toilets were out in the back yard, so that was where we went on frequent occasions for a smoke or even to throw a load of sawdust over the top of a cubicle door onto some poor unfortunate soul who was sitting inside and who would itch for the rest of the day with sawdust emerging from every orifice! It was quite a prank to seek permission for the toilet and then to run up the lane at the side to the Albion for a very swift pint of beer. If challenged on my return for taking a long time, I would say that I was constipated but I'm not sure whether Harold believed me or not - he never said!

In the evening class we would be instructed in theory and setting out techniques, the marking out of cut roofs, Hips and valley rafters etc. which was valuable teaching and along with the humour of our instructor, John Morley, made for a good night's entertainment John was a great personality, his easy way of teaching was a delight and he usually had us in stitches at the end of the class with some yarn or funny story. By day he ran his own small building business and the Clifton Hotel on Douglas Promenade. I think he was probably a 'workaholic' achieving much in his life, including later on, the total rebuild of the Empress Hotel during the day, whilst running the place as well and waiting on tables when necessary. I don't know when he found time to sleep and I had the greatest respect for him as he always had a smile on his face but sadly he died when still quite young in the late 1990's.

Another evening tutor was none other than Godfrey Cain who later became the first Manxman to be Fire Chief. I enjoyed his teaching as well and found that it was easy to learn when things were explained by a tradesman rather than a school teacher and the light hearted mood of the whole place was like a breath of fresh air. A few of the names I remember from those very happy days were:- David Lancaster, Brian 'Rolter' Crellin, Brian 'Bunny' Quirk, Brian Heaney, Dave Pitts, Wesley Brew, Louie Kelly, Michael 'Rittles' Corlett, Juan Mylchreest, Alan Rise and David Christian.

There was great music at the time and I kept an old 'Ever Ready' transistor radio with me at work, listening to such great stuff as The Kinks, The Hollies, The Beegees and of course the Stones and Beatles. Cat Stevens was great with 'Matthew and Son' etc. and I well remember a rather talented Pat Roberts making up alternative and very funny substitute words of his own to various hit songs of the day. Needless to say that most of them would be unprintable even now! But others such as 'Thank you for the days' would become 'thank you for my pay' etc or from the film 'The Graduate' 'Here's to you Mrs Robinson' became 'Here's to you Millie Robinson' in honour of our own famous manx cyclist and signwriter.

I mentioned a great character called Al Lewin or Percy as he was also known at home in the Crosby area. He worked for J.T. Skillicorn Ltd for over forty years and travelled from Crosby to Onchan each day by motor scooter, complete with 'L' plates as despite numerous attempts to pass his test, he never did and alleged there was a conspiracy against him at the testing station! I think his first machine was an 'Auto Vap' autocycle with pedals for assistance which were often needed as he was not very mechanically minded and frequently failed to start the engine for one reason or another. He would arrive at his destination very red in the face but it kept him fit! This was succeeded by various Lambretta scooters and I think his last machine was a 125 Honda motor bike but he will be best remembered perhaps for his old blue 'Pudding Basin' crash helmet! He rarely took this off on cold winter days and could be seen down trenches and even in the firm's vans still wearing it! At one stage he had a thing called a 'turbo visor' attached to it and this was most comical when in the upright position as it spun round on top of his helmet and resembled a helicopter. This, along with the cast in his eye and the ever present pipe in his mouth, was to say the least, quite bizarre! Along with this he had quite a 'swarthy' or brown complexion and dark hair and he once told me that he got locked up with the Italian internees in Port Erin by mistake, after a dance there one night during the war. Taking into account that he spoke in a rather 'garbled' manner which was quite hard to follow unless familiar with his way of speaking, I am not surprised at this, as he could easily have been taken for a 'foreigner' when he started his "says he, says I to meself" routine, which nobody really understood!

In the late sixties there was a great variation of work and from being in the workshop one day with the workshop joiners, the very next day things could change dramatically and I could be out in the rain or even working alongside one of the masons or plasterers, such was the flexibility of the apprentice in those days. I worked for a while with one of the older men who was already past retirement age but still very fit and with a wealth of experience. Tom Howland was his name and to say that he was a character was a great understatement! Tom had a reputation for never being wrong and any ensuing chaos which followed him was certainly not his fault or caused by him in any way. It was quite an experience to work with him and he had some wonderful tales to tell about his years at the 'White City' amusement park at Onchan Head where he spent many winters splicing the rotten timber framework on the huge 'Figure of Eight' roller coaster. He had a metal plate in his skull as a result of a motor bike crash when he was a young man but despite this he continued to work well into his seventies. There were many funny incidents where Tom was involved or indeed had just walked away from, Always denying any liability or knowledge or the chaos that followed him as it was never his fault!

One day we were fitting a new cill to a bedroom window in a commissioner's house in Ballachrink estate and we had successfully removed the large double glazed unit when the elderly lady shouted "Coo-ee Mr Howland, cup of tea?"… we were standing upstairs on some 'parquet block' patterned lino, on which the lady had laid some sheets of newspaper - "about time too" muttered Tommy in his usual ungrateful tone and he chucked his Stanley claw hammer down on the floor where it slid under the bed assisted by the lack of friction caused by the paper and this was followed by a loud noise of metal meeting china as a full chamber pot was demolished and deposited urine all over the floor! The old lady was mortified as Tommy took the tray of tea from her and told her that it wasn't his fault as she should have emptied the piss-pot beforehand! He continued to have a cuppa and a biscuit as I tried to help the lady mop up the mess around Tom's feet as he sat on the bed!

On another occasion we were working at the old 'Theatre Royal' pub in Wellington Street where the big timber lintel over the front window was being replaced with a suitable piece of steel instead. I remember Tom and myself, Charlie Beattie and a quite grumpy mason called Hughie Condra, lifting the steel beam into place and awaiting Hughie's verdict as he held the spirit level. In his usual grumpy way, Hugh advised us that one end was indeed a bit too high and that he would have to scrape away some of the cement bed from underneath as we lifted up the heavy beam. Tom inserted his crow bar and lifted the steel as Condra put his fingers underneath just as old Mrs Groom, the landlady shouted 'Tea up'! Well - all hell broke loose as Tom simply removed the bar and let the steel beam down on Hughie's fingers amidst a tirade of foul language and insults about Tom's sanity!

"Stupid fool" said Tom, " Yer shouldn't have had yer fingers under there" and he proceeded to free the trapped man by re-inserting the crow bar and lifting the very heavy piece of steel. This he successfully achieved but unfortunately he raised the unfortunate Hughie's fingers as well, among screams and expletives which were not very complimentary to the 'helpful' actions of Tom! We took Hughie to out-patients at the hospital and I think Tommie's last word on the matter was that it was a good job that he had been there to free Hughie's hand and that he thought he was a very bad tempered man!

This brings us up to the late sixties when Tom spent a lot of time working at the Palace Hotel and Casino with myself, John Boyde and young John Quirk. John Boyde had a good sense of humour which was absolutely vital when working with Tom, as when one day John was almost permanently deafened. The construction of the place was mainly 'in situ' concrete and a quick method of battening walls for shelving etc. was with the use of Hilti guns and Rapid Hammers which, with the use of various grades of shots would fire a nail into the wall or indeed through a steel girder with just the squeeze of a trigger. Nowadays, health and safety would demand ear defenders and goggles for the use of one of these rather dangerous tools but in those days we had never even heard of ear protection and with goggles you couldn't see properly anyway! Well, the noise was like a shotgun going off and was bad enough out in the open air let alone in the confines of a windowless concrete cellar about 3 yds square when Tom would fire a shot without any warning, as in this case right next to 'Boydie's' head, to fasten a shelf unit to the wall. "What's wrong with you?" asked Tom as John was clutching his ears with both hands and with his head cringing in agony, tried to voice his protest but to no avail as Tom said " You shouldn't have been so close you silly bugger!"

John left some time later and went to work with Terry Fargher and George Peake in a new venture - a specialised glazing firm called 'Manx Thermoseal' which incidentally still trades today as Manx Glass and Glazing Ltd. Hitherto unheard of as all the glazing up 'til this time had been carried out by the building firms or possibly some plumbing firms or painting and decorating establishments.

It would be the winter of 1969 when we worked on the conversion of the beautiful Palace Ballroom into what was to become the 'Palace Lido'. In hindsight, it was a wonton act of vandalism and undoubtedly spelled the 'beginning of the end' for this beautiful building from the Victorian era. A quick facelift or 'make over' as they say today, was the order of the day as the short sighted greed of the Palace Company came to the fore and we proceeded to smash away lovely plaster casts to instal timber framing for the panelling over of all the ornate balcony area. Cherubs and gargoyles alike were struck with claw hammers and loaded onto the old Bedford WMN 649 for their last journey to the tip at Port-e-Chee by the Douglas Rugby Club. Lovely cast iron columns supporting the balcony were 'boxed in' and everything in sight was covered over 'Cellotex' sheets. Our 'gang' included George Gregson, Alan Stone, Lyn Quayle, Ronnie Goldsmith, Kenny Kneen and myself and we had some good days with lots of fun, such as the discovery of a whole barrel of Guinness that had been overlooked when the bar stocks were removed and was 'liberated' to an upstairs toilet cubicle complete with air bottle and tap for further evaluation! The Guinness lasted a few days as we would fill a couple of 'Dewars' water jugs and share them around as and when the thirst was on us!

Scrap dealer - then disaster

This was around the time of my '21st' birthday and after a good celebration at the Hawthorn at Greeba, things for me were going well including winning a few trials with Phil Tasker in the sidecar and generally enjoying myself. I met a nice girl called Cecilia Tomlinson and I went out with her for the rest of the summer until she emigrated to Africa to work. We had lots of fun and I missed her when she went but life goes on and I became a part time scrap dealer instead!

This came about with my friendship with an exiled Yorkshire man called Roger Sutcliffe who came to live and work in the island, at that time 'living rough' with an old friend Bill Bancroft, while they renovated Bill's bungalow at Handley's corner. A quick story about Bill's outlook on life comes to mind as one evening we called to see them and their bachelor existence first hand. Roger had told us about Bill's culinary skills and how he sliced potatoes still covered in soil and simply dropped them in the chip pan, declaring that the scum would float to the top and anyway "A bit of dirt never harmed anyone!" Well we arrived at the back door and were halted in our tracks by two small dog turds which were lying on the step, on seeing our hesitation, Bill came out to see us muttering something like 'dirty bloomin dog' and promptly scutched the offending turds off the step with his good foot. The funny thing was and much to our amusement, he kicked them into the kitchen rather than out into the yard! "Come on in lads - a bit of shit never harmed anyone!"

I mentioned his 'good' foot and this is because he had suffered an horrendous accident as a young man. He told us that whilst motor cycling on some moorland in his native Yorkshire he and a friend had actually ridden over the edge of a quarry in thick mist, his friend escaped with minor injuries but Bill had a close to death experience shattering his hip and pelvis which left him with a pronounced lameness for the rest of his life. He was a real character and sponsored many T.T. and M.G.P. riders over the years, including Roger himself.

Roger and I became good mates and shared a common interest in Ford Thames 15cwt vans which in their heyday, were undoubtedly the 'must have' vehicle for any motor cycle enthusiast. We dabbled in these for some time becoming most adept at repairing them and selling them on again. We made many trips to Yorkshire with cargoes of scrap metal (copper, brass and aluminium) carefully weighed and loaded into one of the Thames vans to be cashed in at a Leeds scrap dealer who was prepared to give us twice the price we could get locally. We stayed at the old farmhouse, occupied by Roger's mother, which was right by the runway of the rapidly expanding Yeadon airport and was ear marked for demolition soon afterwards. We had some real good weekends with Mrs Sutcliffe's warm hospitality and big feeds of bacon and eggs! This was helped along by a pocket full of money from the scrap dealer, resulting from loads approaching two tons on occasions, which was no mean feat in a van meant for 15cwt.

While we were there we would visit our old mate Peter Edmondson at his Dalesman bike factory in Otley and generally enjoy ourselves socially at such events as the Pately Show, meeting up with the Rathmel brothers, 'Killer' Kendrew, Terry Wright and all the other mates we knew through the world of motor bikes. These were good days indeed and could have gone on forever as far as I was concerned but were brought to an untimely end for me through an unfortunate accident at work.

It was around the end of February 1970 when I was working at the Trafalgar pub at the bottom of Gas Works Hill. Myself and Billy Brew were clearing rubble from the old gents' toilets for refurbishment and this included knocking down the old lath and plaster ceiling. The method for this was to pull your hat well down for protection with a handkerchief tied around the mouth and nose for a mask and then simply whacking the plaster down a bit at a time with a shovel, waiting for the dust to settle for a minute before a quick inspection and then carry on. Well you can imagine these dingy old smelly toilets with the smell of urine and dry rot and their obvious attractions for

Charlie Moore   Howard   Phil   John Kissack   Stuey Clague   Colin Harrison

Adrian Hundleby   Peter Christian Geoff Cannell Alan Newton Derry   Dave Baxter Eric Hargreaves   Norman Pallister
Bill Knightingale   Chris Kennaugh   Ian Gale

vermin in a one hundred year old building. We made good progress until after one 'hit' with the shovels and the consequent fall of plaster and lime mortar, I chanced to look up at the result a bit too soon and the reward for my enthusiasm was a face full of damp, stale smelling lime and hair mortar directly in my eyes. In those days of no safety equipment it was not uncommon to get an 'eyeful' and after some careful work with the corner of a hanky and a sluice under the tap things usually returned to normal quite quickly. This time however it was a bit different. Old Billy did his best with the handkerchief but said he thought I should get a proper eye wash as it looked bad to him. I remember being in agony as I drove quickly up to the Railway Shops in Peel Road where, in those days, there was a chemist shop and I bought an eye bath and a bottle of 'Optrex'. Back at the Trafalgar I repeatedly washed both eyes with the stuff and thinking that that would suffice. We sat down for our morning 'cuppa' as usual. It was then that Billy told me that there was blood on my face and that I should go to Nobles' Hospital as soon as I'd drunk my tea!

This I did and shortly afterwards as I sat in outpatients on one of the old green metal chairs, I was quickly spotted by Ella Harding the sister, who was of course the wife of Ken, my mate from Gilbert Hardings. No messing with Ella, I was whisked straight in to see the doctor, bypassing the whole queue in the process. After the necessary details i.e. name, date of birth etc, they moved rapidly and after further cleansing and the application of ointment my eyes were securely bandaged over like a war casualty with the advice of the doctor "Don't remove the bandage or you could be blind within 48 hours and come back tomorrow". With that I was shown out of the treatment room and left to my own devices!

"What now?" I enquired and the nurse asked who had brought me in? "I drove myself, I've got the van outside". She was quite shocked and told me that I shouldn't have been driving in this condition, adding that I must phone someone to collect me, then sitting me down on the green chairs and walking away. I must have said something like "How?" or "Help!" and she returned and saw the funny side of it and offered to dial the old payphone for me. I spoke to Bob and Niels first and explained the situation and they arrived quickly, collecting the van and taking me home to Crosby.

Mum was understandably worried but at that time it didn't seem too serious and we thanked Bob for his care and thought no more of it until around midnight when I wanted a wee. I remember finding my way to the bathroom by feel and then feeling an excruciating pain as I tried to pass water. It was agony and defying the doctor's advice I lifted the bandage to have a look and was horrified to see blood dripping out instead of water! Still with the agony of a full bladder I waited 'til the arrival of our family doctor, Dr Rolfe, who immediately ordered an ambulance and I was rushed into hospital with the bell ringing on the Austin FG type ambulance which Howard told me later was 58 MAN!

I was in Ward 5, upstairs above the main entrance of the old hospital with my eyes still covered, given some pain relief injections in the leg and instructed to drink lots of water to flush me out! Over the next few days the waters started to flow again albeit with some pain and much discomfort and my eyes were eventually uncovered but still looked quite horrific with their bloodshot appearance and crusty eyelids, the frightening part though, was that I began to ache in every muscle and my joints were painful with every movement. I continued in this state for a couple more days and it was evident to me that something was definitely amiss as I had started to soak the bedding with perspiration because of the now considerable pain. Pain killers, injections and antibiotics were tried but only seemed to make things worse, in fact, it was at this time I discovered I was allergic to penicillin when it reacted in my mouth, gums and throat, leaving my tongue badly swollen with white lumps!

The last straw was a painkilling injection in my right thigh one night and as soon as it was in my leg it felt as though I'd been hit with a hammer. The pain was excruciating and the last thing I remember before I passed out was being aware that both feet were pointing outwards in the 'quarter to three' position as my leg muscles twisted violently like ropes.

Some three days later I came round to see my Mum's tear stained face as she held my hands and she hugged and kissed me as only a mother can saying "Thank God, thank God".

Well I wondered what all the fuss was about and probably wiped away the kisses as young lads do, only to be told that it had been 'touch and go' and that I had nearly died! The official line was that I had contracted, probably through my tear ducts, a disease similar to Weils disease brought on by rat droppings and urine from above the ceiling of the toilets. They thought it may be called 'Rieters' disease but they never seemed sure and I think the file remains open to this day. The upshot of it was that I spent a further three months in hospital, now being moved downstairs to Ward One under the care of Dr Bourdillon, whilst they attempted to find a cure for the chronic arthritic condition which had developed. It was very painful in all my joints but especially the knees and they would swell up like footballs with fluid which had to be drained by syringe. Despite losing over three stone and leaving hospital on two sticks with the warning that in the long term I could be in a wheel chair by the time I was thirty, I was determined to prove them wrong and made a remarkable recovery. This was again largely thanks to my dear mother and her excellent feeding and kindness as only a mother (or loving wife) can provide and I was soon nearly back to a normal life, that is except for my knees which have never really been right since.

Stockcars, the wedding and three funerals

Summer time 1970, I'm out of hospital on two sticks and doing well, although I have lost three stones in weight, I am eating well (thanks to my Mum's broth and good cooking) and I am determined to prove the doctors' wrong by making a full recovery.

I remember having to assist my left leg to depress the clutch pedal of the Thames van, by pushing my knee forward with my hand, such was the weakness of my thigh muscles. I don't think the Police would have been too impressed had they known that I was driving around in the physical state that three months in hospital had reduced me to! Despite this I recovered quite quickly and about a month later I was able to compete in the 'banger' class of the stock cars, along with Roger and Howard, driving three old cars we bought for £20 (six pounds, six shillings and eight pence each!) Roger's car was a Mk I Ford Zephyr, Howard had a Standard Ensign and mine was a Farina type M.G. Magnette.

We had great fun with these cars and won quite a few races through the remaining weeks of the summer, driving under fictional names, as the A.C.U. at that time, frowned on 'unofficial' motorsport with the threat of a ban for anyone caught competing in an event organised by a non-affiliated club. Using these nom de plumes, Roger was 'Bentley Brown', I was 'Bertie Bloggs' and Howard called himself - oh! can't remember!

We converted the old Austin L.D.O van to a stock car transporter by cutting off the back, extending the deck and adding a makeshift ramp made of two stout planks. Three trips to the venue at Onchan Stadium would then be made in quick succession before and after the meeting, with the last trip home at night often via the Manx Arms to celebrate with a few pints! The summer ended well with Roger winning the Senior M.G.P. and I met my future wife Karen, sadly though all the old cars went to the scrap!

The following autumn and winter began with the sudden death of Karen's lovely mum Anna, at the young age of 58 and left Karen living alone in the family house 'Kenwyn' in Summerhill Road. Instead of this option she moved in with her brother Niels and his wife Tova and little daughter Heidi. "Trust Kissack" it was said at work to be going out with the boss's sister! It was however, said in good humour by my mate Lyn Quayle, who I was working with at the time and we had many good nights at the Wheel Bar as a foursome together with his future wife Brenda. Karen and I set up home together in a nice flat at the top of Elm Drive in Onchan and we were married the following August in Onchan Parish Church by the 'new' vicar of Onchan Canon Dennis Baggaley. He was a 'larger than life' character and left us laughing after our visit to see him at the Vicarage when he had enquired 'Are you on the pill my dear? I do hope so!' His candid and forthright manner was indeed quite blunt and to say the least he was a very 'modern' clergyman for 1971!

The wedding day was on a Monday because we wanted to give our friends a day off work and it worked out really well with a lavish reception at the Palace Hotel (now the Hilton) with lots of humour and good cheer. In fact Dennis always remarked in the following years that he had never been to a 'do' like it and hoped that all Manx weddings would be as good, this being partly down to my mum who topped up his glass when necessary! We had Corkills' cars for the day, organised by Gladys Hall and beautifully turned out. Three Austin Princess limousines driven by Dougie Bell, Snowy Cowin and Bill Sterling made a fine show with CMN 111 leading the way with Bill driving and Karen and myself in the back like royalty. Niels was best man and after a suitable amount of whisky he performed his task to perfection (even indulging in a cigar which made him ill later as he wasn't at all used to smoking!) This was followed by a lovely honeymoon in Magaluf, Majorca, quite trendy for those days and the first time abroad for me, I was amazed by the heat and the noise of the crickets. Magaluf was a new resort then and there were more empty plots than hotels unlike today with its hectic and thriving holiday industry.

We returned home from honeymoon to the start of the Manx Two Day Trial which was run by the Southern Club because 1971 saw the I.S.D.T. being run in the island for the second time. It was all a bit hectic as our flight home arrived at Ronaldsway airport at 9.00am and by then of course the event had already begun. This slight problem was overcome with the help of Karen's brother Bob, who met us from the plane in his Volkswagen camper with my Barbour suit and boots so that I could change en route to the first group of sections at Ellenbrook Pig Farm! It was pre-arranged that Phil Tasker would start as normal and ride the outfit out to meet us and it worked a treat, albeit with lots of ribbing from the lads who soon found out where I'd just been!

The rest of that year went well and Phil and myself went on to win our first I.O.M. Centre Championship with the B.S.A. sidecar outfit with a last gasp victory at West Kimmeragh, which brought to an end a hitherto unbroken record of wins by Roger Quayle and George Kewley. I think Keith Shimmin won in 1972 passengered by Adrian Hundleby on a nice 500c.c. BSA outfit, repeating their success again the following year.

In 1972 I remember starting work on the new Ashley Hill Primary School in Onchan, with Mike Corris on the J.C.B. 469 OMN and myself driving one of the two D800 Ford wagons, this time 634 GMN. This wagon was ex Roy (Strawberry) Stowell and had a two speed axle fitted. The first entrance was made through the hedge at the first right hand corner of the Ballachrink farm road, leading to the farm from the Little Mill Corner. The top soil was stripped back and we were laying hardcore to form a working area for the site hut etc when my cousin Wendy along with my brother Howard came on site to tell me of the sudden death of her father, my beloved Uncle Henry. I remember being numbed by this devastating news because he had seemed so well and active with never a day's illness in his life. It transpired that on the previous day he had attended the launch of a substantial yacht at his work in Peel Engineering Co. for Dr Ewan Corlett a marine surveyor. All had gone well and he had gone home to bed and died in his sleep, a 'nice' way to go perhaps but not at the

The 1971 Manx Two Day Trial for sidecars run by the Southern Motorcycle Club

comparatively young age of 59. He had led a very busy life, to say the least, was very well known throughout the island and beyond, leaving his mark in many areas. In the 1930's he was renowned for his grass track racing and his use of the 'studded tyre' which was an old tyre for his bike which would have bolts fastened through it for extra grip and legend has it that at the Greeba sports he was winning hands down but there were some complaints about him cheating. On pointing out to the officials that there was nothing in the rules to prevent the use of bolts through your tyre, it was decided to run the next race in the opposite direction to make it fair for everyone, undaunted, the story goes that he still won but the 'studded tyre' was duly banned from then on.

His interest in motorbikes followed him though his life and while serving in the R.A.F. in the Middle East in Mesopotamia, towards the end of the war he 'obtained' a BMW flat twin from a German who, apparently, no longer wanted it!

He sent it home to the Isle of Man in two crates but only one arrived (which in itself was no mean feat) some months later. It contained the engine, petrol tank and some other small items but the other crate containing the frame and wheels was lost. He would know that it was surely a 'long shot' in those troubled times in 1945 to expect anything to reach home from halfway across the world but try he did!

1972 had started on a sad note and it got worse for our family when in May my dear mother lost her life in a car accident on Crosby School Hill. She was returning home one afternoon in an Austin 1300 (on loan from a friend) when she failed to negotiate the corner near the bottom of the hill and went straight on into the wall. She had recently been suffering from blackouts and fainting spells and it seems probable that this is what happened to her. My lovely mum died that evening in Nobles Hospital without regaining consciousness.

We were all devastated at this huge loss and understandably things were never to be the same again, but, as they say, life has to go on and my dad asked me if I would like to return to Crosby to work with him in the family firm.

In one way it was a big wrench for me to leave J.T. Skillicorn Ltd and all my friends and work colleagues where I had been so very happy with a wonderful apprenticeship, for the past six and a half years or so.

On the other hand, I wanted to work with my father who meant so much to me and my mind was made up.

Just prior to leaving 'Skillies' my last job was the total gutting and conversion to two flats of the house on the corner of Summer Hill Road and Ridgeway Road in Onchan, known as 100 Summerhill Road. We had a lot of fun working on this house which had been empty for a long number of years and still had a lot of its contents inside and undisturbed as in those days vandalism as we know it today was then unheard of. In fact apart from a lot of dampness caused by missing slates and the ingress of water, the place was largely untouched without (so far as I can remember) so much as a broken pane of glass.

The big garden at the rear was duly cleared by Mike Corris in the JCB along with John Quilliam and Brendan Noone and the two Ford wagons. The fun started when we began to clear the inside of the place and anything and everything of any value was removed and 'flogged' for beer money! I remember a big marble fireplace in the front room being carefully removed and sold to Bill Black of 'Blacks' Fireplaces for about £20 - and no questions asked! All the scrap and non ferrous metal including the wiring and brass door knobs, plumbing etc was cashed in as well - in fact the word 'cashed' rings a bell when I remember Bob Skillicorn asking what had happened to the back boiler. He was told (by Mike I think) that it had been cast (as in cast iron and worthless) and his reply was something along the lines of cast or cashed? I wonder which? I think it was round about then that we changed the subject rather quickly and being the good boss he was, no more was said on the matter but we knew that he had our card marked!

Most of the contents went on a bonfire or to the tip, but for a bit of fun one day on one such trip to the tip (in Brendan's wagon I think) we put six matching spoon back dining chairs on the top of the load and thought we would stop at the antique shop on the Quay near Riley's and have them valued. I should mention that these chairs were in a hell of a state from water damage and woodworm but as a joke and knowing how off-hand and bad tempered the woman in the shop could be, we decided to offer them to her for sale! Carrying a chair apiece Brendan and I took them off the wagon and proceeded to enter her shop. Well, I never even got inside, as Brendan in his wonderful Irish accent had enquired as to the possible deal with our merchandise only to be screamed at to "Get out of this shop with your rubbish and woodworm - I wouldn't give you tuppence for them now GET OUT!" to which Brendan's reply was "Well what about a penny then?" Her reaction to this was explosive, as her voice rose even higher with some unprintable expletives uttered as she pushed Brendan backwards out on to the Quay! Still grinning and with his cheeky smile he said "I take it you don't want them then?" just as she slammed the door in our faces! - We never went back.

I made for this house a complete set of 'lookalike' sash style windows but with special deep glass rebates for the then 'modern' double glazing which was rapidly catching on for it's insulation properties. I am proud to say that most if not all of these windows lasted very well and I think they may well be still there some thirty five years later if not replaced by the new PVC type.

Lyn Quayle and myself built a new dormer window into the roof at the back and the whole roof was re-slated by Herbie Minnis. With the mention of dormers, Lyn and myself also constructed an 'eye brow' dormer on a new bungalow in Birchill Grove being built for a Mr Robson. These 'eye brow' dormers are not a common sight in the Island and I know of only two others, one on Rose Villa at Crosby and the other on Pine Lodge at Crosby which I was building at the time for myself and Karen.

With the mention of Mr Robson's bungalow it brings to mind the 'crucifixion' of Eric Crellin! Eric was a new apprentice mason at the time and although a nice lad, he was very cheeky and this of course led to his being hung on the cross! A piece of 3 x 2 was slid through his sleeves with arms

A broken down P50 on the back of the Tonner

outstretched and nailed to another piece shoved vertically up his jacket! The whole effigy was then reared up some ten feet in height and roped to a concrete boundary fence post. Amid his protests and bad language he was left there till 'the cheek drained out of him'. Well, as with the best of plans, something always goes wrong and while Eric swayed around on a flimsy piece of 3 x 2 about eight or ten feet off the ground and all the while shouting obscenities, who should arrive on site but the boss, Bob Skillicorn!

The result as you may imagine was yet another 'bollocking' for us and Eric, for being so cheeky in the first place!

These were good days indeed and it was at Birchill Grove that I watched with sadness the departure of the 1930 Centenary steamer 'Lady of Mann'. I remember hearing all the ship's sirens blowing as the 'Lady' left Douglas for the last time and admit to a tear in my eye as she was a personal favourite of mine. It seems quite ironic now that I was connected with the building work in Birchill Grove and watched the departure of the ship from the rooftop of the bungalow - because some ten years later I built a bungalow there myself and lived there for some fifteen years.

Back home to Crosby and Kissack Bros

They say all good things come to an end sometime and I remember these as my last happy days at J.T.S. Ltd, so I moved on and went to work at Kissack Bros. of Crosby, joiners, builders, blacksmiths and undertakers to the parish of Marown since 1715.

As I mentioned, I had already started to build a 'dream house' for myself and wife Karen, and this was to be on a plot of land to the rear of Crosby House owned by retired blacksmith and gardener Charles (Charlie) Clarke. Charlie was one of the characters of Crosby Village at the time and although he sometimes came across as rather a surly and grumpy man I became great friends with him and soon discovered a very kind and well meaning man behind this 'facade'.

He was something of a legend for his expertise in the baking of wonderful cakes and pastries for which he had won many prizes at the various shows throughout the island. A giant of a man he was well over six feet tall and very fit although nearly seventy years by this time and worked full eight hour days in his garden or that of one or two customers in the Douglas area.

Charles lived a solitary existence in this large house which, even by this time 1972, had never been wired for mains electricity and relied solely on gas light. The house was equipped with some electric wiring but this had long ago been abandoned when the old gas engine out in the garage packed up in the mid 1950's leaving the D.C. generator redundant.

He lived mainly in one room at the back of the house which never got any sunlight but was always warm and cosy with a good coal fire burning in the York range and the additional warmth of the unprotected gas mantle hanging above the big square table in the middle of the stone flagged floor.

All the rooms were festooned with thick cobwebs, not unlike the 'Munsters' house! As things had obviously got too much to bother about or possibly were not too high on his list of essentials! In himself he was always clean and tidy and in the house also, everything was in it place and neat but he did say that it was a waste of time dusting as the cobwebs and dust would only reappear in a few days anyway, making the whole thing a waste of time!

As the house I was building started to progress I eventually paid off the sum of money still owing and I was very grateful and indeed indebted to this man for his kindness and patience. The money in fact seemed of little importance to him as he said to me he hadn't much need for money being almost self sufficient with his gardening and cooking etc. I was treated to a nice tea each Saturday throughout the building of the house as he would try out on me various new cake recipes as he strove for perfection in his baking. I remember his cutting each individual raisin and currant with a small pair of scissors when making his own wonderful mincemeat at Christmas time because he believed the flavour had to be released into the pies! Never have I tasted better fare and I'll remember his kindness always.

He did have one or two of the neighbours 'up in arms' however as he persisted with some dreadful garden fires with their thick and acrid smoke leaving a heavy cloud over the village and blackening many a line of washing! I think in hindsight and knowing the twinkle in his eye, that this was sometimes done for devilment after someone had annoyed him but he did insist that it was essential to put the ash back into the ground as part of his compost. His produce was certainly a testimonial to this belief as his vegetables and flowers were second to none.

He always seemed so fit and well and it was with great sadness that I learned of his death some four or five years later on returning from a short holiday. I think it was the only Saturday tea that I had missed sharing with him and being winter, he had suffered a rare chill and taken to his bed in this big freezing cold house. This kind but lonely man had died of hypothermia after falling out of bed and I sometimes wonder that had I not been off island then I would certainly have looked in on him and things may have been different.

Charles told me, during one of our teatime chats, that his family had been the last occupants of the cottage that still stands amidst the gravestones in the Douglas Borough Cemetery and had left it in 1936 as the graves started to encircle them and his mother had felt a little uncomfortable among this ever growing silent 'crowd' that had begun to join them. It was at this time that they had bought Crosby House in the middle of Crosby Village. He also told me that during the war years he had worked in the Vickers Shipyard at Barrow and at the Selkirk Iron Foundry in Scotland doing essential work for shipping and munitions. He had lived alone for much of the 50's, 60's and 70's and after the death of his parents, soon after his return from the war.

I think his somewhat 'gruff' nature often saw him being misunderstood by many but I can honestly say that I am honoured to consider myself his friend. Thank you Charles.

My return 'home' to work was, I have to say, a bit of a culture shock, coming as I had from a comparatively large firm of some forty men, to being one of five. The others being my father, my brother, Jacko Gelling and his labourer Alec Karran from Glen Maye.

We were very busy at the time with possibly a bit too much work, including the building of the new warehouses for Crosby Wholesalers to replace the last of the World War Two huts (from Andreas Airport) which had served so well for nearly thirty years. We were also starting a new bungalow for a Mrs Jacob at Greeba Castle as well as all the regular jobbing work which was mainly looked after by Jacko and Alec. The plant and equipment side of things was to say the least 'better than nothing' but really quite ancient! Howard was doing his best with this side of things and we did have a decent lorry, a Bedford TK

Tipper that he had rebuilt from spare parts. We had a grey Ferguson tractor with a front loader which helped a bit and he was buying a derelict Steelfab digger which was based on an International 275 tractor.

We certainly didn't have the money to buy a decent digger so he did the next best thing by rebuilding one from scrap! This machine was from the mid sixties vintage and was well past it's best. It was brought to the Island circa 1963 - 1964 by the Murtagh family who were in business at the Union Mills Garage formerly owned by Mr Slater, from where I had bought the Austin Seven some years before. This garage was renamed 'Cumbria Garage' and Murtaghs' traded there for some years before it was bought by Jack Kaneen and his family. Ironically Jack had worked as a mechanic for Murtaghs' and was involved in a near fatal accident while working on a repair to this very machine. He had been standing at the back of the digger between the control levers and the back acter when he became trapped. The back acter slewed round and Jack received serious pelvis and spinal injuries which left him with a severe limp for the rest of his life. Despite these dreadful injuries he went on to build the successful business 'Union Mills Garage' as it is still known today nearly forty years on.

Anyway, back to the plant and equipment situation, it was pretty desperate stuff and in need of investment as indeed was the book keeping system - or lack of it!

The problem with the book keeping was that father was running the business out of one trouser pocket and living his own life out of the other! Or so it seemed. He was, I remember, having trouble with the 'tax man' and couldn't separate the business accounts from his own so it was at this time that we formed a limited company to try and separate the two! So for the first time in nearly three hundred years the business became 'Kissack Brothers Limited', standing on its own merits and with much less confusion.

We rumbled along and I very much enjoyed working with my father and spending quite a lot of time in our joiners shop making all the stairs, windows, doors and of course - the coffins! The funeral side of the business was thriving as well as the building work and despite working long hours I was in need of some help to try and keep pace with things. This help arrived one day in the shape of Alan Graham Seed.

Graham or Seedy as he was known around the village, grandson of Seymour Corkill who worked for the firm all his working life and younger son of Lenny and Millie, had come to work with me for what was to be the next fourteens years or so. He had been a visitor to our yard on Saturdays for a number of years as he attempted various car and motor bike projects and, being a likeable lad, who said he fancied a change of job from Marown Engineering, I agreed to give him a start to see how he fared.

I will set the scene by saying that Graham was one of the best workers I have ever seen, extremely punctual, absolutely honest, very able for almost any task, very wiry and strong and full of enthusiasm and eagerness to learn…. but…..probably his biggest problem was that he suffered (still does) from dyslexia.

In fact I think he would probably agree with me when I say that in those days he was a 'bit back to front'. Always full of suggestions and alternative ideas, most of which were alien to good practice and absolutely fruitless, but just occasionally almost borderline genius would emerge! He was indeed an alternative character. Certainly not stupid, as had been his 'label' at school, through a total lack of understanding by his teachers.

In the firm at this time we were running a little Austin LD Truck which had been a brewers 'dray' at Ind Coope Ltd. And Howard had made it into a very useful tipper with the use of a 12 volt electric motor from an Onchan Head dodgem car! This was a very early form of the electric/hydraulic units that are so common today on most pick up/tippers and tail lifts, but back then almost unheard of - most innovative and ahead of its time. However, this little 30cwt capacity truck was no longer big enough with the coming of our newly acquired 'Steel Fab' digger and was sold on to a friend, Henry Sloane. Its replacement was to be a

Bedford T.K., bought in a derelict state from Patrick Carrol at Manx Metals. It arrived as a Cab/Chassis with a knackered 4 cylinder diesel engine which was soon rebuilt and refitted and ran very well. Considerable work was needed to 'resurrect' this lorry and indeed many more in subsequent years, but partly inspired by the lack of available funds and partly by a unique desire to create something 'bespoke' and more suitable for our needs, a very smart and useful vehicle was made. It was re-registered MN 1984 and over the years it had many changes including the fitting of a 6 cylinder 330 engine from a J type Bedford bought from Harold Craine who had just built a new garage between Ballasalla and the Airport (now the Total garage). I think that the remains of this J type were swapped for a BTD6 'Drott' from north side haulier Duncan Black and his sons Nichol and Malcolm.

Money was tight at the time and this mention of the 'J' type range of Bedfords was the start of a long association with the marque for me in particular. With the coming of the more modern T.K. alot of J's became available at knock down prices, they were a very good truck and above all I liked them and still have one to this day.

One of our first jobs with the T.K. was to lay hardcore roads in the new campsite at Glen Dhoo at Hilberry for the Cain family, for whom we had worked for many years on the building side of things. The 'hardcore' was to be Foxdale 'Deads' from a spoil heap opposite the entrance to Eairy Ploydwell and belonging to the Quaye family. A deal was done and it became apparent that another lorry was needed, so we 'hired' an old J type from Billy Collister who had a yard nearby with his wife Jean. It was an ex Forestry Board wagon 4498 MN, 4 cylinder diesel and it went like a rocket!

So it went on, with these two 4/5 tonners we hauled literally hundreds of tons of this lead coloured material to Glendhoo, via the Braaid, Glenvine, Union Mills, the Strang and the Scollag Road until the job was complete. The wagons were loaded with the Steel Fab digger and at the other end the material was spread with our old grey Ferguson equipped with 'Mil' loader and front bucket. These roads seem to have stood the test of time some thirty five years later, although the rows of tents that they gave access to have diminished dramatically since the halcyon days of tourism.

"Go back when I tell you!"

I think it was around this time that I came across an horrific accident one evening at Marown Church. Karen and myself had been, from our home in Elm Drive in Onchan, on a visit to Crosby to see my mum and dad. I had a blue and white Austin A60 Cambridge at the time and it must have been 10.30 - 11.00pm when we left Crosby and set off home. On rounding the Church Hall corner and approaching Marown Parish Church we spotted what seemed like total mayhem, with two cars seriously damaged and steaming and blocking the roadway. We were literally first on the scene of a dreadful head on crash between a green Mini and a pale blue Morris Minor 1000. I remember stopping the car with the lights shining on the crash scene which was right outside the church gate and war memorial. I got out and said to Karen to stay in the car because I could see what appeared to be a body lying in the road close to the most westerly gate of the church (near this house with 'twisted chimneys') and possibly 30 yards from the first car in view - the Morris 1000. I think it was round about this time that the Crosby 'Copper' at that time, Alan Nelson arrived and was doing his best to administer first aid to a lady passenger in the green Mini who was losing lots of blood. I offered my help and Alan asked me to stop the traffic on the Peel side and divert them around the top road. I didn't have to do this for long however as more Police arrived with the ambulance, so I decided to go home and I think shock was setting in a bit when I started to realise that I had counted around five seemingly lifeless bodies altogether and I remember an eerie silence, at least until more people had joined me. Yes, I think it was shock and I was still stunned next day when I learned that two people were already dead and the others were critical, one of which was a mate from my Braddan School days - Malcolm Magee. Malcolm was brain damaged and lingered on in a coma for some years before his eventual death. It was all very sad and I still see the incident clearly, not a pretty sight!

On a lighter note, I remember one of the first funerals I did with father on joining him and Howard and it was at Lezayre Church on the morning of a Manx Grand Prix race. Needless to say timing was to be most important because of the imminent road closure and Lezayre Church being literally land locked in its own section of roadway which is totally cut off during these closures. Anyway, all went well with the ceremony which was for Crosby character Billy Yewdall and I was to go back to Onchan with John Moore who was that day driving the little Austin A55 hearse (Man 50). John decided that we would have enough time to beat the road closure by going 'with' the course through Ramsey and over the mountain. By any standards we were perhaps cutting things a bit fine but we were cruising along nicely, much to the amusement of the crowds along the hedges and after the long pull up the Mountain Mile we reached the Black Hut with what we thought plenty of time (about 10 minutes) still left to get to Creg-ny-Baa, we were most surprised to see our way ahead blocked by the long arm of the law! Sergeant Arthur Quirk was blocking the road and flagging us down and to our utter amazement he was telling us to turn round and go back to Ramsey! John tried to explain that we only intended reaching the 'Creg', that we did have time and in any case it would surely be an act of lunacy to go back against the flow with possible unthinkable consequences should we encounter a pre-race travelling marshal for instance??

We got our reply 'GO BACK WHEN I TELL YOU'! I leave the readers to decide for themselves on the wisdom of this decision but I have to say that I remember John and myself being rather 'anxious' to say the least as we went back down the mountain in this little hearse on the fastest trip it ever did! We both breathed a sigh of relief when the Hibernia turn off came into view and a policeman dropped the rope and got us off the course in the nick of time. He had a look of utter disbelief on his face when John explained what had happened up at the Black Hut - 'Unbelievable!' he said shaking his head whilst I think we were just shaking (with relief) as the large crowd at the Goose Neck gave us a huge cheer and a round of applause! I still meet John sometimes and we nearly always recall that day and the comical outcome which could easily have turned out so differently!

Rover the dog! 'Pine Lodge' Dad!

At this time, socially, we were very friendly with Glen and Billy Clelland and along with Glen's sister Betty and her husband Henry Sloane, we had many happy evenings out and indeed lots of suppers in the old farmhouse at Lanjaghan, Abbeylands. We had great fun on treasure hunts and at most of the dinner dances for the motor cycle clubs and the various farming related 'doos' as well as riding in all the sidecar trials, in which Henry and Billy had recently started and were doing very well. We rode many of these trials with Philip and myself and Henry and Billy almost as an unofficial team, which turned out to be beneficial to us all and achieved some good results.

Meanwhile Karen and myself had acquired a new pet, 'Rover' the dog! He was a black and white smooth haired sheepdog/collie type from the M.S.P.C.A., who at the time were operating from a house at the bottom of Quine's Hill at Port Soderick before the days of Ard Jerkyll and the fine sanctuary at Foxdale. Rover, was to say the least, a bit of a legend. Right from the start, on his first day we knew that he wouldn't be easy, especially as at this young age of about nine months he was already trying to mount our cat Fluff! He was very bright and obedient and learned tricks easily and in fact he probably would have had a much longer life if he hadn't caught that awful disease of dogs called distemper. He nearly died of it in fact and he was never quite right in the head afterwards! Gwyn Davies the vet was quite amazed that he survived at all as distemper was usually fatal then and it certainly wouldn't have happened today with the M.S.P.C.A. insisting on vaccination for all the animals in their care.

Anyway survive he did and for the rest of his life he would run everywhere never walking and all the while looking skywards and snapping at imaginary flies or such like! Also being an 'entire' dog he cocked his leg anywhere and everywhere on frequent occasions throughout the day!

One evening whilst we were at a working party on Douglas Head preparing for the 'Grand National Scramble', the lads were taking a break and had formed a rough circle discussing the nights work and generally having the 'craick', as Rover ran round and round (rather like a red Indian circling a wagon train) when he suddenly stopped and cocked his leg on Dave Baxter! Dave was blissfully unaware of what was happening to start with until he was eventually alerted to his plight, partly by the soaking wet effect and partly by the growing roar of laughter surrounding him! Not content with this, very soon afterwards, Randall Cowell arrived in his V.W. Pickup truck and out jumped his pedigree Boxer bitch and yes, you guessed it! Rover was in there like a rat up a drainpipe and 'nailed' the Boxer! Much to the annoyance and indeed angry protests of Randall as he tried to chase Rover away, the dog 'stood his corner' until the job was well and truly consummated! He was most annoyed with Rover but also the roar of laughter from the assembled audience seemed to make things worse for him as he shouted at me something like - 'This is a pedigree animal and I paid alot of money for her!' 'Oh really' I replied 'You should have got a dog like mine, I got him for nothing!'

There were many such incidents with Rover and one of his favourite ports of call was Ballaquinney Farm at Glenvine where he would hang around for days when one of Arnold and Geoff Kinvig's collies was in season, eventually with him arriving home like a skeleton or being picked up by me after a friendly phone call from Arnold tipped me off as to his whereabouts.

Not all farmers were as patient or compassionate however and I think Rover's eventual demise was brought about by his being in the wrong place after a bitch, when a farmer had his gun handy and wasn't going to chance a possible sheep worrying incident. In fact the last time I saw the dog was as he struggled out through the small quarter-light window of the Morris 1000 van in Onchan one day. This in itself showed his desperation to copulate and it was indeed no mean feat for a full grown collie to squeeze out through such a small aperture albeit breaking the quarter window in the process!

Despite many appeals in the press and on Manx Radio, Rover was never seen again, but in the ten years that we had him he had certainly left his mark and an unknown number of offspring!

By this time around 72/73 I was well into building our 'dream house' Pine Lodge situated on land at the top of Charlie Clarke's garden next to our yard in the west of Crosby village. It had been a struggle to obtain planning permission even in those days and we had to present a case at the review to be held in the old 'Drill Hall' at Tromode, which was being used as Government Offices whilst the new ones were being built in Buck's Road. With the help of Neil Hanson, we must have presented a good case and common sense prevailed so building could begin at last, after nearly 8 months of hold ups! With little funds but lots of enthusiasm I managed to salvage enough second hand bricks to bring the footing up to damp course level at the lower end which was to be the garage of the split level design.

The house as it stands today measures sixty feet long by thirty feet wide and at the time, we put all the very best quality materials and fittings that we could afford into it as we fully intended to be there for a long time. Inflation was a factor around this time and when I ordered all the floor and ceiling joists and the roof spars from Peter Simpson of Quiggin and Co, he told me 'on the quiet' that timber was to increase in price by a huge 40% on the 1st of January, such was the rampant nature of inflation in the early seventies.

Pine Lodge

With the building well on the way, my old friend Stuart Clague and his partner Teddy (The Death) Kelly and John Marlow, the hod carrier, would crack on with the brickwork each weekend as a 'foreigner' from their weekly employment with McCormick and Davies. They were a superb team with a first class result and with everything clean and tidy at the end of the day so unlike some of today's 'cowboys'. Peel clay bricks were the order of the day and in my opinion they remain the best possible material for house building with little or no problems experienced in expansion or burst rendering. These bricks at the time cost £21 per 1000 and we used around 38,000 of them all told.

The site is split level and entering from the lower level these bricks had to be raised to the higher level somehow! In those days when working on a shoe string an old dumper and a grey Ferguson tractor provided the answer to the problem with the 'Fergie' pulling the dumper up the steep site, both on full power and the dumper loaded to capacity! It was a stirring sight! Not to mention the smoke and noise of these already ancient machines. As they say 'where there's a will there's a way' and this ambitious project eventually began to take shape with long hours spent each evening after a normal day's work was over at 5pm. A good mate to help me at the time was Nigel Kermode, who, many years previously had bought my first Austin Seven from me. Nigel was always cheerful even on wet days and his help was, and still is, much appreciated.

In life it seems that there are good times and there are bad times and for some reason we seemed to be going through a very bad patch in those days.

I had been working at Nigel's parents house in Stanley View on Broadway one day with Nigel but on my return to the yard at Crosby at five o'clock I was devastated to find that my father had suffered a massive stroke and an ambulance was on its way for him.

It was the day of the anniversary of my mother's death the previous year and it transpired that father had simply buried his head in his work as he tried to come to terms with his grief. He had literally worked till he dropped and he died later that night in Noble's Hospital almost exactly a year to the day of my dear mum's death. It was a very sad time indeed as in the space of three years, Karen and I had lost Anna (Karen's mum), my Uncle Henry, my mother and my father and to say the least we were left somewhat numbed.

The TT Course job and driving coaches and wagons

Life has to continue and somehow we found our feet again and got on with things. It was soon after this sad time that my good friend Ken Harding offered us the job of T.T. Course contractor when Leslie Clarke retired. Les Clarke had his joiners and builders workshop in Victoria Road in Douglas and had done the 'Course' job for a number of years using the haulage services of Donald Fletcher with his Foden and Bedford wagons and later on Max Crookall with his E.R.F. and Leyland. When we took delivery of the course equipment it was quite obvious that much of it was in need of replacement and in fact 'antique' to say the least!

From memory I think that there were three wheeled stretcher carts, two of which had wooden spoked wheels and the other with old style wire spoked wheels, all from the 1920's and in use up to the days of the helicopters. Mainly for the mountain section of the course they would be pushed by the marshals from the scene of the crash to the nearest ambulance access point which could be literally, miles - either to the electric tram at the Bungalow or the Creg-ny-Baa or even the Hibernia for instance. It would say a lot for the fitness of the marshals, not to mention their bravery while they did their best for the injured rider.

At this time Les Clarke had the help of Corlett Sons and Cowley Ltd, who would be enlisted to fill the straw bags that were used in those days before the use of bales. The 'bags' were full size jute sacks with the yellow and black 'Dunlop' logo on them and would total merely hundreds, rather than the thousands of bagged bales used today. In fact bagging the bales was one of the first improvements introduced by my brother Howard on taking over from Les Clarke who had always had whole bales broken down and stuffed into sacks simply because the old Dunlop sacks dated back to the pre-war days before bales and weren't big enough. Simple - thought Howard and ordered new sacks that were big enough, along with a stitching machine to seal the tops and what a difference this made not only in the saving of man hours but also in the loading of the lorries. From these early days nearly thirty five years ago the job has expanded many fold with many more areas of the course being protected for the safety of riders brought about by the ever increasing speeds and health and safety implications.

2007 saw the 100th anniversary of the TT races and it is therefore interesting to note that for a third of these years Kissack Brothers Ltd have been entrusted with the task of not only the building of the course but with the storage and maintenance of the vast amount of equipment necessary for the staging of this truly great historic event. Long may it continue.

It is probably apparent to the reader by now that I have something of a fixation or 'thing' about registration numbers! Well in truth, I really don't know why and in some cases I really don't want to remember them so please forgive me if it bores you! I can't help it!

The numbers WMN 741 and 742 come to mind as I recall my coach driving days as part time/relief driver for Michael Marshall. Mike was married to Karen's sister Bette and knowing that I had my H.G.V. licence he encouraged me to take the P.S.V. test as well and help out with the then busy summer holiday trade of the early seventies. He was a major operator in those days with his very smart fleet of coaches 'W.H. Shimmin' or 'Shimmins' the Crescent' as they were known based at the Empress Hotel on Douglas Promenade and with booking offices at the Peveril Hotel, Reece's Billiard Saloon and Shimmins' Garage on Queens Prom as well.

Mike introduced the first 'twin steer' coach to the Island - the Bedford VAL with two front axles MAN 615 driven for many years by Jack Looney. Other drivers at the time that I remember were Joe Kneen, Norman Mills, Bill Christian, Fred Bell (who was a partner with Mike) 'Jumbo' Joughin, Alan Richardson and his father (whose first name escapes me) and a true professional and probably the 'Daddy' of them all, Albert 'Togo' Corkill. I think Albert was well into his sixties himself and he seemed to 'cash in' on his maturity by specialising in the older traveller and the 'Saga' tours. He had some wonderful patter and a wealth of experience especially with the ladies! And could often be seen assisting their entering and alighting the coach with a friendly pat on the bottom! A charmer indeed he was much sought after and usually filled his coach first and got away on time. As for myself I would sometimes get a full load but usually just ended up with the stragglers and was always away last - if at all!

WMN 741 was the first coach I drove for Mike and it was one of a pair bought new by Clagues Coaches and inherited by Mike when he took them over, along with the strip of land by the Empress Hotel. This eventually became part of the Hotel when John Morley built above it and extended in the 1980's.

My first trip was to collect a party of T.T. fans who were arriving at Ronaldsway from Castle Donington in the Midlands and along with a guy called Marty who had WMN 742 we set off to pick them up. It was a dark overcast day and even then at 8am the weather didn't look good but we got everyone on board including some women and young children and set off for Creg ny Baa.

The first drops of rain started almost as soon as we parked up at the 'Creg' alongside all the other coaches and it soon became apparent that racing would be postponed. It then set in for the day and with all the windows misted up, most of the men in the pub and with bored children groaning and later on being sick, it turned into a bit of a nightmare. With crisps scattered seemingly everywhere and a coach full of increasingly hungry people with 'Brummie' accents asking me when were we leaving? I remember thinking 'so this is coach driving - eh?'

Anyway I think the race organisers finally decided to open the roads around 2.30 much to my relief and on our return to the Airport the last man to get off the coach handed me 2/6d and said 'Thanks son'. Great I thought but I suppose in hindsight they really didn't have a very good time! I remember mopping up the sick off the floor and sweeping out the debris and returning the coach to the garage on Barroose Road behind the Liverpool Arms with mixed feelings but decided not to be beaten at the first hurdle.

Subsequent trips were much better I'm pleased to say and I enjoyed many a Sunday afternoon or early morning round the course during T.T. week where generally tips were very good.

Without doubt the name of Bedford was by far the most popular make of coach and of the ten coaches in the fleet, nine were Bedford and one an A.E.C. which was a beautiful 41 seater eventually being sold in Ireland.

Two destinations I liked were Rushen Abbey and the Sound Cafe at the Calf of Man, where the drivers' received a half crown tip, a cup of tea and a jam sandwich, made of course with the famous Rushen Abbey strawberry jam!

On the subject of part time driving jobs I helped out at the agricultural shows with Eric Leece for a couple of years and the wagon I drove was his 'spare' an Austin FF, HMN 748, with a Jennings cattle body. Eric used the 748 number on a few of his wagons at the time with his own Leyland/Carmichael being LMN 748 and another Austin FF used by Albert Crellin was 7483 MN. I think it would be the Royal Show at Ramsey in the fields opposite the

Grammar School in Lezayre Road around 1970 that I remember most. An early start, as always, around 4am I picked up the wagon in Crosby Station and nearly jumped out of my skin with surprise when Eric appeared out of the pitch black and said 'God lad, I was just making sure you were up'. He certainly ran a very efficient operation, leaving nothing to chance with the smooth running of the business. Customer satisfaction was (and still is) paramount, especially in a small island as it's not so much a case of 'what you know' but 'who you know!'

The show day was a long one usually starting at 4am and finishing around 10.30pm by the time everyone was returned home safe and sound and very tired to say the least. On this particular day I remember a young cow making a bid for freedom from the field with perhaps as many as half a dozen lusty young lads trying to prevent her liberty as she dodged them all in scenes reminiscent of the 'bull in a china shop!' Eventually this half wild and probably scared stiff animal launched itself at the wire mesh chain link fencing on the Lezayre road side of the field and bursting through it with apparent ease, was last seen heading for Ramsey at top speed! I can't remember where or when or by whom she was eventually apprehended but it certainly was an hilarious sight at the time!

I can remember however being treated to a nice lunch in an old fashioned restaurant in Parliament Street. I can't recall the name of it but the food was very nice as we dined upstairs as Eric's guests and I think Glenn and Gary (Eric's sons) were there along with myself and the other drivers of the day - Fred Clague, Lennie (Leo) Kerruish, Albert Crellin, Jack Clague and Roy Lightfoot - who was helping out in the old Austin belonging to Dan Creer. I think also present was a young Michael Crellin, Albert's son, who now runs the Corporation stables and is farrier for all the tram horses. He has also looked after my own Shire horse Tom for many years shoeing him and trimming his huge toenails! Some thirty years later.

Greeba Castle - lager and a chaser!

Around this time in the early seventies, I was working at Greeba Castle along with 'Rentokil' the dry rot specialists as they replaced various windows and joinery items. Skillicorns at that time did quite a lot of their work for them and Rentokil seemed to take the credit for it, or so it appeared to us. Many a staircase or window expertly made in our workshop was bashed into place with a big hammer by rough 'tradesmen' wearing 'Rentokil' overalls, much to the disgust of our own craftsmen, all of whom had served a proper apprenticeship and were proud of their skill.

An interesting job one day was the removal of the flag pole from the top of the tower for repair and painting, a difficult manoeuvre as there was very little room on the small roof for the lowering of a pole in excess of 30ft in length. Kenny Kneen (son of Percy) my apprentice at the time, and myself and possibly another man who I can't remember, struggled a bit with the sheer weight of it, but with a little bit of cunning and patient thought, a fair bit of strength and a smattering of bad language, we not only lowered it to the top of the tower but got it down the 70 odd feet to the ground using just a piece of rope. No mean feat for those days but I wonder what Health and Safety would have to say now?

At the main entrance to this beautiful castle is an impressive terrace and this is bordered by a fine timber balustrade with Newell posts at either end and accessed by a short flight of stone steps leading up from the sweeping driveway. I'm not sure who built Greeba Castle but I do know that Kissack Brothers of Crosby had a hand in it and did some considerable work and repairs to it. With this in mind one day, the owner, Charles Gill arrived at our yard with two of the fine Newell posts from this balustrade which were obviously quite rotten and with a tale of woe he explained that his effort to find anyone with a lathe capable of producing replicas had come to nothing.

My father immediately put his mind at rest and unearthed the necessary Headstock and Tailstock of an ancient machine which could be made to literally any length required by the simple addition of two stout planks to form the 'bed' or base. Apparently this machine would have originally been powered by our water wheel and could well have been used to make the originals! Who knows? But a few hours later and with the cunning adaptation of an old electric motor instead of the water wheel, we were in business!

These Newell posts are 16 inches square at the base and around five feet tall so the reader can imagine the sheer vibration and spectacle as they revolved for the first time and a cut was taken off them!

Anyone who has turned timber on a lathe will know that the first few minutes are the worst and the whole thing soon 'settles' down as it becomes mainly cylindrical but believe me a piece of clear Columbian Pine of this size and weight spinning round is quite an awesome sight until it has been 'tamed'!

From memory I think there were two Newell posts and also three or four ordinary balusters measuring around 6 inches square and possibly three feet long and once started, I thoroughly enjoyed making them for a delighted Charles Gill. I often wonder if this lathe was used for the originals all those years ago? Wouldn't that be something!

1973 was a year of mixed emotions in many ways and whilst doing well in my sidecar trials and socially, I found the going tough working with the family firm. As I said previously, we had rather too much work in hand and an argument a day seemed to be the norm, as the pressure started to show.

I think it was around this time in 1973 that I bought a piece of land in the village of Higher Foxdale, known as the Brookfield. The land at that time had some outline planning permission for a couple of bungalows and thanks to my old friend Andy Sykes, he organised a meeting on site with the owners Hugh McCanney and Pat Barret. Two Northern Irish characters - if ever there were!

I remember a warm sunny evening - a brisk walk round the site and an adjournment to the 'Baltic' across the road to talk business. An agreement was quickly reached, a price thrashed out and then the serious stuff began!

I can honestly say, even thirty three years or so later, that I have rarely seen so much alcohol drunk so quickly! I don't think we were in the pub for more than perhaps three quarters of an hour and we seemed to have swallowed about five pints of lager apiece and a whisky with every one! Truly a super way to do business!

I was approached soon after this transaction by the neighbouring land owner Harold Craine, who offered to make an entrance to the site complete with access road in return for a right of way to his land to enable him to build a house behind the Foxdale Filling Station.

Harold and his brother Alfie of course, I have already mentioned as hauliers of the sand and gravel which came to our yard when I was a little boy and true to his word, he built a nice driveway for me, saving me a considerable sum of money. Things seemed to be on the 'up' again and I was successful in changing the permission so that a small terrace of four dwellings could be built instead. However this didn't happen due to pressure of work and a start was delayed for almost another ten years.

The Clelland adjustable wheel! Club dinners

Around this time, in the evenings I was building a new sidecar for the old B.S.A. as a replacement was sorely needed. The bike frame was badly twisted as well and that was replaced by another one supplied by my old friend, from our days at Ronague mountain, Geoff Comish. Geoff's frame was (and still is) painted bright orange and looked quite 'garish' for 1973 as everything in those days seemed to be painted black! A brand new sidecar was designed and built by my good friend Billy Clelland at the workshop up at Lanjaghan Farm, Abbeylands. This is fitted with the 'Clelland Adjustable Wheel', a revolutionary invention which allowed for the raising and

The Clelland adjustable sidecar wheel in action

Henry Sloane and Billy Clelland

lowering of the sidecar for different cambers. There was a bit of 'chuntering' from some of our competitors but Billy's answer was that there was nothing to stop their copying it and also that there was nothing whatever in the rules either!

We worked on the outfit for quite a while to get it right and all the way through the 'head scratching', Billy's wife Glen would make a nice supper for myself and Karen in truly Manx hospitable style! A good natter was essential and we were often joined by Glen's sister Bette and her husband Henry Sloane and possibly, George and Margaret Kissack as well, making a wonderful jovial atmosphere! Good friends indeed and much appreciated and happy days!

The new sidecar outfit was a great success and this was crowned in 1973 with a great (and unprecedented) 3rd place in the National Two Day Trial that

September. I remember well riding back from the Grandstand to our Flat in Elm Drive on Onchan with great pride and emotion and thinking that my late parents' would have been so proud. In hindsight, I think that their untimely deaths at such a young age (Mum was 57 and Dad was 59) fuelled my determination to succeed at this and indeed everything else!

Along with Phil Tasker (who went on to passenger for me for 30 years) we went on to win the IOM Centre Championship for 1974 but things were changing fast in sidecar trials and the writing was on the wall for the big British made A.JS, B.S.A., Ariel and Triumphs, as the Spanish Bultaco started to make inroads into our sport.

I think that I had my head in the sand a bit at the time because I remember ridiculing the lightweight new outfits and calling them 'Fairycycles'. We were on a roll at the time and winning a lot of trials but it was soon to change with the rapid improvement of the two stroke Bultaco, Montesa and Ossa machines and I had to eat my words and make the transition, moving with the times and, eventually, even buying a Bultaco for myself! I couldn't bear to part with the old B.S.A. though and I still have it to this day, unrestored but still a runner!

The change over to the much lighter 2 stroke machines wasn't easy for us however and we ended up completely upside down on more than one occasion as can be seen in the photo, much to the delight of the youngsters who were watching the trial!

The nightlife at the time was good with the club dinners and social events such as 'Treasure Hunts' which were very popular. On a Saturday night the 'place to be' was the Majestic Hotel in Onchan where our crowd would gather for the 'George Ferguson Disco' held either in the big ballroom or possibly downstairs in the Nightclub, a lovely friendly atmosphere was evident with never, so far as I can recall, so much as a cross word - good times indeed!

The Majestic Hotel was indeed the venue for the 'Gold Jubilee' dinner and dance of the Peveril Motorcycle club in 1973 and which was, if I remember rightly, also a year of some disruption because of an oil shortage and possible petrol rationing. I seem to remember all car rallies and motorcycle events having

a ban slapped on them 'for the foreseeable future' although the Island seemed to have no shortage of actual petrol. There was however doubt over the supply of heavy oil as used at the power station and being as stupid as ever, the politicians of the day, didn't know the difference! (Some things never change!)

Well, it so happened that the guest of honour at the dinner was none other than the head of government or Chairman of Exco (as it was called then), one J.B. Bolton. He stood up and made a speech in the most eloquent fashion, praising the club for its forbearance in this matter, in the sort of patronising way that only politicians can! He was stopped in mid flight however by Neil Kelly who stood up and said something like "Absolute rubbish!" or words to that effect and he went on to explain to this 'Elder Statesman' that heavy oil was used at the Power Station and not petrol! And in any case there were absolutely no restrictions placed on football matches or darts matches where most of the players travelled the length and breadth of the island weekly in their own separate vehicles, thus clocking up far more miles than the small band of trials and moto cross riders on whose behalf he was speaking! I seem to remember at this stage that one or two of the more two faced 'old fuddie duddies' cried "Enough" on Neil and something like "Not the time or the place son" but Neil would have none of it and amid the cheers of the rank and file, he continued to press home his most valid point - and then he sat down!

Some days later, despite the obvious embarrassment caused by his impromptu outburst, Neil was some kind of hero as an announcement was made by the Government, that off road motorcycling could now proceed!

The annual dinner/dance and prize presentation evenings of the Peveril, Ramsey and Southern Motorcycle Clubs have been the social highlight of the year for me for over 40 years and I can recall some hilarious moments. The first of the dinners I attended was the Peveril in 1965 at the Metropole on Douglas Promenade and I remember being very proud to receive the Novice award - a club tie, emblazoned with the club logo and I still have it although I have never worn it!

As a young lad of only 16, the committee or 'elders' seemed quite ancient to me, they weren't of course, and I spent the next seven years amongst them on the committee as Club Captain and later general committee, seeing in those years, the purchase of Knock Froy and the formation of a limited liability company to protect the directors of the Club.

Back to the dinner/dances and on one occasion at the Southern Dinner, held in Ronaldsway Airport, a loud scream came from a waitress and a mouse could be seen darting across the parquet floor (probably more afraid than she was!) and banging its nose on the skirting board at the other side of the room before disappearing behind the radiator. Later that evening the bar ran out of beer! A typical night out!

Once at the Ramsey Dinner at Ravensdale Castle in Ballaugh, a nice meal was enjoyed by the assembled crowd in a most amicable way, followed by the presentation of awards and speeches - and then nothing! Someone had forgotten about both drinks extension and the Band! Well despite attempts to find a record player and smooth things over, there was nearly a riot when the landlord Mr Smith point blank refused to serve anymore drink - he was aptly named 'Heir Schmit' for his actions but I suppose he was only obeying the law and everyone made their way home sober and grumbling!

It was usual at one of these dinners each year for the chairman of that club to allow himself to become inebriated during the evening and for his lady wife, always resplendent in a long black dress, to dance the night away with the lads - the younger the better it would seem, as she held them close and whisked them round the floor and it mattered little that hardly any of us could dance properly and often stood on her toes! Without so much as a grimace on her face she would carry on undaunted as she attempted to regain her youth and get to know us 'better'! A lovely woman!

The Kawasaki days, Southern MCC

In the world of off road motorcycling, there was a closed season in the summer months mainly brought about by the fact that many of the lads had summer jobs in the very busy days of tourism, so after the Peveril Club's big event 'The Grand National Scramble' on Douglas Head, there was a complete lay off till the Manx Two Day Trial on the first weekend of September. That meant that from the start of June till the start of September the bikes were 'mothballed' and the land and tracks got a welcome 'breather' to let them recover. I still think this was an excellent arrangement and when the Two Day came around it started the winter season off with everyone full of enthusiasm and champing at the bit! I am of the opinion that these days with twice as many clubs and goodness knows how many more events each week, things are being 'stretched' a bit, with over use of land and indeed the land owner's patience, with events on Saturdays as well as the traditional Sundays taking things a bit too far.

However, as they say, it's a case of supply and demand and there certainly is a huge demand for off road sporting events throughout the year. I share the view that it's much better to cater for the needs of these budding 'world champions' in organised properly insured events, than to let them ride 'willy nilly' all over our lovely countryside every weekend.

Throughout 1976 Phil and I rode a 250 'grey import' Suzuki RL on our sidecar outfit but I just couldn't come to grips with it at all, having probably our poorest year ever and almost losing the plot over it. Never being a defeatist however led me to the conclusion that it might not in fact be totally my fault and on a chance meeting with our Kawasaki agent George Short a deal was done for the coming season. Up 'til this time no one had had much success with the Kawasaki KT250 in trials and although one similar machine was being used locally by Gary Owen and Colin Bell, it really hadn't attracted much attention. All that was about to change however and after we had swapped the sidecar from the Suzuki and done a few little modifications we 'jumped in at the deep end' by riding it at Cornelly Mines the very next day without any practice at all. The outcome was amazing with a runaway win first time out for us dressed in matching green Kawasaki one piece suits! In his weekly report in the paper Geoff Cannell described us as the 'Green Meanies' and we went on to win every event in the 1977 season bar one, when my good mates Trevor and Keith Moore beat us by one mark! Great competition indeed!

This little Kawasaki was so good that by the end of the season it was indeed the 'must have' machine and no fewer than ten outfits at the time were replicas of our own, much to the delight of George Short and S & S Motors! The ensuing success led to oil sponsorship from Duckhams Oil following an article in the Quest magazine written by Doug Baird who was their local correspondent at the time - almost famous!

It was around this time that I changed my allegiance from the Peveril Club to the Southern Club and joined the committee at their A.G.M. in the George Hotel in Castletown. The meeting had come to a full stop during the election of officers with no one willing to face the many tasks and events for the coming season. The big problem was the lack of help in the running of scrambles (motocross) events at the Braaid course and the stalwarts of the club committee, whose allegiance was mainly towards the 'Southern 100' were fed up with putting on scrambles with little or no help from the scramblers themselves. The 'southern 100' had (and still has) a fairly large band of helpers and supporters and really was a quite separate part of the club, although coming under the same 'umbrella' of the general club for accounts and the A.G.M. In fact it was all rather vague as over the years the road racing had gone from strength to strength and had become almost 'religion' in the south of the Island, whilst the off road side of the club was just 'ticking over', in short the two functions of the club had grown apart.

I had this in mind when I stood for the committee, along with Dave Cubbon, Juan Bimson and Juan Crebbin and along with the exisiting

The Kawasaki and trophies

'stalwarts' - Phil Taubman, Hoss (Gordon) Clague, John Byrne, Graham Clark and Doug Beaumont, we formed a committee so the club could continue. I thought that the writing was on the wall and things had to change and so I proposed a new club be formed called the 'Southern 100 Ltd' and that we should go our separate ways in an amicable fashion with a proper share out of assets. This proposal was adopted a short time later at the 1981 A.G.M. but not before I was almost lynched by an angry 'mob' of Southern 100 supporters! I had with careful thought prepared my proposal which said that - the Southern 100 should become a separate limited company at the expense of the club and should retain all the equipment and ropes including the hut at the Bypass. My proposal however was mislaid by the secretary and another 'set of words' was printed on the agenda in my name! It read - 'The southern

Suzuki in 1976

The Kawasaki and trophies

Motorcycle Club shall no longer run the Southern 100' - well I arrived at the A.G.M. full of hope only to be glared at by a room full of Southern 100 supporters who thought I wanted to scrap the event! I had to stand up and make a very hasty and well thought out speech and explain to these understandably hostile people that it was never my intention to stop the event. In fact I was trying to do the best thing for both sides and to help them prosper, but believe me I had my work cut out that night to convince the meeting of my good intentions!

Anyway despite the 'cock up' by the secretary the meeting did indeed calm down and common sense prevailed. History shows that it was the right thing to do as a new club was formed and has prospered, likewise, the original club has also moved on to be very successful instead of just 'ticking over' and has never been short of a full committee since.

I think I may have been forgiven by some of the irate people from the road race side that night as time has proved me right but it certainly wasn't a pleasant evening thanks to a complete loss of my proposal which I know would have paved the way for a much nicer and more friendly split.

The problem of apathy among the scambling fraternity didn't improve however and that side of things lurched along to a new course at the top of Strenaby at Abbeylands, where access was poor for the ambulance and vans in bad weather and once again the committee of the day cried 'enough!' It was then resolved that the Southern Motorcycle Club would no longer run scrambles or moto cross as it is known now, but would concentrate on solo and sidecar trials and the 'new' concept of Enduros.

Rover at the MSPCA!

On the work front in the late seventies, we were as busy as ever having built a new Club House for the Cronkbourne Cricket Club in King George Park after being invited to tender for the work by my old friend Mike Deane. They seemed very pleased and honoured me by making me a Vice President of Cronkbourne Cricket Club! This building still stands as the office for the Sports Centre but Cronkbourne moved on to Tromode road and built a new and much grander building with the help of some government funding. I have a photo of the 'topping out' ceremony which appeared in the local press, with the late Ian Brown who was the architect, Mike Deane and committee members and our workforce which included Mike Corris and Allan Phillips for the digger work, Graham Seed, myself and of course Rover the dog! In the background is the old J type Bedford lorry which I still have today.

A mention of Rover reminds me of a job we did for the M.S.P.C.A. at Ard Jerkyll in Foxdale. The MS.P.C.A. was to say the least, the craziest organisation I ever worked for! They (the committee) were obviously a well meaning crowd of dedicated people but they all had different opinions and all seemed to be pulling in different directions! The job was to build a new cattery for the ever increasing cat population and Bob Teare, who was the inspector for them, told me that his bungalow was absolutely full of cats and could we please build the new accommodation as soon as possible. This we endeavoured to do and following the plan of the architects Partington, Nixon and Kinrade we began the brickwork only to be stopped almost straight away by Marge Joughin who said that it wasn't big enough! We assured her that it was in fact exactly to the specification of the plan and proceeded with caution, only to be stopped again soon afterwards by a man with a red nose called Colonel Ramus who wondered why the front side of the building was wide open? I explained that on the plan, this elevation was to be chicken wire for ventilation for the cats in an open run. He then told me that he wanted the front built up in brickwork

Cronkbourne Cricket Club

so I pointed out that this work would be extra and would have to be approved through the architect at which he said rather angrily - "Do you know who I am?" and started to lay down the law to me in a very excited fashion. After some minutes of this ranting he calmed down a bit and said something like "You'll do as I say!" I replied that, no matter how much he shouted, I still couldn't deviate from the plan without approval and anyway, I thought he had been very rude to me and the title 'Ignor Ramus' might be more suitable than 'Colonel Ramus!' He didn't react too well to this and his face quickly changed to the colour of his nose as he raged about his army days and that I should have been court martialled for my insolence! On this note he stormed off the site and we carried on with our work. Rover meanwhile trotted happily around the place and did whatever he had to do. I should mention that he had a habit of hoisting his bottom up as high as possible and then doing his business on top of a big stone

or something similar. I think it was possibly the same day as the Colonel Ramus incident when Rover came skidding round the corner of the kennels closely followed by a very angry Bob Teare shouting "Keep that dog under control can't you?" when I enquired what was the matter, Bob insisted that I follow him round to the front of his bungalow to see what my wayward dog had done - and there for all to see was a large collecting box made of glass fibre in the shape of a begging dog (a golden retriever I seem to remember) with a medallion round its neck which had the words 'Please give generously' painted on it. The words were partly obscured however by dog pooh, still soft and steaming, sliding down the front of the dog - and apparently Rover was the donor! Bob was very cross and said something of the order that 'if he had a gun he'd shoot the bloomin thing!' I apologised and washed down the plastic dog for him and even he had to laugh when I pointed out to him that maybe Rover could read because he had certainly given generously! On hearing the story later, Marj Joughin was horrified, not about the pooh but about Bob's remark said in the heat of the moment that he would shoot the bloomin dog! "For Gods sake" said Marj "this is an animal sanctuary!"

And so it continued 'til the cattery was eventually completed albeit with many 'modifications' - then the hard part began - the final payment! I had submitted the final bill and it was approved by the architect but some nine weeks later there was still no sign of a cheque. I held the trump card however as, with all the hiccups along the way and suspecting something like this may happen, I had at my own expense, fitted good quality 5 lever locks to both doors and held on to the keys. True to form, I had received quite a few phone calls requesting the keys be handed over to the secretary Marj, so I explained that when I received the cheque, they would receive the keys! Well, I think all this must have become too much of a strain for poor Bob Teare and his wife because he eventually called to see me and paid me the two and a half thousand out of his own bank account! "I can't stand it any more" he told me, "It's a mad house, my home is full of cats and it's driving us mad too!" I remember handing over the keys to this elderly man and feeling sorry for his plight, I enquired as to whether he would ever be reimbursed by the society "God knows" he said as he left me"! God knows?? A crazy organisation indeed!

Derry Kissack Ltd

This would be in March or April of 1979 and sadly it was to be my last job with Kissack Brothers Ltd. It was a very unhappy time for me and in a 'less than friendly' split I decided to start a new company of my own called Derry Kissack Ltd and I bought a disused workshop in Queen's Road, Onchan from my brothers in law Bob and Niels Skillicorn. This property was semi-derelict but it was just what I needed to start afresh and it already had three phase electric for the joiners' machines although about half of the roof was missing! It was at this time that Karen and myself decided to move to Onchan and I embarked on building another bungalow at Birchill Grove on a plot we also bought from her brothers Bob and Niels. It was, as far as I was concerned, to be a temporary or stop gap measure, quick and simple design to provide some thinking time whilst we found our feet again following the turbulent times of the split up with Howard and his wife Helen. I think it was probably one of the very last buildings in the Island to be built with the old Peel clay bricks, as the brickworks had ceased production and delivery, so, being a traditionalist and a great believer in the qualities of these bricks I undertook to both load and haul them 'home' myself. Tom Clague was 'brickie' working on a good set of footings laid by Irishman 'Dixie' Dean - a real character who seemed to work 24 hours a day and never got tired! I remember one warm evening he was stripped down to his underpants while mixing batch after batch of concrete and he would never bat an eyelid as he worked like a horse! The plasterers at the job were Brian 'The Moot' Moore, his brother Roy and Ross Jones, and besides the cups of tea and good banter it was memorable with the good craick always associated with the building trade in those days. This 'temporary' bungalow turned out very well and was to be our home together for the next sixteen years.

And so to the start of a new life and business venture in Onchan and in hindsight it would seem that I have spent much more of my life there than I ever did in my birthplace of Crosby, so much so that I now consider myself an Onchan man!

It was a big wrench to make the move, as day after day Graham Seed and myself carted first the building trade machines and equipment and then all the furniture to begin again in the unknown! Well not exactly the unknown, we had only lived in Crosby together for some four years and the old workshop was well known to me having repaired it many times during my apprenticeship. The business took off well and my old mate Mike Corris asked me to help him with quite a large job he had secured at the old Crescent Cinema in the centre of Douglas Promenade. The building needed to be gutted and a complete new floor was to be added right through from front to back to replace the existing balcony level. This was to be good 'inside' work and keep us going all winter right through in fact 'til T.T. week with Graham Seed going in early on in the autumn to strip out the existing ceiling and stage area with Roy Moore and Ross Jones. I think Graham saved a considerable amount of expense on the site with his 'bravado', somewhat foolhardy approach to demolition 'good practice' and total disregard for health and safety! I remember going down there one day and on hearing a chainsaw high above me, I looked up some seventy feet to the ceiling to see Graham standing in a rope sling with the revving machine almost at arm's length while he cut away a huge portion of the timber and Celotex ceiling! As that came crashing down I think he shouted something like "Timber!" as a warning to anyone who may have strayed beneath him! I did remark on the total lack of any scaffolding whatsoever but he assured me (after his bollocking) that it didn't matter as he had nearly finished anyway, and finish it he did, which opened the way for the erection of the new steel by Wilson and Collins Ltd, supervised by Percy Wilson himself who remarked on the accuracy of our footings and wall pads which he said made his job much easier. Leading Percy's gang was Dougie Corlett, a jovial character, who worked for Wilson and Collins for many years and did his bit to add to the general humour already abundant on the site. When all the steel was in place, an 'Omnia' floor was laid over it with concrete beams and infill blocks by the gang from Rural Industries at Braddan led by 'Bo' Lyons. We were joined some time later on, as work progressed rapidly, by plastering gang

Crescent Cinema

Ray 'Lofty' Hardinge and his team - more humour - with none other than Nigel Walton who nearly started a riot one day whilst working at the front of the building! It must have been around Easter time because the horse trams were operating and there was quite a number of visitors (mostly pensioners) waiting in queues for the Tours Coaches parked on the forecourt of the cinema and certainly within earshot of our site. To cut a long story short as they say, there had been some discussion and controversy in the local press and radio as to whether it was cruel to allow a horse to pull a tram. Nonsense of course, as the horses have always been well treated and none other than Jimmy Saville proved the point by pulling a tram along he Promenade himself, it was being stirred up by fanatics and a local dog loving lunatic who had a heart of gold but often held the wrong end of the stick! With his radio switch on to the 'Mannin Line' and listening to one of these 'phone in' discussions, Nigel, in a very loud voice said "Well. I don't think they should clout the tram horses!" He was of course joking and doing his own stirring to provoke a reaction and it certainly worked because before many more minutes had passed someone must have picked up on this and phoned in to the Mannin Line! It caused quite a storm and had repercussions for quite a few weeks until things eventually calmed down again!

By 1979, which was Manx Millenium Year, the new Fire Station had been commissioned in Peel Road and so the old fire engine garage in Lord Street was now redundant. It came about that Bill Corkish the builder (and councillor) of Kingswood Grove, had the job to demolish this building and tidy up the site opposite the old Hanover Street school. At that time, Mike Corris did most of Bill's ground works and haulage, often calling on me to help out and so it was that we took down what had almost become a landmark in Douglas. Although by now a bit shabby, but still with its bright red doors facing the street, this garage which dated from 1936, had seen lots of action such as the big fire at Woolworths and of course, Summerland, which I suppose may have been the turning point when it was realised that the equipment of the day, including the station and this garage, desperately needed to be updated. So a new station was built and Mike and myself demolished the old one and I am pleased to say that many years later, this same garage is now my workshop at Ballakissack Farm! In fact it sometimes seems to me that things are or are not meant to be, well in this case it was almost uncanny because this building was almost a guide to my future.

The old roofing and wall cladding sheeting was disposed of to a few farmers who thought they could make use of it and all the steel frame was carefully stored in the Queens Road workshop waiting for the day when a suitable site could be found for its re-erection. It was to 'reside' in the workshop for another ten or eleven years however, often being tripped over and cursed for the lack of space whilst a new site was sought. I thought at one stage in the early 1980's that I had it

'cracked' when I bought some land at the 'Butt' in Onchan which is now the Village Green behind Welch House, but I changed my mind and sold it again. I suppose it was put on the 'back burner' for a while after that and I contented myself with the fine workshop that I was fortunate to own in the lane off Queens Road.

Quite a lot seemed to be happening around this time after my move to Onchan, not least the challenge of 'going it alone' and the formation of the limited company with the help of my old mate Mike 'Waller' Kennish. The gathering of necessary equipment and plant that would be needed began in earnest and a small digger was bought in a derelict state from Henry Costain at the Moorhouse Farm in Colby. It was an International 2275 industrial machine with a Wainroy back acter which really was in a dreadful state but as ever and with Howard's help it was rebuilt and lasted for about six more years albeit with many modifications along the way. These mods included fitting a front bucket from an old J.C.B. that I bought from Rob Brew in Peel and a hydrostatic steering head, also from a J.C.B. which only turned the steering to the left! This piece of equipment had been thrown out as useless at E.B. Christian's, White Hoe Garage and the lads there had given up trying to make it work, so this meant a challenge and we fitted it to our machine anyway! We must have spent many hours trying to get it working properly, as must our predecessors at E.B's, and then, just as we were about to give up on it, Graham Seed decided he could fix it. As I have said before, Graham suffers with dyslexia and struggles with some fairly simple problems in life but when it comes down to complicated situations he really does surprise everyone with his apparent 'genius'! He took the weighty hydraulic unit home with him one night and stripped it down on the kitchen table, much to the delight (I'm sure) of his mother and father! With oil, nuts and bolts, washers, springs and ball bearings all over the place he eventually fathomed it out and reckoned that a spring and a ball bearing had been assembled wrongly, probably from new at the factory. "Never" I said, but my scepticism was severely shaken when he refitted the unit, started up the machine and - hey presto- it worked!

Graham worked with me for fourteen years and in that time I never

The old International 2275 digger

Working at Margy and Jim Lace's property in Greeba

remember him being late for work and he was always the last to leave at night. Just like his grandfather Seymour Corkill who had worked for the family firm all his life, he was truly loyal and very hard working and always applied himself 100% to whatever we were doing. Indeed often was his enthusiasm so intense that he would take the very tools out of my hands and not content to merely assist me he would push me to one side and take over! This was all very well when it was a job that he understood or was good at but needless to say on some occasions he came unstuck and things didn't just work out!

Anyone who has ever driven a wheeled digger (or JCB as all diggers were once called by many who knew no different!) will tell you that they are quite an ungainly and clumsy machine when manoeuvring in a cramped space. Well - a back garden behind a house in Sunningdale Drive in Onchan was one such

cramped space and in true form Graham worked hard with the old digger and J type wagon (which only just fitted up the narrow drive with inches each side) while he stripped off the top soil and dug out the footings for a new extension. A very neat and tidy job was the outcome with all the soil carted safely away and with no damage to either vehicle or property which was no mean feat in such a tight space and then....... I think I made the mistake of praising him and his expertise as, over the noise of the engine, he shouted something like "What did you expect?" and in this moment of glory at the rarely given praise, he stuck the machine in gear to leave the site on a 'high' only to forget all about the confines of the garden as he swung round towards the road and almost totally demolished the garage of the house next door with the back bucket! The side wall teetered for a split second before it fell into the garage, leaving the roof hanging

The J5 on the scale at the Point of Ayre

precariously and a Triumph Herald inside covered in bricks and pebble dash! To be fair, there wasn't much holding the wall to start with as it was built of the old Scotch bricks and lime mortar - no match for a digger in full flight!

Accidents will happen as they say but some are waiting to happen, as was the case one day when I returned to the workshop to be confronted by the sight of our five ton Bedford J type sitting on top of four forty gallon oil drums while Graham worked underneath it! "What the f.... are you thinking of?" I shouted at him as he scrubbed away with a wire brush beneath the swaying wagon. I was genuinely alarmed at what I saw but more so, I was dumbfounded and amazed at how he had actually achieved such a feat entirely on his own with only a garage jack at his disposal! I can't remember what his instructions for the day actually were all those years ago but I think he was probably just asked to

adjust the brakes and apply some grease where necessary but being Graham and always eager to please me he must have decided to do a full overhaul and repaint as well. So without any thoughts of health and safety and armed with four rusty tar barrels or oil drums, some wood blocks some aluminium beer kegs and an old jack he lifted the whole wagon some four feet in the air so he could work in comfort underneath it!

This particular wagon was bought as a replacement for our old 'J' 138 JMN and although a bigger model J5 it looked much the same to the uneducated, so much so that they shared the same registration for a few years, the two never being out at the same time however!

Graham has always been a 'character' and long may he be so and he has achieved much in life, coping well with the dyslexia which has dogged his progress and would surely have stopped a lesser man in his tracks. As I have mentioned previously he worked with me for fourteen years 'serving his time' as an apprentice mason/bricklayer which included slating and tiling and just about everything else in the building trade along the way! It seemed a long hard road for me at the time and I do admit to shouting at him on frequent occasions when I became frustrated by his 'back to front' approach but generally we got on well and a lot was achieved, including his building of a fine house for himself. It was with sadness for both of us I think when he left the firm in the late 1980's to work at the Majestic Hotel where he had been offered a lot more money in wages than I could pay him. A good man and a good friend.

The 'Hot Dogs'

aving previously mentioned the Southern MCC and my joining their committee in 1977 when things in the club were generally at a low ebb, it became clear that their finances were also pretty low. For many years the club had run a very successful 'Scramble' at the Braaid course by kind permission of the Watterson family on 'Mad' Sunday but things became difficult there, especially with parking problems on the main Foxdale road. Help was offered by the Ramsey club to run the event at their course at West Kimmeragh at Bride as a joint venture and this seemed a good idea at the time. After a couple of years however the Ramsey Club adopted the event as their own and the Southern club were more or less told that they were by now surplus to requirements! This of course meant that the Southern club had lost one of their main sources of income and something needed to be done to provide an alternative.

I made a suggestion that maybe we could charge an entry fee for spectators to watch a trial during T.T. week and that I thought that Scarlett, with its natural amphi-theatre could be the ideal venue. I envisaged maybe guest riders and even some catering facilities to try and build some atmosphere. We gave it a try and it turned out to be very successful at around 25p a head, although one or two 'tight' locals refused to pay on the grounds that there was a public footpath running right through the land! On the catering side, I decided to make a 'Hot Dog' stall for the benefit of the club, the punters and of course myself! I had some limited experience along those lines, having transported a young chap called Filson out to Tynwald Fair some years ago with a proper stall which belonged to Onchan Stadium and with which he seemed to be very successful.

From memory, I designed a replica of the 'real thing' and using an old industrial battery charger and an aluminium side panel taken from an Austin van, a 'stop me and buy one' type thing was created and mounted on a pair of pram wheels! I now needed the cooking part of it and for this expertise I turned to my old friend Nigel Kermode. Nigel, resourceful as ever, came up with an old 'Bain Marie' with four cooking pots, complete with lids, so I discarded the electric heating elements from underneath, mounted the top part on my battery charger and opted for gas rings instead - bingo - success! He also thought that I may be able to sell some soup as well, so a big aluminium pot with a tap was pressed into service, also using gas and mounted beneath the 'Bain Marie'. I painted the whole thing with some 'Tekaloid' yellow paint and adorned it with some T.T. stickers to complete the effect. Now all it needed was a trial run!

The Scarlett trial was scheduled for the Thursday night so I thought that if I was to get some experience first it may help. This I set about doing by going to the Monday races of the T.T. and with the permission of Mr Walker from Glen Roy I positioned my Ford Thames van 9491 MN at the Windy Corner and waited for the spectators to arrive. I had spent time on shelving the back of the van, making sure I had everything, including water cans, gas, finger rolls, greaseproof paper, 'Westlers' sausages, mustard, onions and sauce - phew! - I even had a canvas awning tied to the ladder carrier on the roof and draped over a makeshift 'roof' which kept the two back doors an even distance apart and covered me as I stood between them. So the scene was set, I had been to Craines the bakers in Peel Road and Peter had baked me a fresh batch of finger rolls and wished me luck, Nigel had given me a catering pack of lentil soup (which was nearing its sell by date but it's label professed to make five gallons when diluted!) what could possibly go wrong?

The weather that's what! The race was postponed and my only company besides some bedraggled sheep was a young constable called Simon Mann and yes - you guessed it, he had a flask and sandwiches and absolutely no need of my 'Mobile Catering Services'! The racing was eventually called off that day and I remember being somewhat disillusioned and feeling let down by my choice of venue when I passed the Creg-ny-Baa on my way home with a van full of stuff. Whilst I had been hardly visible in the mist at Windy Corner, the Creg for much of the day had been basking in sunshine, so, not to be beaten, I sought permission for the land by the car park above the pub for the next day.

I rang Trevor Baines, the owner, who was most co-operative, he granted me permission and merely requested a few complimentary hot dogs for himself and guests who would be there spectating from their open topped ex Douglas Corporation A.EC. double decker bus. Karen came with me along with young Johnny Marshall, her nephew, and we had a great day of it, selling absolutely everything we had, including nine gallons of soup! Quite odd you may say as the packet said five gallons! The answer being that I had to thin it right down to get it through the tap and it was in so much demand at 10p a cup that no one seemed to notice me unclogging the 'works' with an old bike spoke that had been lying in the back of the van! Johnny was very handy at procuring water and refilling the cans behind the Creg at an outside tap, until the landlord caught him and told him to 'buzz off' or something similar as he was

completely stopping the supply to the pub! I learned later that there is no mains water supply to the pub so from then on I used to bring 25 gallons of water with me - sorry landlord!

The great thing was that this home made contraption actually worked and worked very well indeed so much so that I used it for many more years without any modifications whatsoever.

The Thursday night at Scarlett also went off very well and from memory I think that Mick Andrews was guest rider and that the club made some £300.00.

Karen and myself had some good days on the 'hot dogs' at the T.T., always treating ourselves to a big steak at Jurgens restaurant afterwards. Our old dog Rover often accompanied us, usually lying quietly in the van doing nothing more than having an occasional scratch which nowadays would probably be frowned upon by the health inspector, but for some reason at Scarlett one night, he decided to have a run around. We were very busy and couldn't keep an eye on everything at once but I remember a very large German visitor buying some hot dogs and retiring to lean on the stone wall by the van when he suddenly started swearing at the top of his voice in his native tongue and which I didn't understand but seem to remember the words 'Fudge Dogg' or something like that! It was no wonder as there was a roar of laughter (which didn't help) because Rover was cocking his leg in the crash helmet which belonged to the German with the now purple coloured face! The laughter was not fully understood by the man, who had put his expensive helmet on the ground while he ate his food and a further witty remark by Keith Marshall brought the house down when he said 'Are you potty training your dog?'

As I said, the German gentleman didn't seem to think that the laughter of the crowd was entirely warranted and up until then I don't think he even knew that the dog belonged to me, so when Karen offered him a full kitchen roll to mop out his helmet he began to soften a bit and thanked us for our concern, taking a complimentary coffee and calming down nicely, that is until Rover hopped up in the van, after all our efforts to discreetly shoo him away as a stray dog and the poor man, despite our apologies, walked away muttering something in German and I never saw him again.

I suppose we had some ten years selling hot dogs to hungry people but possible only about half of those at the T.T. and the rest at local motorcycle events to try and add something to the fun and atmosphere. One such event was the annual fancy dress trial on the 2nd January at Glen Lough where the hot dogs were given away free as a good will gesture along with a 'compulsory' pint of ale for the adults (and pop for the kids). On the closure of Craines bakers I went to Crellins in Grosvenor Road and the manager Pat Goodby became a good friend, always ready to supply me, even though he must have been busy with his regular orders, he never batted an eyelid when late at night I would order 1,000 finger rolls for the following morning 8.00am. In hindsight he may well have been glad of the extra business as at that time many local small bakeries were going out of business and in fact Crellins also eventually conceded and amalgamated with Ramsey Bakery where Pat now works.

I eventually gave the old hot dog stall to the Southern 100 club courtesy of their chairman Phil Taubman, but I don't know what happened after that. What I do know is that I had many good days with it, it was hard work and quite exhausting but very lucrative and we enjoyed many a good steak on the strength of it!

Wensleydale and the Cover Bridge Inn

I mentioned a Ford Thames van 9491 MN, as my transport in the venture and I think it is worthy of a mention as it was to be the last of many such vehicles I had owned and enjoyed the use of. It, like the J type Bedford wagon, had belonged to Bruce Mackie the builder of Allan Street in Douglas and I bought it for £5 with the engine knackered. It received another engine and a respray in green with a yellow roof in the colours of the John Deere tractor range - why? I just liked the colour! I should say that these vans were a 'must' for any real motorcyclist! This leads me on to my first trip over to Wensleydale in Yorkshire to compete in the Richmond (Yorks) MCC two day sidecar trial. It was a super event on the lines of the Manx two day but in the wonderful Dales, taking in Coverdale and Wensleydale and centred around the lovely market town of Leyburn. The Yorkshire connection was forged by Dougie Beaumont who, with his wife Maureen, had a static caravan at West Witton and he had 'pioneered' the event for a couple of years and extolled its virtues being enthusiastically supported by Trevor and Keith Moore who persuaded me to have a go.

So it would be May of 1979 when we loaded the Ford van with the Montesa sidecar outfit, petrol, spanners, baggage, Phil Tasker, his wife Erica, their new born baby Cheryl, Karen, myself and of course Rover the dog! This was quite a cramped load indeed with the front wheel of the bike in between two makeshift seats, forming an arm rest and with the carrycot on top of the engine, we set off on the Manx Line sailing on the Friday afternoon, eventually arriving late at night in Leyburn none the worse for the experience but wondering about a slightly larger van the next time! We had a great weekend in wonderful warm weather and became totally 'hooked' on the event and the friendly nature of all the people there, so much so, that it became almost 'religion' with another twenty years of top class competition and unequalled craick and fellowship that were to follow.

We never won the event but were quite well placed on a number of occasions and were actually 'overnight' leaders on the first day once in the early nineties! Speeches were made in the Golden Lion at one of the memorable Saturday night suppers laid on by the landlord Richard Wood, and the scene was set for a Manx win next day - what could possibly go wrong? In hindsight I think that fourteen or fifteen pints of Theakstons XB had something to do with our slide from fame the next day and we finished tenth!

New and lasting friendships were made and continue to this day, with a great 'overseas' link each year which developed into other Dales holidays for us and likewise T.T. trips and suchlike from the 'other side'. It was not uncommon to see possibly ten or twelve vans and or cars/trailers passing over Ingleton Tops to Hawes in the lovely Wensleydale, for the annual pilgrimage of Manx sidecar competitors, wives, girlfriends and supporters who were just there for the beer! 'Hot spots' in the evenings were the local pubs which had 'quite flexible' closing hours to say the least but we were amazed when the local constabulary would merely look in, nod at the landlord and say something like " Don't be long " before disappearing into the night! In hindsight, I think that the various landlords were either known to keep a 'good house' or simply knew someone 'higher up' because it was a great arrangement and a brand new experience for us. I think it is fair to say that never before or since, has a landlord anywhere perfected the art of 'late tasters' to equal the late Jim Carter of the Cover Bridge Inn near Middleham! Jim. Along with this wife June, ran a fantastic pub with really tremendous portions of mouth watering home made food where the gammon covered the big oval serving plate completely with the chips, eggs and pineapple all piled up on top. They marinated the huge steaks with a secret recipe that had no equal, their prices were very low and all you needed was a good appetite! The scene was set for a 'lock in' and a dozen or more pints of Theakstons before the short drive back to Leyburn in the early hours. 'Lock in' is not the correct terminology because I never remember Jim being the slightest bit flustered

by threats to close him down and he continued to break the law so blatantly that he had to 'cool it' a bit on one occasion when the local magistrates took away his licence and banned him from the premises! His answer to this was to buy the bungalow next door and to put the licence in June's name. She slept in the pub as the designated official and Jim lived next door for a couple of years until things eventually returned to normal.

I remember one night when it was well after midnight and a policeman entered the unlocked door, Jim offered him a drink to see him on his way but he wasn't having any and he warned Jim that if his light was still on when he came back that way then he would book everyone and out he went on his rounds..... Well it seemed the end of a good thing for us and we began to empty our glasses when Jim said" Do you want another lads?" When we looked at him in amazement and knowing his history of losing his licence, he laughed and said "He won't be back!". We took his word for it and carried on as normal and I think it was around this time that we more or less adopted the 'cover' (as it 's fondly known) as the Manx Embassy. This unique 16th century Inn with its quaint lifting latch on the door as you enter has been a great favourite of ours, spending many evenings there and indeed staying there on many trips, in the cosy en-suite accommodation above. Jim was a time served joiner and had attempted to upgrade some rooms to en-suite and this he made a fair job of but it has to be said that he was no plumber or heating engineer! In these early days of en-suite, which was becoming fashionable, Jim had split two areas with a well made partition wall but had left a large radiator spanning both rooms! The new partition simply butted up against the radiator with the woodchip paper roughly lapped over it where necessary and so it was shared by both rooms! Such was the charm of the place but some time later it was put right when Jim found a suitable plumber and bit by bit the place was upgraded but never losing its character. A wonderful cosy bar with a big open fire was patronised for many years by a local character called Ted Banks and he had his own spot by the fire most nights of the week, sitting on an old high backed kitchen type arm chair albeit with one of its arms missing but woe betide anyone who dared to sit there without his permission.

I mentioned the Golden Lion in Leyburn Square and I must say that for the twenty odd years we rode in the 'Gerald Simpson Memorial Two Day Trial' (as it was formally known) we made it our first port of call and it was an unwritten rule that we would all meet up there at 4pm on the Friday prior to the event to begin the social side of things with a few pints of Theakstons XB and a good natter. With all the English crews who had travelled up from all over the mainland. It was however the Saturday night that became the main event socially, taking over from an organised film show that was laid on in the early days by the Richmond Club. That seemed to 'die the death' and the do at the Golden Lion became very popular with the majority of crews and their followers, largely thanks to the landlord Richard Wood. He would concoct a wonderful 'Manxmans' menu and the place would be packed for an evening of superb hospitality.

I got to know Richard very well over the years and he had at one time lived in the Island in the Glen Roy area of Laxey, but at a very young age, possibly around fifty or so, he collapsed and died at the funeral of his mother. A sad loss indeed but ironically it seemed to coincide with the demise of the trial around 1999 and he, like the event is much missed by all of us.

New business - new workforce

By this time in the early 1980's, we had settled nicely into our new workshop in the lane off Queens Road in Onchan. We had done many repairs to the place including some steel beams to support the roof and had generally made ourselves at home. We had the big circular saw, planer, morticer and cross cut all wired up and some lights installed by my old mate Phil Taubman. We then added an air compressor and an overhead hoist for the lifting of heavy things where needed in the joiners shop on the first floor. It seemed at this time that there was a bit of a down turn in the island and a shortage of work for the building trade in the trend of 'Boom or Bust' that we had become used to, but I have to say that if anything, it suited me because some good men became available and being very busy myself I was able to take them on. Dougie Forster was the first of these, bricklayer/mason and comedian would probably be a good description of him and an excellent tradesman he certainly was. Among other jobs, we were building an extension on an hitherto derelict cottage near to the Highway Board depot at Glen Duff. It belonged to Mike Roddy who, along with his partner Jim Derbyshire, ran the very successful D and R Joinery Manufacturing business at the fine workshop in Dalton Street previously owned by Douglas builders J.K. Brearley Ltd.

I learned a lot from Doug and I became his 'apprentice' when learning the finer points of bricklaying and stonework. I always enjoyed his company at work and he was never short of a good story to tell me. He once told me that he had had a very tough childhood with little or no money and had been brought up in poverty, living for a while at 'Social Cottage' near Axenfell plantation at Lonan. Social Cottage was owned by the people of the parish and this remote 'hovel' was in fact the 'poor house' of the Laxey and Lonan area, without electricity or mains water. His diet as a child was mainly rabbit, pigeon and even nettle soup, such was the hardship of that time for him. Doug was a first class tradesman and I well remember him building a bungalow in Birchill Grove in Onchan for J.T. Skillicorn Ltd, entirely single handed and without a labourer. This was an amazing feat as he mixed all his own mortar, laid all the bricks and obviously handled everyone of them twice as he first loaded the scaffold and then built them into the walls, not to mention the lifting of all the lintels. I think it also worthy to say that this particular bungalow had a dormer roof with a very steep pitch and a substantial chimney stack, so it needed three full lifts of scaffold and I have to say that never before or since have I met a more determined man who, as well as being very strong physically, was resolutely focused on the job in hand and would never be beaten.

He was with me for about three years and in that time we had also started a new apprentice joiner, Neil Christian who was the elder son of Peter and Brenda. Peter, from the world of motorcycling asked me one day if I could give young Neil a try and I'm very pleased to say that he was probably the most able lad I ever had a hand in training. He learned quickly and, thanks to the wide variety of work that we tackled, he could turn his hand to anything. One day he could be bricklaying with Dougie and the next he could be making a staircase with either myself or Bobby Fick. He was a very versatile lad and could even be found on wet days possibly welding and spraying one of the vehicles which needed repair or refurbishment. A true 'all rounder' he was school-boy Moto Cross champion as well and a first class trials rider which he continues to be to this day. We were involved with 'Ind Coope' brewery through the 1980's and as such, Neil gained experience in bar fitting and fine joinery work, which I'm sure has, along with his other grounding and versatility, stood him in good stead for the running of his own building business today.

Bobby Fick had joined us at around the same time as Neil and had stepped into the 'breach' when Ed Burrows decided to leave for a while and work with his brother Johnny as a partnership. I was very pleased to be working with Bobby again after quite a few years and he stayed with us for around five years and the end of Neil's apprenticeship, at which time he had also reached 65 and wanted to take things a bit easier. In fact we had a very good work force and could tackle quite sizeable projects as well as the day to day jobbing work which often included haulage and digger work for other small building firms such as P.V.T. Ltd (run by Steve Taylor), Howard Corlett, Norman Caley and brothers Ed and Johnny Burrows.

Because of this I had started to look for a bigger wagon and eventually bought the Ford D800 that I had taken my test on, 193 PMN. It was by now in a sorry state after some twenty years of hard work with J.T.S. Ltd and we set about rebuilding it. The old workshop has a very awkward doorway and it proved very difficult to enter with the larger vehicle, so much so that it nearly ended in disaster on one occasion. Neil was helping me to tow another similar Ford we had bought for the necessary parts for the re-build and we were easing it through the very narrow doorway with the help of the towing vehicle - the 'J' type. This Ford was to go in forwards with Neil steering it and with the old 'J' type back to back with it, which I was driving and awaiting a signal from him to begin pushing. With the driver's door of the Ford already removed Neil was able to see better and we started the tricky operation with just inches to spare on each side when Neil spotted a wood block by the front wheel of the Ford. Thinking that the block would hamper our progress, he jumped out to move it just as I started to reverse and he became trapped between the door frame of the workshop and the cab of the broken down lorry. Not being able to see him by now owing to the angle of the doorway and the position of the mirrors I continued slowly back and feeling a slight resistance which I thought would be the wheel passing over the wood block, I thought no more of it until......a distraught Neil staggered into my view by the side of my wagon holding his left arm! His left fore arm had snapped like a twig he told me later as he held it across his chest to protect himself from worse injury to his head and upper body. He was obviously in agony but being a strong lad and certainly no wimp, he got into our old transit van and I drove him down to Nobles Hospital, doing my best to avoid too many pot holes along the way, whilst going as quickly as I could.

It certainly was not a nice experience but being young and strong he recovered well and eventually got some compensation from our insurance - the doorframe was undamaged!

The summer cabarets

During the late seventies and early eighties we had a great time socially with nights out such as the 'Grumble Weeds' at the Palace Lido which were comparable to the very best light entertainment anywhere and to this day I have never been to a better show than the very last night that they performed at that wonderful venue, now sadly demolished. A big gang of us would sit near the front at a table especially reserved for us by Brian Murray who worked there at the time and actually took part himself as an 'outrider' in a fantastic tribute to Elvis Presley, where a real army Jeep was flanked by the motor cycle outriders right through the centre of the wonderful ballroom! The atmosphere was 'electric' to say the least and this was evident by the appreciation shown by the packed house as they applauded non stop, refusing to sit down during a prolonged standing ovation which seemed to go on and on with the 'Grumble Weeds' by now quite exhausted after numerous 'encores'!

We would be like 'V.I.P's' thanks to Brian, who is of course the brother of my friend from school days Phil, as we took our places right at the front of the 'Lido' which would be packed to capacity every single night of the summer season in those days of mass tourism in the Island. We would be with our friends Vanessa and Kevin Cubbon and Phil and Pauline Murray and the humour and fun was second to none! Another great show at the time was at the Villa Marina Garden Room and it was a full cabaret show promoted by Billy Cain the joiner and Dominic Delany the scaffolding contractor. Top of the bill was a Liverpool comedian 'Al T. Cosy', ably supported by our very own 'Salamander, the Escapologist and Mystical Magician from the East!' (His real name was Percy Cowley and he kept a boarding house on Douglas Promenade!) The music was provided by 'Nelsons Crew' lead by the laid back and ever cool John Nelson himself.

I well remember one evening when we were sitting near the front and thoroughly enjoying the show, 'Salamander appeared dressed in full Arab turban and cloak and was duly introduced as 'Salamander, the Mystical Magician etc etc' and looking quite 'eastern' to say the least, complete with gravy browning for a fake tan, he commenced his act by climbing a ladder of swords and laying down on a bed of nails, when Kevin Cubbon shouted "Hey Percy! - All right yisser?" - and to this all the locals in the crowd who knew Sal's real identity erupted with laughter! Salamander however being a true professional never batted an eyelid and continued his act which really was very good! Dominic asked us to 'be quiet' and the show went on. This included a very good version of the escape from a straight jacket which 'Sal' certainly had off to a fine art but I'm afraid that we could never take it seriously as we knew that he wore a toupee! Well, this was funny enough in itself but when he donned a black 'Ballaclava' to hide the pain on his face (as he put it) while he escaped by writhing around on the floor and sweating profusely in the process for five minutes, it was obvious that the hood was just to keep his wig on! But escape he did to a huge round of applause and laughter - a great show indeed!

Al T. Cosy was very funny too and, unlike 'Sal' he was meant to be! He did a wonderful comedy routine and being from Liverpool he was one of the 'Scousers' who were so popular as comedians at that time, also appearing as landlord of a pub in the hilarious T.V. series 'Boys from the Blackstuff'. His name made mockery of a very poor quality wig that he wore and this would usually end up on a very jaunty angle as he inevitably became the worse for wear with the drink as the evening progressed.

The show would play two 'houses' and we would often make a night of it and sit through both performances because it was so good, with Al often becoming 'legless' by the end of the night as he reduced the crowed to tears of laughter. We were indeed very lucky in those days of tourism in the Island and were spoilt for choice with really good cabarets and entertainers at a large number of venues throughout a long summer season.

Another scrap digger!

By now in the mid eighties it became apparent that a better digger was needed and true to form, I managed to buy one that needed a hell of a lot of work done on it to make it useable. It was indeed a sorry sight as it lay in a gateway on the Summerhill Road in Jurby, totally out of action with no steering or drive and with the buckets down. Quite a challenge as we had no heavy lifting gear or low loader with which to move it. It was a Case 580B model that had belonged to northside firm Lacey and Evison and looked as though it hadn't seen a grease gun for years. With some thought about how to move it back to Onchan I eventually hatched a plan that would involve Trevor and Keith Moore, the old 'J' type, a piece of telegraph pole and some lengths of chain! We picked a nice fine day and set off for Jurby with a full box of spanners, some clean diesel and a battery, and on arrival we were greeted by a local sheep farmer and his son who were attending to their flock through the very gateway where the derelict machine was partially blocking their access. Our arrival seemed to brighten up their day as we reversed our wagon up close to the front of the stricken digger and began to make ready for it's removal. They came over straight away and in a friendly, if not nosey way, they began to enquire who we were? What were we doing? And something like are you mad? "You'll never shift that the son said with his hat pulled well down on his head and grinning from ear to ear, so we assured him that we would! "Betcha won't" said this somewhat comical figure who was a rotund man in his early fifties with bright red rosy cheeks, a big smile and most comical of all - just one tooth in the centre of the top row! His father on the other hand was of slight build and quite elderly and unlike his son didn't have much to say except that some other people had tried to shift it previously and they had all failed.

Meanwhile Trevor had wedged himself in the side of the engine cover and was attempting to pump some fresh diesel through and bleed the pump but his efforts were being seriously hampered by 'junior' who also had his head (complete with hat and one tooth) crowded in beside Trevor's and while watching his every move continued to advise us that "If Jimmy Faulkner couldn't shift it, I don't think you fellas stand much of a chance!"

We had a battery on it by now and it was obviously vital that we start the engine to activate the hydraulics and move the crippled machine but the battery didn't have enough 'clout' although nearly bringing success and blowing some water up out of the exhaust pipe. "Told yer" said our friend once again showing us his one and only tooth as he grinned and shook his head, but he stopped grinning temporarily as we started up the wagon and left it running whilst borrowing its battery to put on the digger - "Look at that dad! The wagon's still goin' without a battery!"

Well, this time with the fresh battery, the old machine coughed a few times and spluttered into life as Trevor gagged the air intake and nipped up the bleed screw only to get an impromptu shower of dirty water sprayed over him from the exhaust pipe! It soon picked up on all four cylinders and we were able to raise the back acter and chain it up along with the stand legs so now we were in with a real chance, as the two sheep men became silent with mouths open as they watched in amazement as the front bucket was raised and the wagon reversed underneath it! We then put the piece of telegraph pole between the front board of the wagon and the bucket to stop it sliding forward when braking but also allowing it to turn slightly like an articulated trailer. The front axle of the machine was now off the ground with lowering the bucket down onto the flat back of the truck (which had the side boards removed) and was chained securely to the towing hitch. The digger engine was now turned off and the battery returned to the wagon and Hey Presto! We were ready to go!

"Well I never..." said the father. " 'can ell" said the son as we said goodbye and 'set sail' for Onchan, while laughing our heads off all the way home! It was quite some trip too as we headed home through Ramsey, negotiating the

Case 580B in the workshop for resoration

The finished machine

many steep climbs on the coast road when a sigh of relief was the order of the day, certainly after cresting Slieu Lewaigue and of course the Corony, but the little old Bedford 'J' never missed a beat and proved yet again to be the ideal vehicle for the job in hand! Many onlookers stared in amazement as we trundled along with the digger 'piggy backed' behind an already ancient Bedford doing its best with around seven tons trailing along behind it. On reaching Onchan we still had to manoeuvre the whole lot up Queens Road and turn the 90 degree left turn into the lane by the workshop, not to mention the notorious workshop doorway - quite a challenge indeed but no match for us - a piece of pole and some chains and of course, the old J-type Bedford!

During the following few months this digger was renovated and restored to working condition including many new parts and a full re-spray resulting in a very smart little machine with the absolute luxury of a cab! Trevor and Keith Moore were involved in many such projects with me and we remain great friends to this day, knowing that if needed, we are at the end of the phone for a speedy response!

Life was soon to change direction for me however, mainly brought about by an accident at work one day. I was cutting some timber on the big circular saw in the workshop when I was struck in the right eye by a tiny piece of metal which I believe was a fragment of one of the tungsten tips on the blade. For anyone who has had a similar injury I am sure they felt, as I did, a cold shiver down their spine with the reality of the situation and some panic with the thought of possible loss of sight! I went to A and E at the hospital and an elderly man in a vicar's collar called Dr Sarkies had a go at me, poking about in my eye and eventually giving me an injection in it which was excruciating to say the least and I nearly passed out. He said to rest up for a few days, put in the ointment and wait and see what happens. Well! What happened was that the pain was quite severe and as for taking time off work, that was impossible because we were so busy, so after a few more visits to him I was left partially sighted, still in pain, very sensitive to daylight and quite disillusioned knowing I would have to 'live with it'. It did however make me think seriously about my work in general and although I enjoyed some of it the rest was quite stressful and a real chore. I think it was at that moment that I decided to try and get out of the building trade or to at least change or wind down a bit. The next step was not so easy and took quite a while to bring to fruition.

During this busy time in the 1980's projects included a new clubhouse for St Georges A.F.C. at Glencrutchery Road in Douglas, an extension at the Hailwood Centre nearby for Vagabonds R.U.F.C. and an almost total re-fit at Douglas Rugby Clubhouse in Port-e-Chee Meadow.

A large part of our time was taken up with Ind Coope, the brewers at their depot at Diamond House in Westmoreland Road and their many outlets and wine shops which they had taken over form the old Manx firm of James Kissack Ltd. We did lots of bar fitting and roller shutter work including a little job at the Airport to make the first duty free shop, as well as many new bars and alterations in numerous private hotels in Douglas. I would also plan these bars and appear in Court before the licensing board, for the Company, where new licences were sought.

A little sideline at the time was the purchase of some of the beer wagons when Ind Coope were finished with them. We would convert them to tipping bodies and repair or replace the engines as a 'wet day' job before selling them on to the building trade. I think, between Graham and Neil and myself, we did three Bedford T.K's from Ind Coope and a Ford D series from Douglas Steam Sawmills.

Meanwhile in the world of sidecar trials Philip and I won our fourth Island championship on an Italjet four stroke outfit and I consider myself lucky to do so as we were already in our third decade together and the competition was fierce to say the least. This seemed at the time that it would be the last championship we would win as the eye injury certainly didn't help my judgement of depth and distance, both crucial factors when riding observed sections in motorcycle trials!

I had at long last, started to develop the parcel of land in Foxdale called the 'Brookfield' opposite to the Baltic pub and by this time around 1987 - 88, Neil Christian was by now out of his apprenticeship and the last of my employees. I had vowed to change course after the eye injury and had let everyone else go as their particular projects or jobs came to an end and by now there was just myself and Neil. We were progressing well with a nice split level bungalow on the site and had just traded in the Case 580B digger for a brand new machine from Brian Shaw in Bolton when out of the 'blue' one day Neil announced that he had been offered a new job elsewhere. Everything seemed to be falling into place at last and although I was very sorry to see him go we parted on good terms. I think we trained him well and he now has his own business with his vehicles painted in same red livery as 'Derry Kissack Ltd' which makes me rather proud!

On my own now at work - Joe Cain

As if by magic a buyer appeared on the scene for the half finished bungalow the very same week and a deal was struck which included the site hut, all the scaffold and the mixer. No turning back now I thought, I was at last free of the building trade and decided to pursue the plant hire trail with my new Case 580G digger and the wagon.

Rather like a weight lifting off me and with my responsibilities at least halved, my new 'career' was an instant success with loads of work coming in from existing contacts and fellow builders as well as new jobs from the government departments. One of these was for Douglas Corporation when one day, after a chance meeting with Joe Cain, I got a job carting wrack off Douglas shore alongside some real characters such as Norman Mills, Ray Purvis and Alan 'Laddo' Douglas. I enjoyed this work and the craick or fun that went with it although being a tidal operation it sometimes called for a very early start, albeit with a nice early finish as well. It was quite a smelly job to say the least, especially near to the sewer outfalls such as the Metropole and Crescent end of the bay and after a day of moving this seaweed laced with the 'ozone' that went with it, my neighbours questioned the wisdom of my parking the Ford lorry outside the house in Birchill! To be fair to them the stench could be pretty strong and seemed to 'linger' in the air for a while - thank goodness for the 'Iris' scheme you may say!

One of the 'Corpy' men, usually Geroge Hogg, would be stationed on the top of the cliff edge out by Keristal at Port Soderick on the Marine Drive, where a big baulk of timber right on the edge of a 100ft drop was all that stopped the back wheels of the wagon from going over the cliff! He would have to remain there in all weathers for safety reasons to make sure each driver inched his way back far enough for the load to be discharged into oblivion and cascade downwards to the rocks far below! I sometimes wonder what 'Health and Safety' would have to say about that nowadays! In hindsight I suppose

The man who takes his trials ultra seriously — trouble is his driver doesn't!! Derry Kissack and Phil Tasker with their Italjet plot.

that what followed was a bit like perpetual motion because the tidal currents seemed to fetch all this seaweed back to the shore again for us to move the next week!

Joe Cain was something of a legend in his own right in Douglas and knew the Borough 'inside out' as the works foreman and then as Clerk of the Works for many years. He seemed to be everywhere at once as he raced around from job to job in his fairly new, but already 'clapped out' red Ford Escort! Indeed on one of his surprise visits, when he took delight in catching the unwary man who might be having a sly cigarette or 'skive', I remember picking up a stiff brush and pretending to sweep up around the 'road closed' signs at the top of

120

Drinkwater Street, just for fun, only to be spotted by my old maths teacher from the High School, none other than the fearsome Fred 'Jakey' Hogg! He was in the first car of a line of traffic which was temporarily halted by our 'stop and go' board and whilst I'm not absolutely sure that he recognised me after some 25 years, the words "Kissack! You'll end up sweeping the streets" came flooding back to me as he impatiently waited his turn and seemed to be scowling at me with the same sanctimonious look on his face from all those years ago! Very funny! He was right! Sadly when Joe retired some months later his retirement was cut short by an untimely death and ironically, the Corporation tried but failed to replace him and all their functions of road works were handed over to the D.H.P.P. where numerous people tried to achieve what he had done single handedly but with only mediocre success. Joe Cain, one of the old school, a good man who undoubtedly helped to keep down the rates in Douglas with his endeavours - an unsung hero!

Well on the way in haulage and digger hire by now, with a nice new Case digger and the Ford lorry, the old 'J' type was left in the workshop in a sad state or repair after many years of hard work, so I decided to restore it. When the work was nearing completion I took it up to 'Ballacain' in the Little Mill Road in Onchan for my friend Chris Kennaugh to spray paint it in the 'works' colours. It had by now received a replacement cab from my old friend Billy Clelland at Lanjaghan, front wings from a little bus of Parkinson the builders care of David Gleave at Barroose Farm at Baldrine and countless hours of loving care! It was well worth the effort and I still have it and use it to cart in the hay.

Buying a farm

It was an eventful and fortunate trip to Ballacain because while I was there I noticed some derelict buildings behind Chris's workshop and discovered that they had been farmed until 1974 by Chris's father Peter, when he then decided to sell them and the 50 acre farm they belonged to. He had sold up to a man called Robbie Martin, an Irishman and by all accounts a real character! Peter and his wife Barbara had decided to leave farming and turn the farmhouse, Ballacain, into a guest house. This they did, most successfully and Chris, having served his time at Mylchreests Motors, started a very good motor panel repair shop on his own account in the lovely grounds of this fine house. I was to say the least, almost enchanted by the derelict farm which had by this time descended into total ruins - just the thing for a joiner and builder to renovate! It transpired that Mr Martin had died and that he had left a wife and four children who apparently couldn't reach agreement on what to do with the property. Obviously my workshop in Queens Road was by now unsuitable for my change of work and I desperately needed more room - could this be the answer?

Negotiations were started with the executor of the estate, a nice man called Bill Beattie, who noted my initial offer and said he would pass it on to the family. Things were progressing well and after the surviving children of Mr Martin had all agreed that they would be prepared to sell, it was all down to the price! An agreement was almost reached when a third party came on the scene and started to bid against me! He eventually turned out to be a 'bullshitter' but not before he had pushed up the price by almost 50%, at which stage he suggested to me one day that possibly we could share the land because all he really wanted was to build a dwelling for himself as he wasn't that interested in the rest of the farm. I gave consideration to this, as money was tight at the time, and we agreed that if and when I could obtain planning consent for a house then he would have just the one field and I would have the rest and we would pay half each of the asking price. After initially being refused permission by the L.G.B. planning committee and going to review

Russell Moore watches the brand new machine

The Triumph Stag at Birchill Grove

supported by Onchan Commissioners, I eventually secured permission in principle and rang Ken to tell him the good news. I could tell by the silence at the other end of the phone that something was amiss and after some lame excuses he told me that he would have to back out of the deal leaving me to face the full cost of everything!

In hindsight I now know that he did me a favour in one way as the permission was in my name and all I needed was money! But he certainly cost me plenty of that and I struggled to raise it by selling almost everything in sight!

One of the first to go was a lovely Triumph Stag that I had lovingly restored to a very high standard and this went for a good price to Peter Jenkins the builder who had just bought the land and bungalow at Foxdale from me. The old workshop in Queens Road was next to go with a 'sitting tenant' who now used the joiners shop. Lee Partington, cabinet maker and 'character' had been introduced to me by Peter Kelly and now used the machines to make some beautiful bespoke pieces of furniture. He was to stay on when the new owner, local business man and famous pet shop proprietor Bill Black took over. The local bank manager in Onchan branch also played a part, with a loan to make up the shortfall and as one of the last 'proper' bank managers, Geoff Quayle and myself got on very well.

The purchase went through at last and I began to move everything up to the farm, a lorry load at a time. At the farm I managed to patch up the roof of

Stevie and Keith marshall - the new house

the small cow house so at least I had some cover for the tools and welder etc, the only snag was the absence of electricity with which to use them! Everything else had to be stacked outside and covered with tarpaulins, so it was a race against time and the elements to rebuild the old fire station building that I had kept in storage for so long just waiting for this day to come along. Things weren't so rosy at home however and Karen felt, I think, threatened by this new dimension to our lives. She had become very fond of the little bungalow in Birchill Grove that I had considered just a temporary measure and couldn't understand my lust for the countryside! But, being a country boy, I just couldn't settle in the very pretty but suburban estate and I think, in hindsight, this spelled the end of our twenty five year marriage. I

battled on with the marriage in the old fashioned way, thinking 'It'll get better, it'll be alright' but sadly it didn't get better and it certainly wasn't alright! We were clearly pulling in different directions and something would, eventually, have to give!

At this time Karen's nephews Keith, Steven and John were of great help to me and every Saturday morning great progress would be made repairing the derelict buildings of the existing farmyard and the rebuilding of the old fire station on the new site.

Meanwhile in the world of 'Trials Sidecars', Phil and myself had been 'granted' one more Manx title in the 1991 centre championship. The leading rider at the time was Adrian Beale but he had gone on holiday to Australia or New Zealand or somewhere! Who cares?!! And it fell to me to show 'em a bit of old fashioned riding grit! (one more time perhaps). In the end we had a great battle with our good friends and rivals Andy (Bobba) Greggor and his passenger Chris Molyneux and it went right to the last round or to the 'wire' as they would say now.

The final round of the championship was in King's Forest behind the lovely 'Highlander' Inn at Crosby and 'Bobba' - always a good sport, was most gracious in defeat and made me feel almost humble with his warm congratulations! A good lad!

The presentation of the 1991 Championship Award from Peter Kneale

1991 Champions again!

'Bobba' Greggor   *Nikki Keig*   *Derry*

A few beers with Ffinlo and Brenda.

The 1991 Manx Two day Trial at South Barrule

Tarmac, reclamation and motorbikes

At work in those days, I was very busy with the tarmac project at Ronaldsway Airport which was to be the first time (I believe) a runway was laid in tarmac instead of the usual concrete at our national airport. It was to be the last time that four wheeler wagons would be used for such a large project in the Island and as such it was the last time that real 'piece work' or 'ton mileage' was to be used as the method of payment. Some good fun was to be had with the humour of the drivers' and some of the names that spring to mind include Tommy Kinrade (Highway Board); Andy Clarke (Frank Jones Haulage); Jimmy Gribbin (Nelsons Haulage); Tony O'Sullivan and Cliffie Costain (A.V. Craine & Sons); Alan 'Laddo' Douglas (Nelsons Haulage); John Kissack (Kissack Bros), owner drivers' Howard Kissack. George Havercroft, Alan Watterson and myself with possibly one or two more on different days to maintain a 'nucleus' of around ten wagons.

The men at Poortown Quarry were led by Sid Taylor who was quarry manager at the time and unfortunately lost his life some time later in a 'hang gliding' accident. Alan O'Connor was in charge of the weighbridge with Les Walker operating the tarmac plant alongside an old friend of mine from Braddan School - Dougie Corkill. In hindsight, I suppose it was quite an achievement for such small lorries and such an antiquated tarmac plant when compared with todays' super new quarry at Poortown and the 'eight wheeler' trucks with their automatic load covering sheets which save the driver from the necessary covering over of the very hot load by literally walking over it to unroll the canvas sheet by hand. I remember one day when Alan Watterson and myself were 'marooned' at Castletown Promenade after the road was temporarily closed by huge waves crashing over the sea wall and making it impossible for us to reach the airport gate which was further on towards Derbyhaven on the left hand side. In total contrast to this the weather could be very hot with the tar stuck to everyone's boots! Manx weather!

A 'Pre-65' Trial at Dhoon Quarry

'Brew' time!

Also around this time, talking of bad weather and big waves, it brings to mind the night that 'Gansey' sea front at Port St Mary was nearly washed away by the high tide and gales. A big fleet of lorries was pressed into service and worked through the afternoon and well into the early hours of the next day, hauling big rocks from South Barrule Quarry to be tipped into the breached

On the runway - K444 MAN

sea wall while the huge waves crashed over the wagons and the machines which were doing their best to combat the elements. Some of the road was washed away along with a big piece of the sea wall but thanks to the prompt action of all concerned, the sea front properties were largely undamaged. I think it true to say that a kind of 'Dunkirk' spirit was achieved by a team effort and the kindness of a householder who made cups of tea for us in the early hours whilst his property was under threat!

Back at the new farm, now renamed Ballakissack instead of Ballacain, things were moving along nicely and I had mains electric and water to help with the huge task of rebuilding and restoring the six old buildings. As well as these six there was of course, the old fire station building to be re-erected which would give me some cover for the wagons when maintenance and servicing were due. Bit by bit things started to come together at the farm and good friends Paula and Phil Kelly from Ballamodda in Baldwin joined with me to reclaim the fifty acres of farmland from the ravages of nature. Much of the place was invaded by gorse and bracken with a covering of rough grass in tufts like wire wool. With a total lack of fencing and not a single gate in sight, the place resembled a prairie until it was transformed back into a farm by

On 'Gansey' Beach for the new sea wall

countless hours of work - ploughing, sowing barley and re-seeding, along with a liberal dose of lime from Billown.

Phil, and Ian Walker who worked for him at the time, got 'stuck in' to the task and they enlisted the help of a real character from Ballaugh called Stan Teare, who was a fencing and ploughing contractor for a number of years after spending a long while in the building trade with Parkinson Ltd of Braddan. Stan was a big jovial man with an almost total absence of teeth! I enjoyed many a 'cuppa' with him and his son on some cold misty days in the winter when they took shelter with me in the old cow house which was at that time the only building with a roof!

More roofs were to follow however, as one by one the buildings were sorted out, the first being a nice joiners' shop which was essential to the re-building

A classic trial on Ariel H.T.

programme. This was to be occupied by Lee Partington who moved from Queens Road, bringing with him, not only his jovial disposition, but some much needed rent as well! This rent was most welcome at this time and enabled the purchase of timber and roof trusses to be used alongside the stone and slates being re-cycled on site and this, coupled with the generosity of the Kennaugh family next door, really got the 'show on the road'! Each Saturday morning, Keith. Stevie and John would work away with me 'til ten o'clock when meat pies from Caleys would be enjoyed with our 'brew' for half an hour. Work would then continue till lunchtime when some 'Rennies' or similar would be needed to combat the indigestion from the very rich pastry!

1993 saw the first T.T. visitors to the farm and a new friendship was made with a 'larger than life' Yorkshireman - Frank Buck, trucker and all round 'good egg' from Leyburn. He was introduced to me by old mate Mike Gaines from Spennithorne also in Wensleydale, who I had known for many years and was an inspiration to me on the renovation and restoration of buildings, having completed a really nice holiday cottage complex himself at his home. Frank brought his mate Peter Wilson with him and they must have enjoyed themselves, having returned each and every year since, bringing many more friends and acquaintances with them. So much so that around T.T. fortnight, the farm becomes the North Yorkshire Embassy! I've always enjoyed the ambiance and atmosphere of the T.T. period and feel that people who dodge it with a trip 'across' are really missing out on a lot of good fellowship, fun and entertainment. As far back as the seventies, I made a good friend in Adrian Moss who would travel over each year bringing with him classic bikes and parts for the 'Auto Jumble'. Then going on to organise the first beach races on Douglas foreshore, when I helped him with the haulage of railway sleepers and posts to fashion the jumps over the timber groynes which are set at intervals to retain the sand. He was also responsible for a Classic Two Day Trial in the eighties in the true spirit of the big four stroke bikes such as the Royal Enfield, Ariel, B.S.A., Matchless and A.J.S. which were often sidelined by sections too tight for them to negotiate but suitable for smaller, lighter machines. Adrian had recognised this problem and he laid out some 'real' stuff for the big bikes with the Saturday at Rushen Mines and the Sunday at Billown

Glen. He also brought a large following of able riders and their machines over with him, ensuring a great weekend's sport for all the older riders who still could 'ride a bit' but were no longer in top competition on the modern bikes.

A great organiser, entrepreneur and indeed pioneer - thank you Adrian.

The bombs

October 1993 and a job from Housing Maintenance Manager at the Department of Local Government and Environment - Peter Hughes, at the Threshold, Jurby turned out to be quite eventful to say the least! The job was to clear the debris, gorse, old vehicles and indeed everything else including an old kitchen sink, from a large piece of land behind the back gardens of the houses on the Sulby or east side of the estate. The idea was to use this waste land to extend the gardens behind the properties to prevent it from being just a dumping ground for anything and everybody. I spent around four weeks there, working on my own, removing many derelict cars to the scrap yard at the old airfield at Andreas and gorse and other rubbish to the tip at the Point of Ayre, even digging up an almost complete (less the wheels) grey Ferguson tractor! Such was the range of 'crap' being unearthed I don't think I was unduly surprised when I first saw what looked like a small bomb! I was intrigued however and took it to show Reg Skillan who was caretaker and key holder for the remaining Jurby Camp and barracks and he laughed and said it was an incendiary or tracer bomb, he often came across them and didn't think I needed to worry my head. Sound advice indeed, so I just carried on with the work and when I dug these little bombs up I just took them to the tip in the wagon with the rest of the rubbish! The job was nearing completion and just required a rotavator to be passed over it prior to the fencing being erected. A local man called Richards (whose first name slips my mind) had a rather smart little Massey Ferguson and rotavator parked at the side of his

house which backed on to the job, so I asked him if he would do the necessary for me. He did a nice job but must have unknowingly disturbed a couple more of those rusty little WW2 explosives! Then someone found one of them and called the Police! Well! The whole place was cordoned off with tape and a young P.C. left to guard the 'Danger Area'! Some of these little bombs were gathered up and put in a plastic laundry basket next to the Police Landrover and, being by this time quite late in the evening, everyone retired leaving the constable (who shall be nameless) on guard. Sometime in the night he must have dozed off and in the morning he awoke in a panic - the bombs had been pinched! They were recovered later having been taken by children - some to school and some to their homes! Meanwhile, the Bomb Disposal Squad had arrived and I was summoned to return to the site with the digger to assist Ft. Sgt. Richard Hughes, Bomb Disposal Officer! This man seemed to know his stuff and he equipped his men accordingly, each being issued with protective body armour, face shield and helmet along with the metal detectors or Geiger counters or what ever they were called - but hang on a minute - what about me? I enquired as I leaned out the back of the machine in my normal working gear complete with old cloth cap! "Oh don't worry" said Richard as we both looked at a much larger bomb that had just appeared, "if that one goes off, none of us will know much about it anyway - it's full of T.N.T.!"

He seemed to know what he was doing and drawing on his confidence I continued to dig 'gently' when and where requested, the bucket often emerging from four or five feet down, top full of these much bigger bombs! It seemed to be raining incessantly to add to the drama and the place rapidly deteriorated and began to resemble the battle of the Somme with its own bomb craters! I remember suggesting that as they had lain quiet since the war ended, then perhaps these dormant bombs would be alright left in peace till the rain went off? "Not a bit of it!" said the sergeant as his men floundered around in the thick mud being generated by the action of the digger - "Job to be done!" By this time we had dug lots of holes all over the site and amassed quite a pile of the small bombs and as many as sixteen of the bigger T.N.T. filled ones. I explained to Richard that I had already disposed of a few dozen incendiaries previously and he was eager to know where "Why?" I said wondering if I was in for a bollocking - "well, we'll have to dispose of these somewhere - any ideas?" he enquired.

Some of these bombs were in remarkably good condition and looked quite dangerous to me but the sergeant explained that as they were without detonators they would be 'reasonably' safe, so I loaded them on to my wagon, spilling the bucket forward very slowly just in case! With the lorry now loaded, I was joined for a 'cuppa' in my cab by Gordon Garret, the man responsible for the housing maintenance at these houses and he looked rather nervous when Richard the Sergeant handed me a little metal box of detonators and asked me to mind it carefully while he went to the telephone. I placed it on the dash board of the old Ford and noticed that Gordon looked rather pale as he said something like "I hope that doesn't explode!" "So do I" I replied, "these Ford D series cabs are quite scarce now, I wouldn't want anything to happen to it!" "You're mad, you are!" he muttered and then realising that I was joking joined me in a good laugh! The drama wasn't quite over yet and after numerous phone calls, all of which proved fruitless, as one after another passed the buck, we decided to go to Ramsey Police Station and enquire there as to where the hazardous load could be blown up. Whilst parked on the reserved police parking space outside Ramsey Courthouse, a young police woman became quite 'shirty' with me and told me to move the lorry "Now!" so that she could park her Panda, only to drive away again in a great hurry when I explained that the truck was full of bombs! A decision was eventually made and permission was given to detonate them on Ballaugh Shore where they were lifted by hand from the back of the wagon into the back of a Land Rover and ferried along the beach to a 'Bund' which had been dug by hand to contain the blast - and what a blast! Probably quarter of a mile from the wagon, the shock waves rocked the suspension as the stones and seaweed flew high in the air and rained down again in what seemed like an 'after shock' - Phew!

No going back

Meanwhile back at Ballakissack the new house was well on its way up and I was thinking about slates for the roof when passing the old Villiers site one day and a chance meeting with the demolition contractor Cliff Cowin provided the answer. A deal was done and I was to leave the Ford Wagon 193 PMN on the site, where it would be filled with slates direct from the roof to save double handling, then to be unloaded straight onto my roof without their even touching the ground. There was a great feeling of satisfaction on seeing, not only the house, but also the big stone barn covered in and slated with the help of Eddie Burrows who had been invaluable, working away at the farm whilst I was gainfully employed elsewhere with the wagon and digger.

Things at home however, had gone from bad to worse. A very very hard decision had to be made and on July 26th 1995 I left home and went to live in the 'office' in the cowhouse at Ballakissack Farm. It was the hardest thing I have ever done in my life, moving from the warmth and comfort and good food with a very high standard of living to a very tiny room in the end of a cowhouse on a semi-derelict farm! I was very lonely for a long time and very much aware that Karen was feeling much the same but there could be no 'going back' for me now, I had 'made my bed' so to speak. We managed - eventually - to sort out an amicable agreement and have gone our separate ways, even managing to remain on friendly terms, both having remarried since.

Eddie Burrows

The office in the cowhouse

Steve Colley and the Purple Helmets

In hindsight, 1995 was a very sad year all round as my very good friend and chairman of the Southern MCC, Les Jones had, in February, been taken seriously ill and died in the I.T.U. at Nobles Hospital, leaving everyone devastated and mourning the loss of the man who had really 'fathered' the enduro scene in the island. For around five years, since the untimely death of his predecessor Mervyn Caley, Les had led the Club very well but finances weren't great and I suggested that we should have a fund raising 'show', possibly featuring Steve Colley, the young trials star. Some years previously I had proposed that the Club should donate some money to help the obviously talented youngster with his blossoming career and the sum of £1,000 was unanimously agreed upon by the committee of the day. Steve and his father/manager Brian, have never forgotten this generosity, albeit from the then smallest and poorest club on the island and he readily agreed to perform a stunt show on the 8th June with the proviso that he could take a few intervals during the evening to rest his wrists between stunts. A supporting act was needed! This was to become the birth of a legend as the gang of local lads who were mainly part of the enduro scene and known as the 'Sheepskull Enduro Riders' were approached through their 'leader' Steve Collins and friends Keith Moore and Chuck Bregazzi. After some discussion amongst themselves it was agreed they would do the show and someone said it would be a bit like the famous 'White Helmets' Royal Signals Display Team. "More like Purple Helmets!" said another and so a legend (although not known at that time) was to be born, I had got them into 'show business!'

The show was a huge success for entertainment value but not financially as intended. This was mainly due to the venue which was good for the performers but almost hopeless for the spectators! We had chosen the test track used by the vehicle testing station at Tromode because of its new tarmac surface, little knowing that so many people would turn out on the night and the few good vantage points were quickly occupied leaving the vast majority to stand on tip toe on the sloping ground at the side. The sloping ground was not that of a natural amphitheatre but just the reverse, sloping downwards rather than upwards and making viewing almost impossible! Par for the course you may say!

A modest sum of money was collected in buckets being passed round and all in all, a wonderful night's fun was had, with Steve riding over everything in sight and the 'Helmets' making people laugh as only they can! The commentator for the evening was Roy Moore, who, of course is very well known as a T.T. and M.G.P. 'voice' for many years since. Thanks Roy!

Was this to be the start of something much bigger?

I was lonely on my own so I worked long hours both at work and back at the farm, where I would work late at night making all the windows and stairs for the new house. I was however, kept company during the days but it was the nights I found most difficult so I either went out or worked each evening. By now I had made a couple more buildings watertight and let them out as workshops and this began a good friendship with Mike Duke and his wife Lorraine who were very kind to me. I even travelled with Mike to the Scottish Motorcycle Show in Edinburgh for a weekend helping him with the 'Duke Video' stand there. Having a good time but getting rather cold and tired in the process!

I think this coincided with the demise of Phil Tasker as my sidecar passenger after some thirty years, over which time we had won countless events and five Isle of Man Centre championships. He saw fit to end the partnership with a mumbled message on my answerphone one day and went on to be a Jehovah's Witness or something! Thanks Phil, for your support at this time!

Every cloud has a silver lining they say and I wasn't passengerless for very long as Jim Davidson stood in with me for a few events and said that a friend of his called Nikki Keig fancied a go. So after a shaky start Nikki rode with me for the next nine or ten years with some limited success but always with lots of fun, eventually seeing my retirement in 2005, from competition through failing health/injury after some 40 years at the 2-Day Trial.

Coming up to Christmas of '95 was particularly hard and despite the kindness of friends I must admit to feeling a bit low and decided to take a trip to Sheffield with old mate Ffinlo Crellin, on a coach excursion organised by Brenda Jones. Brenda, the long time, brilliant secretary of the Southern M.C.C. had put the trip together to go and watch Steve Colley in action at the indoor arena, so Ffin and myself put our names down and boarded the 'Tours IOM' coach, ably driven by John Webster and bound for Sheffield in thick mist and rain on 6th January. It was to be an eventful weekend, firstly the show was really good and then Ffinlo and Brenda got on together very very well! - For the next twelve years or so! I, meanwhile had arranged for Frank Buck to travel down from Leyburn and take me back with him for the following week. He really helped me to lift my spirits as we travelled around North Yorkshire in his Volvo FL7 Tipper with me riding 'shotgun' and learning about 'trucking UK style' while enjoying such treats as fruit cake with Wensleydale cheese! It was a good break lifting the darkness a bit and 'charging my batteries', ready for the rest of the winter wet and snow.

The passage of time sometimes sorts things out and I was kept really busy with the D.O.T. both on the highways and at times up at Government House which I particularly enjoyed, working with the gardeners over a period (in total) of around 20 years having some good fun along the way. Another interesting job was at Langness Lighthouse working for Malcolm Teare and Sons Ltd. And this involved ducting work for the eventual automation of the light and the removal of the compressor engines which powered the huge fog horn. These engines were eventually to power canal boats and I took three or four of them down to Gloucester on the Ford Cargo I had just bought from McArd Builders in Port Erin, picking up a return load of farm equipment in Leominster for Mr & Mrs Sanders who had just come to the island to farm at Ballalough in Baldwin.

I think by now that the Purple Helmets had more or less 'adopted' me and I got caught up in the excitement of it all with T.T. fast approaching. Preparations were under way for a real show this time at Onchan Stadium, much bigger and better and to be called S.M.C.C. 'Big One' again featuring Steve Colley and - 'The World Famous Purple Helmets!'

It was 'mega' to say the least, a huge crowd of people were thrilled by a great show and this time everyone could see the action! Roy Moore was again the commentator for what was to be his last time with us and through pressure of other commitments he decided to quit, leaving us without a 'voice!' So, this is where I was persuaded, somewhat reluctantly I have to say, to take over and I made my debut as commentator soon afterwards at our first off Island appearance at Oulton Park in Cheshire.

The old A.E.C. Regent double decker bus which had spent its working life on the streets of Douglas was now really coming into its heyday, having already been driven all the way to Poland in 1995, it was now going off island for a weekend trip to Knutsford and Oulton Park for the 'Make a Wish' charity to raise money for sick children to travel to Disneyland and the like. All the bikes had their wheels removed and were stacked in the lower deck, where the seats had been removed, along with the famous 'big coats' and helmets and all the lads travelled upstairs with the ale!

It was to be a truly 'Mega' weekend as we stayed at the 'posh' Cottons Hotel in Knutsford where the old bus was parked up alongside the Bentleys and Rolls' cars of the celebrities who were to join us for dinner that evening. I think it is fair to say that they had never had a double decker bus in their car park before as it snapped off more than a few branches from the flowering cherry trees that lined the drive! I remember also that we went in to Knutsford town on the bus and I drove it for the first time, right through the town centre where a few eyebrows were certainly raised by the sight of the bright yellow bus with it's Douglas Corporation transport livery. We parked outside a pub and had a great afternoon in preparation for the evening celebrations.

The A.E.C. Regent

Onchan Stadium

Leaving the Railway Inn!

134

On our return to 'Cottons' sometime later we were greeted by a sign in the lobby which said "The management wishes to apologise to its guests for the presence of the World Famous Purple Helmets!" Fame at last! We had arrived!

That evening we dined in our coats and helmets, with celebrities from sport and T.V. such as Richard Thorpe who plays 'Tubby Turner' in Emmerdale, 'Bill Webster' from Coronation Street, some 'loser' from a motoring programme called Berry and so on. The great Steve Hislop was with us too and joined in the fun which went on into the early hours making it a truly memorable occasion. We were made very welcome by the representative of 'Make a Wish', a lovely girl called Heidi along with T.T. commentator and old friend Charlie Williams who helped us to make the following day at Oulton Park quite special, inviting us to lap the circuit on our Hondas! Richard Thorpe who plays 'Tubby Turner' in the awful soap opera called Emmerdale was a good sport and took part in the wheelie bin race and a wonderful weekend was capped off with our first T.V. interview for 'Men and Motors' to be screened on their programme reaching a very wide audience!

Despite the loneliness there was to be no going back to Karen and we sold Pine Lodge at Crosby, came to an agreement on assets and money and managed to stay on friendly terms. It may sound easy now, but believe me, it wasn't!

Meanwhile the lads in the Helmets were keeping me going and around Easter of '97 Dave Rielly arrived at the house with a 600 Yamaha, full face crash helmet and boat ticket for the following day for a trip to Donnington for the Superbike to watch Steve Hislop! Talk about spur of the moment! Well, the best is often unexpected and this was no exception with a fantastic gang of lads having fun and a few beers! Dave had organised hospitality on a grand scale with a private suite and balcony overlooking the start straight, courtesy of Everards Brewery, complete with a truly sumptuous buffet, champagne and nearly enough beer!

I remember never saying 'No' to any challenge and so I was off island quite a lot that year, going soon after this to represent the island at the Inter Centre Team Trial in North Yorkshire. Another great weekend, the team rode well and I remember enjoying a pint of Theakstons bitter after the event while lying in the bath at the Golden Lion in Leyburn. My old mate Robbie Lace decided that while he awaited his turn for the bath, he would treat us to a well deserved pint. Well done Robbie! And thank you!

The big show at Onchan Stadium went from strength to strength and I remember making a 'shabby start' with the microphone but I soon got used to it and there didn't seem to be too many complaints. I had got myself a job whether I liked it or not!

The highlight of the summer was undoubtedly my first trip abroad with the Sheep Skulls and Helmets, to Italy for their annual trip to the International Six Days Enduro or I.S.D.E. This was to be an incredible adventure, where we had loaded all the bikes, helmets, coats and a few tools onto the Wilson and Collins Ltd Isuzu truck which was to be driven out to Brescia in Northern Italy by Dave Rielly, Keith Moore and the main man himself Steve 'The Bear' Collins. The rest of us were to fly there and await their arrival with the whole thing being well recorded on video - hilarious! About 8 days of tracking on the little Hondas over most of the actual route of the event, after the competitors had passed through, proved to be quite an exhausting experience especially wearing an ex Army 1941 Trench coat in the midday heat of Italy! To combat this, 'the white Tables' of just about every bar or 'taverna' in the area were sought out, often having their entire stocks of beer decimated by the 'men in the big coats!' It was indeed a stirring sight to behold when following the long line of the Big Coats stretching far into the distance on some of the long straight roads, with the sound of the engines resonating in a chorus - magical!

Big Thomas - shire horse

During 1997 I had completed more stables at the farm, with the great help of Eddie Burrows, and had some new liveries to occupy them. This paved the way for me to have a horse of my own, even after some forty years since I had ridden one but still game, I decided to buy a Shire cross Irish Draught gelding from a yard at Jurby. His name was Thomas and he was a five year old grey but almost pure white except for his quarters which were, at that stage, green! He was quite ill with a gut infection and was scouring out at the back end, so much so in fact, that after his blood tests were taken Stuart Angus, the vet, advised me not to buy him and that it would be 'touch and go' whether he could survive or not. Someone had suggested trying him on 'Bio Pro', an alternative bacteria instead of drugs and we dosed Tom for a week to ten days with the stuff, with a remarkable result. He responded almost immediately, his scouring stopped and his eyes brightened up as he tucked in to some good feed and hay, coming 'back to life' as such, in a most gratifying manner and gaining weight rapidly. He was brought on for riding and harness at Abbeylands by Alma Faragher and Hugh McCanney and went on to win some prizes at the Agricultural Shows, where even Stuart Angus himself commented on his fine state of health and congratulated us for our efforts!

I even rebuilt a horse wagon especially for him as his size demanded something quite substantial. I bought the remains of an 'Oakley' timber horse box from Willie and Lynda Christian at Ellerslie, where it had lain in a sorry state of repair and was almost beyond redemption. 'Almost' was the word however and after many hours of rebuilding and alteration to make it fit a Leyland chassis rather than its original Bedford, and with the help of Phil Quayle and Chris Kennaugh, a fine result was achieved in time for the Royal Show at Sulby in August 2000. The new 'cab and chassis' was to be an amalgamation of two old Leyland 'Boxer' ten tonners I had bought from Howard - one with good engine ex Forestry Board and one with knackered engine which was ex T.T. course. The best of both were put together in record time by Phil and myself and sent to Chris and his mate Ian for spraying red. The whole thing was finished on the eleventh hour the night before the show and I'm pleased to say that Tom always travelled very well in it, making it all worth

while. Tom was with me for ten years and it was with great sadness that I decided to sell him to a lady in Warrington who is delighted with him and rides him every day giving him the attention he deserves and which I could no longer manage through injury and health problems. A truly lovely and honest animal - my Tom!

Honda at the farm!

While riding pre'65 trials and thanks to Adrian Moss I had rekindled my friendship with the 1970 2-Day Trial Winner Terry Wright, who introduced me to the T.T. legend Mick Grant and they became regular visitors to the farm, often staying with me when competing in the Classic Two Day event at the end of August each year. Mick had witnessed my rebuilding of a very rare 500cc Ariel over a number of years and arranged the sale of it to the British Motorcycle Museum to be used as an exhibit after their disastrous fire when much priceless machinery was lost. It was a V.C.H. model with magnesium crankcases and many special parts, bought new by Dennis Christian at the old Salisbury Garage in Fort Street around 1950 and successfully campaigned by him in scrambles and trials. It eventually came my way in the late 1980's when I bought it from Willie Cowell the driver of the Mobile Library. Willie had owned it for some years but was just one of many owners over some forty years and everything on it was extremely well worn, not least the gearbox which would hardly stay in any gear without jumping back out again! I spent many hours on it and restored it to fine running order and I can honestly say that, despite it's age, it was a very lively machine.

Mick brought the Sanyo Honda team to stay at the farm to celebrate fifty years of the Marque in 1998 and they occupied the old fire engine garage at the top of the yard, making a very impressive sight when the newly painted floor was laid out in herring bone style with a line of beautiful racing bikes gracing each

The special Ariel V.C.H.

Mad Sunday at our H.Q.!

side of the building! Works mechanics completed the scene in their immaculate white overalls and were using lap top computers instead of the old spanners that I'm more accustomed to! Although some of the bikes were garaged at the old G.P.O. garage at Linden Grove, Mick wanted the peace and quiet offered by the privacy of the farm and it proved to be a huge success, so much so that the following year, being the celebration of Hondas' 40 years at the T.T., Mick and Russell Savoury of R.S. Performance, again took advantage of the seclusion. This time however, I was honoured with the presence of Mr Baba, the senior Honda mechanic and Mr Yoshi, the big boss of Honda Europe, as they worked through the night into the very early hours, on a problem with a single cylinder machine for Jim Moodie to ride the following day. I think it was well after midnight when Yoshi, with his broken English, indicated to Mick that he would prefer to stay 'Here with Derry San!' rather than return to his posh room at the Hilton! I explained that already being host to 19 of the team, the only place available for him would be on a sun lounger in front of the Rayburn in the kitchen! He readily accepted the offer and after one of my bacon toasties he went to bed and slept very well, leaving early in the morning, but not before thanking Mick and presenting me with a lovely solid gold Honda badge! Thus began a long association with Honda U.K. which spilled over to encompass the Purple Helmets, opening the door for many invitations to perform and better still, to their wonderful T.T. parties at local hostelries such as the Castletown Golf Links Hotel and the Villa Marina.

Around this time, the wonderful enthusiasm of Dot Tilbury of Crosby and the Philatelic Bureau came into its own, with the issue of a series of postage stamps featuring the 'Helmets', putting us right up there with the really famous people of the world! A great honour indeed. The irrepressible Dot has a long and happy association with the Helmets, often promoting us with introductions to book signings and general P.R. for Isle of Man Post. Dot has also helped us out on a few occasions with the commentary at our Onchan Shows when I have been unable to attend, bringing her own brand of fun with her and keeping the show on the road at very short notice - thanks a lot Dot!

The birth of the pub doughnut

This was an entirely new concept brought about initially by an invitation to 'drop in' for a pint at the old 'Iron Pier' pub in Ramsey. On Mad Sunday, it was, in the early days of the Helmets, traditional for us to do a complete lap of the T.T. course, possibly stopping here and there for a spot of refreshment and even an impromptu show for the crowd whether they wanted one or not! This was taken a step further, unknowingly, by the landlord of the Iron Pier, Jim Houghton, when he asked me if we would like to drop in for a pint and maybe bring some trade with us to his pub which was well off the course and very quiet. We complied with his wishes by riding our bikes right into his pub, literally into the bar where a rather inebriated 'Lady' sat alone on a stool and witnessed our arrival, as one by one we stopped our engines and leaned the bikes against the pool table! "What the f...k's this?" she mumbled as Jim, true to his word, pulled us all a pint and awaited the onslaught of trade he hoped would follow us. Sadly none ensued and we were never invited back! This however 'opened the door' so as to speak and ride in visits were made to both the Railway at Union Mills, which was to become our H.Q. and of course the Farmers Arms at St. Johns. The Farmers at that time was ably run by our friends Angie and Dougie Christian and the plain wooden floorboards in the bar were to provide the perfect venue for what was to be possibly the world's first smoke assisted 'doughnut' performed on a Honda 90! On this occasion the building was completely smoke logged, causing an almost total evacuation by all except one customer who was a heavy smoker and hadn't noticed the difference as the revving engine delivered its acrid white smoke! Good sports as ever, Dougie just coughed alot and Angie said the curtains needed a wash anyway! We had lots of fun at the Farmers Arms over the years so on behalf of myself and the lads please accept our apologies for the smoke Angie and Dougie, I'm sure it'll make a good story someday! Thank you both.

Meanwhile back at the Railway Inn, we still ride through the pub every Mad Sunday, although there has never been a doughnut performed there - yet! Mine hosts Celia and Ray have been most hospitable over the years despite the total loss of a couple of their carpets, which were worn right through by the spinning rear wheels of the Hondas as the riders fought to control the awesome power of their engines! Thank you Celia and Ray.

My new house at the farm was by now finished and it was very cosy (especially after living in the office for ten months), with a lovely old range and open fire gracing the lounge. I had rescued this antique range from the farm next door, Kerrowdhoo, owned now by good neighbour Brian Cartmell, as he was about to demolish the old farmhouse in readiness for a new one. I had first spotted this lovely old fireplace a few years earlier when I paid a visit to the then owner Harry Goldsmith whose family had farmed there for generations. Although the house was no longer lived in, Harry would light the fire each day to heat some water for use in the dairy and would enjoy the warmth and comfort of the kitchen, along with his old sheepdog, on wet winter days. After extensive restoration which included fresh nickel plating of the oven door and shelf, I fitted it in the new house to a specially built chimney breast designed for this unusually large casting - still bearing the maker's name - Todhunter and Elliot of Douglas, Isle of Man - a real gem! Thanks Harry and Brian.

Good neighbours and Thomas at the Show

With the mention of Harry and Brian it brings to mind the good neighbours in the Little Mill Road. I had by now become good friends with Robert and Barbara Callow and their son John next door in Ballig Farm. Robert was a great character and I spent many an hour with him as he told me stories of his life as a boy in Bride and of his moving to the Howe farm on Douglas Head with his family and all the livestock. For a small boy of around seven or eight years, it must have been quite some adventure in the early 1930's to move from Ballakeigh near Bride Village all the way to Douglas. He said that he and his brothers set off driving the sheep into Ramsey along the road at five in the morning to catch the steam train into Douglas. This would mean a change of train at St. Johns and then on to Douglas where a tired small boy and his brothers would then drive the flock over the stone bridge along Leigh Terrace and turning left up the steep road to the Howe and their destination at the farm. It seems quite a feat when one considers that the same operation would have to be repeated several times for the cattle and household and all the equipment and machinery as well, some of it travelling by road in early motor vehicles before the days of Fred Leece and his Chevrolet cattle wagon. Rob was an expert horseman winning many a ploughing match and when I asked him how he had set about the very steep fields on Douglas Head he said that he had ploughed them in a diagonal fashion with his pair of Clydesdales, both up and down those dangerous slopes, which would have been almost suicidal on a tractor! Incidentally there is a good picture of Rob ploughing with a nice pair of Clydesdales on page 38 of the book 'Harvest of Memories' by Harvey Briggs. Rob was a great inspiration to me and he liked my horse Thomas, encouraging me to show him at the Southern show in 1999, wearing a beautiful set of harness, Rob's pride and joy, which he loaned to me for the occasion. The story has a very interesting link with the present day and is quite an astonishing coincidence - fate maybe?

It goes as follows, I borrowed a large Ifor Williams Horse Trailer from Angela Whitlow, a good friend of my new girlfriend Tricia, and picked up Tom and of course my old friend Robert. We set off early for Great Meadow and without a hitch got Tom settled in his pen made of timber hurdles. Bearing in mind that neither Tom or myself had ever been to a show before and Tom had only been 'Dressed' in the harness a couple of times for practice, I suppose in hindsight, both of us were quite 'green' to say the least! It was a long day, very hot and sunny with little or no shade or shelter from the blazing sunshine and as the day wore on Tom became a bit fractious and uneasy especially when dressed up for the grand parade. As usual there was a bit of a hold up which didn't help and at this stage what he really needed was a good walk round to calm him down. Too late! He'd had enough and decided to have a good shake

and a buck to rid himself of the harness but in the process he stumbled back and flattened the hurdle behind him which unfortunately struck the leg of a young lady who was watching, scratching her quite badly. I held onto him however and with the help of Amy Kneen we took him for his walk and he calmed down enough to continue with the Show. The young lady however was taken for treatment to her leg and eventually made a full recovery and this is where the twist of the story begins.

The young lady in question, whose name I never knew, quite by chance brought her own horse to Ballakissack some nine years later as a livery on our yard. Still none the wiser but knowing that she was by now married to Bob Clague, grandson of Matt Clague who had farmed Ballig next door (Rob Callow's farm). It transpired in a conversation one day that she had been injured at the Southern Show by a collapsing hurdle! "What caused the collapse of the hurdle then?" I enquired as Susie Clague answered "Oh a big white Shire horse that we were admiring at the time". Quite amazing, it was of course my Tom! Thinking back to 1999 I suppose it was quite ambitious or even perhaps just nieve to go to a show with so little experience but with Rob's help and that of another good neighbour Bill McCoubrey, who had been one of the last horsemen with the Isle of Man Dairies in Douglas, we got by! Not to be put off, I decided to try again at the Royal Show a fortnight later, but this time without harness and with Tricia along to help - we had a very good day with a rosette to bring home as well. Robert however admitted to being a bit tired after having a good 'natter' with his friends old and new, and generally a good but long day! Tom behaved well but was not happy travelling by trailer - he was just too big! Hence the Leyland/Oakley horse wagon story mentioned previously. Robert Callow was truly one of the last of the 'old school' and taught me a lot, sadly he died at the end of 2003 but his son John and his family remain our closest neighbours.

Another true Manxman lives nearby, alone now with just his dogs for company since the sad death of his wife Norma, but Arnhem veteran and

Tom at our first show

World War II hero Bobby Quayle has always made me feel welcome in the Little Mill road and we have shared many a good natter over the years. Bobby has told me stories of his youth in the north of the Island working on farms with horses and indeed of nowadays when he still makes loose hay gathered into expertly made 'ricks' in the little fields by his home 'Glen Rosa'. Norma and Bob took a keen interest in my restoration of Ballakissack and took, with an early digital camera, a series of 'before' and 'after' shots of my work which I treasure greatly. They have cared for donkeys and ponies in their last years and at their demise I have helped by using my digger to bury them - the donkeys that is - not the Quayles! Indeed one little donkey was in it's forties and when I refused payment for my work Bobby arrived

next day pushing a B.S.A. Bantam motorbike he had owned from new in the sixties and insisted that one good turn deserved another! Thanks Bob! Now in his late eighties Bob still rides his own motorbike - a Yamaha and can be seen walking his dogs along the road most days of the week, so from farming to sailing deep sea, parachuting into the battle of Arnhem and still leading a very active life indeed, I would say that he's a tough man! Good on yer Bobby!

I think it is well documented that the Kennaugh family, who farmed here 'til the mid seventies, and then retained Ballacain farmhouse as their home converting it to a fine guest house along with a large garage which was to become the business premises of Chris Kennaugh Ltd, were wonderful neighbours to me. Their welcome to me was second to none but sadly around 1997 they felt the need to sell up and move down to Onchan, all the while insisting that they wouldn't lose touch and wouldn't be far away. Well the latter is indeed fact, they're not far away and we do keep in touch with Chris coming up to see me often. I still see his father Peter too, his mum Barbara now sadly gone - but what was to follow could only be described as a nightmare when a dreadful family moved in next door and caused chaos - I won't go into it but the rest is history! Arrogance is a terrible thing and pride, inevitably, comes before a fall! Need I say more!

New girlfriend! Things are looking up.

In April 1999 on a night out at Paramount with my good mate Nigel Collins, I was lucky to meet a 'pretty, little thing' called Tricia Kilmartin who was introduced to me by Tina Kelly, one of her friends and someone who I shall remain indebted to forever. Things progressed well and as my loneliness started to ebb at last, we moved on with our shared interest in horses and things in general, through the 'turn of the century'! Tricia likes the motor bikes and I like the horses so it has been an ideal formula over the years since. I had at the time, an 850cc Yamaha T.D.M. bike for the road and together with long time friend Ffinlo Crellin and his new love Brenda Jones, we had many a good trip across to Ireland and thoroughly enjoyed local nights out to the likes of Ballacallin to watch the sunset over a nice supper and a pint of bitter or two - magic!

It was on one such trip to the West of Ireland in the summer of 2001 when we arrived at Clifden near Galway, on the bikes, thoroughly soaked through to the skin and we sought refuge in a nice pub there for a few days while we dried out our leathers, socks, boots and undies! Well, it just so happened that this delightful little town was absolutely full of French people, students mostly, who had come to soak up some Irish history where that intrepid duo, Alcock and Brown the aviators had landed many years ago on their first successful trans-Atlantic flight. As we chatted to these nice young people who had remarkably good English, I thought this could be my chance to learn the correct French for my forthcoming commentary at the Six Day Enduro in France with the Purple Helmets. The words I wanted were obviously not in the normal dictionary, such as 'roll over man', 'total shite' and 'purple helmet'! So amid great laughter and a few pints I eventually learned some correct translation in slang type French! I was quite proud of my word of mouth translations which were to be used at Brive le Gailliard (close!) some weeks later when we performed a show at the closing ceremony for this great world class event. A near disaster was to occur however when on the day of the show, which followed a fantastic week of tracking and socialising second to none, my big coat caught fire on the exhaust of the revving Honda while we travelled there up the motorway! Not being aware of the blazing coat as the wind kept the flames behind me, it was only when I pulled into a lay by to re-group with the lads that the thing ignited and became quite a serious fire. The removal of my coat was to be hampered by the belt of my bum bag which was very

difficult to unfasten with gloved hands as panic set in. The fire was eventually put out by the lads using their drinking water bottles and indeed anything else that would squirt water - quite literally! I could have been accused of taking the piss! It may sound funny now but I had received a very bad burn at the back of my right thigh with a huge blister forming - around six inches in length and shock was setting in fast as we arrived at the venue for the show. I went straight away to the First Aid team at the tent and they made me as comfortable as possible with painkillers, gauze and bandage and told me to rest for a couple of hours to counteract the shock. I thanked them for their expertise and concern but explained that I couldn't rest yet because of the show which was due to start at any minute! From memory I think their comments sounded like 'crazy man' or something similar, but the show goes on! The shock had really set in by now, along with excruciating pain and worst of all, my French had deserted me, all my lines, such as Roulee Boulei, les casques violet, celebrities du monde and many more had completely gone - I had dried up! Well something had to be done and quick! I had the microphone, the 10,000 crowd had gone quiet and were looking at ME - I had to say something - so I began in my own Manx voice " Hello everybody, we bring you a great big welcome from the world famous Purple Helmets!" The response to which was a huge roar of approval and applause and I reckoned that at least half of them must know some English, so for the other half who should have been treated to a great oratory in my 'excellent' French, I said in my best Renee (from Allo Allo) voice "Allo everyone zis is a great big welcurm from zee purple helmetz!" to which ad lib there was an even bigger cheer - I think I got away with it! I have to admit in hindsight that it was not one of our better shows, the field was very uneven and rutted and the lads, to add to my misfortune, were suffering from the effects of the previous night! So much so in fact, that after they had performed the chest jump - where the bikes leap over the prone bodies of the lads laid on the ground in front of the plank, one of the lads remained in situ on the ground! The crowd gasped - something had gone wrong? - but no - Wig Bregazzi had dozed off to sleep! Absolutely incredible you may say as no one could go to sleep while a revving Honda leapt over him with merely inches to spare? Well top stuntman Wig did just that!

Live on stage! A busy year for the 'Helmets'

Around Christmas at this time I was asked one day to stand on the stage at the Gaiety Theatre for five minutes or so! There was to be a little show called 'Countryside Characters' with proceeds to benefit the N.F.U. Benevolent fund, so after some persuasive talk from Graham Crowe I was 'roped in' to help. I must admit to making a shakey start and finding it quite a daunting experience to stand there alone, staring blankly into total darkness with nothing for company except an old shovel I had brought along! "Why the shovel?" I was asked afterwards and replied "Well I really wanted a bicycle but couldn't find one!" The truth was that I needed something to lean on because my knees were very sore at the time. I have to say that after recognising a few friendly voices from the darkness, I settled down and really quite enjoyed the experience, so thanks are probably in order for a 'kind audience' that evening! Thanks all for laughing at my stories - all true of course!

Certainly 2001 was a big year for me with the 'Six day' of course and started in January with a trip to London for a show at the Alexandra Palace. Our friends Margaret and Robbie Allan who promoted the Scottish Motorcycle Show, invited us to be 'top of the bill' down in that London. We were very well received by a quite 'conservative' crowd who obviously didn't know what a 'purple helmet' was and began their education with a rapid learning curve! It quite surprised me just how ill informed these 'Southerners' were, many of them staring blankly at my mention of the Isle of Man - they'd never heard of it! I think most of them thought the world ended north of Watford, but not for long, as after a few great shows by the 'World Famous Purple Helmets' their education was complete! They were now left in no doubt whatsoever as to the whereabouts of the Isle of Man or indeed what a purple helmet really is!

A serious outbreak of foot and mouth disease in the U.K. was to be a big threat to our next mainland show in Edinburgh the following month and only after some serious disinfection of Glenn Leece's wagon by Ffinlo Crellin and myself, were we allowed to travel. In hindsight we probably faced more obstacles by our choice of transport at this time, attracting a lot of attention as obviously no livestock movements were allowed on the roads. I think it would be around this time that I had the great pleasure of meeting the new Lieutenant Governor and his lovely wife. Air Marshal Ian Macfadyen and his wife Sally were introduced to me by the head gardener at Government House, Dave Musson, whilst I was loading the lorry one sunny afternoon. It so happened that they had heard of the 'Helmets' and wondered if it would be possible for them to appear at Government House! I remember laughing in reply and asking the 'Guv' whether he thought Government House to be ready for such lewd entertainment presented as only we can? He replied that the friends he would be entertaining for dinner were very broad minded and he was sure that we would be appreciated by them as they were all veterans of the first Gulf War in '91 as he himself was - a great invitation indeed and a great show was to follow, the first of many at Government House during the Macfadyens five year term of office.

A disaster was to strike the Purple Helmets in April of 2001 when the Wilson and Collins factory at Balthane was to be badly damaged by fire. All the show equipment and some of the bikes were burnt in a bad blaze that started in the canteen area right next to where all the 'gear' was stored and it was said by a couple of jokers that the fire had caused "thousands of pounds worth of IMPROVEMENTS!" ha - ha - very funny but on the run-up to the big show at Onchan for that year it couldn't have come at a worse time. Luckily most of the lads had their own personal bikes at home for 'fettling', along with their coats, so with 'all hands to the wheel' and work parties switched from Balthane to Ballakissack the midnight oil was burned to meet the deadline in T.T. week.

The T.T. Proper didn't happen of course as Chief Minister Donald Gelling announced that for this year, it would be too risky to allow spectators to invade farmland adjacent to the course. In hindsight I agree it was probably the right decision and indeed a very difficult choice for Donald to make, but a limited number of stalwarts made their annual pilgrimage to the island anyway and luckily we remained free of this dreadful curse which would surely have wiped out the farming enterprise in the whole island.

A few well meaning people donated old Hondas to help our plight and one of these was old friend and sidecar trials man Neil Cleverly who supplied a C90 which became the replacement for the 'Long Bike' and indeed remains so to this day! Thanks Neil. Other such donations were made and we remain grateful to everyone who helped. Needless to say that the 'Big One' at the Stadium went ahead and despite the setbacks it all took place and a busy summer was to follow with a second show at Government House soon after for none other than Royalty, this time with Prince Edward and the lovely Sophie enjoying every minute of the fun. This brings to mind the precision timing of our shows at Government House. I would normally receive a call from Chris Tummon who would explain the schedule for the evening, such as: Helmets to arrive at main drive 6.15; show to commence 6.25; show to end 6.45 followed by drinks with the guests 7.00pm; Helmets to leave and guests to begin dinner. I have to say that I had many a laugh with Chris when I would suggest that possibly a little 'lee way' would be necessary for our 'raggle taggle' outfit to organise themselves? Maybe the show could begin as late as 6.26 instead? Maybe? Possibly??

In the mid summer of 2001 we had great fun doing a show on Douglas Promenade for the closing ceremony of the Island Games. Our good friend Dot Tilbury had passed on the details to Brian Shooter and with his co-ordination a fast and furious routine was performed with lots of smoke, sparks, noise and crashes at speeds approaching one hundred miles an hour! Great fun and entertainment but for one or two Faroe Islanders who just didn't understand. They were overheard by Dot to say something like "Oh! They're not very good, they keep falling from their motor bikes!" to which Dot may have said " I think they're supposed to!" - or something like that anyway. Meanwhile, soon after this in America, the Twin Towers fell down - but it was nothing to do with the Purple Helmets!

We rounded off a great year, after our return from the 'Six Day' in France, with the launch of our first video and D.V.D. which was to be called 'TOTAL SHITE!' and this footage compiled by Dave Reilly has gone on to be one of Duke Video's best sellers alongside such classics as the George Formby film 'No Limit'. Little did I realise at this time that the trip to France would be my last one abroad for quite some time after what was to follow in 2002!

2002 and disaster in the mist

The year started off in fine style with a memorable trip to the Scottish Motorcycle Show in Edinburgh when my good friend Ffinlo Crellin was once again co-driver for the weekend, in fact he was almost an indispensable part of the team by now, always a great help, unflappable and a first class driver and mate. He even donned a big coat and deputised as a 'Helmet' when necessary on many occasions, eventually being adopted as a 'real' Purple Helmet for his efforts, building his own bike and thoroughly enjoying himself along the way. This was followed by a great trip to Port Rush in Northern Ireland for the North West 200 in May, which of course called for two sea crossings each way to reach the Emerald Isle. It was to be a 'mega' trip with an unbelievable consumption of Guinness and a great show on the windswept coastline complete with squally showers to add to the effect! A big crowd seemed to enjoy the show immensely and crashes were frequent, in fact they'd never seen anything like it! On the way back to the pub, the lads unwittingly and assisted by the Guinness, rode up a one way street causing absolute mayhem, with one or two of them actually being ticked off by an off duty policeman. We were never however, asked back for a second performance! I recall that our own Mayor of Douglas Stephen Pitts and his Mayoress wife Dot were present, along with the mentor to the team - Des Collins and his party, adding to the festivities and doing wonders for Isle of Man/Irish relations - true ambassadors.

Next came the T.T. and all was well until Mad Sunday - read on....

Also in May of 2002 and ever mindful of the need for the Southern Motorcycle Club to purchase its own land, Steve 'The Bear' Collins's eagle eyes spotted in the local press an auction for some 100+ acres of land in the Foxdale area. Could this be what we were looking for? At last a chance to purchase somewhere permanent to ride our events presented itself. So Steve and I attended the auction at Cairnagree and started, after a walk around the land, to bid enthusiastically on the divided lots of the place, hoping to possibly buy a reasonable portion of the more mountainous areas. The result however, was to exceed our wildest dreams as lot after lot was knocked down to us and we ended up buying everything we wanted! In total we bought 112 acres including two ruined farms and were very pleased with ourselves and with the price we had paid. The Club already had half the money thanks to the Onchan Stadium shows from the past six years or so and the rest was to be a loan from Des Collins. I should mention the great contribution made to the Southern Club over the years by the Collins' family. Firstly by Nigel who served on the committee for a while, then being followed there by his brother Steve over many years and of course the generosity of their firm Wilson and Collins for making the Purple Helmets ideas become reality through many metres of steel and welding rods! All this watched over by their father Des, a good man to have on side. Thank you all.

Mad Sunday started off well with our usual ride through the Railway then on to the Sulby Glen for some chips courtesy of the landlady Rosie. Then on to Ramsey - one or two punctures to be mended and then an impromptu stunt to clean up our act with a 'ride through' the car wash at Raymotors! Madness!

Quite poor weather was by now being enjoyed by the team with mist and drizzle as we headed up the mountain to the Bungalow only to be stopped by the Police while they cleared away some 'incident' or other further on. As I write this page, some six years later, I still have a vivid memory of what was to follow and I feel that I can possibly reveal a bit more of what actually happened although little was said at the time.

I was aware that the helicopter was above waiting to get some 'footage' of the team doing the 'Nose to Tail' and so we set off along the road with the backlog of traffic from the hold up surrounding us. All was going well and I remember being alongside a khaki coloured Shogun as we gradually gathered speed on 'Hailwood Rise', when having travelled no more than a few hundred yards and probably doing no more than around 35mph, the bike immediately in front of me suddenly ceased its forward motion! Well! Normal riding would have guaranteed a safe distance between us for just such an eventuality but 'normal' this wasn't and swift evasive action was called for! In hindsight if I had chosen to veer to my left then I would simply have rubbed along the side of the Shogun - but - no! I chose to go right, which I believe to be the natural instinct, glancing off Mikey's big coat in the process and thinking 'Oh F...'(or something similar) as I struggled to regain control. Disaster loomed however as out of the corner of my eye I was aware that another bike, which was overtaking our line, was just about to hit me and he had little chance to avoid me as by this time I was blocking his path! Wham! Unbelievable impact - Bang! Ground - sky - spinning over, all the while thinking - 'this is it this time!' Then sliding towards the grass verge and a black and white bollard directly in front of me and remarkably, at a time like this, thinking 'It's OK, it's made of plastic and it'll collapse in front of me!' Luckily it did collapse or I would have had some serious problems with my genitalia as well! I was by now lying flat out on the verge with some of the lads around me and very soon the emergency services as well, as they had sped to the scene from their station nearby at the Bungalow. One of the first on the scene was none other than the Deputy Chief Constable, my old friend Neil Kinrade and, on seeing that I was still alive, albeit with one obviously broken right thigh bone, he said "By Christ you were lucky!" I then replied "How the f... do you make that out?" - to which everyone burst out laughing and one of the firemen saying something like "It's only Derry who could joke about it at a time like this." The truth is I suppose that rather than being a joke it was just a knee jerk reaction to the obvious well meaning but unfortunate choice of words by Neil! I did however get the chance some months later to thank him for his most genuine concern at the time and we had a good laugh about it! It transpired that the other biker, a German visitor had on impact 'flown' somewhat spectacularly through the air as he 'ramped' over my stricken machine but mercifully landed in the soft peat by the side of the road braking just his little finger! His VFR 750 Honda was smashed to pieces as it cart-wheeled down the road but, ironically, my old C90 was hardly damaged at all!

I remember A and E at the old Nobles' Hospital and the wonderful treatment there by Jenny Hill and her team as they proceeded, despite my protests, to cut off my big coat and right boot! Then amidst the good humour I think I must have passed out! It was probably little wonder that I had because it turned out that I had, in addition to the broken right femur, a broken left collar bone and three ribs on the same side and just to balance things up a bit maybe, my right thumb as well. A 'special thank you' is in order for Robbo who sorted things out 'on the ground' so to speak and was a great help to my Tricia at this worrying and stressful time. Thanks Boy!

They did a good job at Nobles' and some six weeks later I was due for release, albeit on a zimmer frame. The obvious pain throughout this period had been eased considerably by the many messages and get well cards and of course by the dozens of visitors whose number included none other than the Governor and his missus! Much appreciated - thank you everyone. I struggled for the first week

or two, still on the frame because of the broken collar bone but ably assisted and chauffeured by Quayley, my mate, who was invaluable while Tricia was out at work. I think it was around this time that I promoted him with the honorary title of 'Estates Manager!' Thanks Son!

Eventually graduating to crutches, I was able to attend the Royal Manx Show at Sulby, always a great 'Manx' day, attended by the rural community or the 'real people' of the island and truly one of my favourite days of the year. Tricia showed Big Tom or to give him his show name 'Ballakissack Thomas' and looking splendid in a set of harness loaned by Michael Crellin he won the harness class bringing a tear to my eye in the process. We were congratulated by Show President for that year Willie Christian, who was host to the Governor Ian Macfadyen, this time accompanied by his mother on a visit to the island from England. At the shows over the years, I enjoyed many a 'dram' of good malt whisky with Sir Charles Kerruish who was undoubtedly the 'Father' of the local Heavy Horse Society. Charlie would always make us feel welcome and share a yarn or two along with the hospitality, which was usually dispensed from a picnic basket in the boot of his car! I always enjoyed his company and sadly although I didn't know it at the time, it was to be his last show as he died the following year.

Things were looking up a bit once more, except possibly marred by a lack of sleep which was caused by the almost incessant barking of two dogs, well into the early hours of the morning, courtesy of some aforementioned dreadful people who lived next door at the time. This we could certainly have done without as it went on most of that summer, eventually being resolved around October when the dogs escaped one day and raided our henhouse, killing off some of our little bantam hens. Enough was enough and after a trying time over the previous months, when after repeated phone calls from us to 'please do something', I wrote a final letter to them with copies to the dog warden and the Police and this brought the episode to a close. Dreadful, irresponsible behaviour but as they say - 'Every dog has his day!'

At the Royal Manx Show with Sir Charles 'Charlie' Kerruish

Thomas in show harness

Air Marshal Ian Macfadyen,
The Lieutenant Govenor and
his mother join us at the show
hosted by Show President,
Willy Christian

The end of an era, Prince William, Steve Hislop

2002 was the end of an era for me regarding the Manx National Two Day Trial, the event I loved and had never missed since 1967 was to be watched and marshalled at, while my entry was to be used by Bobba Greggor riding my TYZ Yamaha in my place. It was to be quite emotional for me as although I made a start in the 2005 event with Nikki to commemorate the Gold Jubilee of the event, I knew that I was never to compete in a 'serious' fashion again, my leg wasn't right and I ended the year with a revision operation which, unfortunately also failed to cure the problem of non union of the femur. Now forced to sit quiet and keep off the leg as much as possible I was faced with two possible options. One was to watch daytime T.V. and go mental and the other was to do something worthwhile like write down my memories, perhaps going mental in the process but maybe, just maybe, having something to show for all my idle hours! So, reader this is how I began to write down all these pages of, well, some may say 'Total Shite', I'll leave you to judge that one yourself!

At the start of 2003 I began taking Tricia out for H.G.V. lessons in the Leyland horse wagon and after a series of lessons with Peter Howe at Motivation, she took her test and we had a new 'trucker' in the family! A cause for celebration at last but it soon became apparent that my leg wasn't right and more surgery was called for, this time at Arrowepark on the Wirral, under Mr Robert Harvey, around the end of April. Just in time for T.T. week I thought! (only joking Tricia!) It turned out to be a big operation to include a plate and bone grafting but all went well and I was able to commentate at the big Show in T.T. week, albeit sitting on a stool but glad to be part of the action again. The highlight of the week was to be Mad Sunday, once more, this time with a show in Peel for Honda as they moved their road show there from the previous venue at Laxey. This went well but that evening we had a mega time at Government House with an hilarious show for none other than H.R.H. Prince William! I think

My Tricia - HGV driver

he really enjoyed his visit, starting with a fast trip over to Peel, riding pillion with expert Police rider Robbie Lace and causing a bit of a panic amongst his 'minders' as Robbie's bike disappeared in the distance amongst the traffic! He was in safe hands however and Robbie got him back in plenty of time for our show, the Prince smiling widely and loving what was to follow! At the end of our show (at around 7.43 Chris?) he was so enthusiastic I think he wanted to join our gang, so I suggested he may like to try on a coat and sit astride one of our machines! "Rather!" he said so Robbo, as ever a gentleman himself, swapped coats with the Prince for a photo shoot! Snag was that Robbo, despite

The 'Helmets' with Prince William

his obvious courtesy, was also rather sweaty so when he himself donned the blue hand stitched blazer belonging to the heir to the throne of England, he would be sure to leave his 'bouquet' in the arm pit area! To add to this, as he rummaged around in the pockets, albeit empty, he said "There's not so much in yer pockets yer highness!" Luckily this was to be well received with the guffaws of laughter all round and not as I had feared, a trip to the Tower of London for us all!

I continued my recuperation and sometime after this I remember a visit one day from Steve Hislop when he told me of his helicopter exploits and how much he was enjoying the thrill of flying them. He wondered if he would be able to land at Ballakissack when coming home to Onchan but I explained that it would be impractical with so many horses around and the obvious risk to their safety. I suggested that he ask at the 'Max' restaurant and clubhouse at Howstrake where a couple of years previously, Russell Savoury of Honda had landed when staying with me. Sadly I think this was the last time I spoke to Hizzy as he was to die soon afterwards, not racing motorcycles but flying a helicopter in the Border area. I still have his Purple Helmet coat and his C90 is in the proud possession of Ray, landlord of the Railway at Union Mills. Good man Hizzy.

More trouble and the 'Helmets' get the sack

My leg was by now gaining strength but there was a new worry on the horizon and I wasn't feeling very well. I'm not sure whether or not the crash had anything to do with it or if it was just bad luck but I was by now experiencing bowel trouble and was soon after diagnosed with cancer. What next, I remember thinking as I was only just getting back to normal after the crash and really didn't need this news. It was almost as if Mr Stock the consultant was talking to someone else because how could I

possibly have cancer? He must have got it wrong I thought! But no such luck, as he went on to explain that I would need a colostomy and it would not be reversible into the bargain. Surgery was inevitable but first I thought it a good idea to pack as much in as I could with regards to work matters and indeed pleasure while I still could.

The year began with a great Helmets trip to Dublin for the Irish Motor Cycle Show at the Royal Show Ground at Balls Bridge. Always a great event organised by good friend Ruth Lemass it proved to be a winner with the Irish people and of course, many gallons of Guinness were consumed by the lads, with the barman at the showground thanking us for our custom as he'd never seen the like before!

Back home to reality and I was involved in a project at the farm to bury the electric supply underground in conjunction with the M.E.A. and to get rid of the unsightly overhead supply and the poles, many of which were past their best. This would later prove to be a godsend, as not only did it achieve its intended goal but also helped my physical fitness with the manual work involved and this strength was to be vital in what was to follow. A date was set at the end of April for my operation but first I was to have the great pleasure of my engagement to my lovely Tricia! It was a lovely ray of light amongst the bad news of late which by now included the sad loss of Tricia's mum as well. We had a lovely 'do' at the Highlander to celebrate this and my birthday too, with all the lads wearing their new black kilts and 'Bonnie Prince Charlie' jackets and the ladies looking their best - as ever!

Could this be the last supper?

The answer to this could be 'very nearly sir!', as all was to start off quite well with the operation taking place as planned. Soon after however I became unwell and began to suffer severe abdominal pain and the next day I was 'opened up' again for more investigation and to release a 'kink' in the bowel or something similar. Well, to cut a long story short, it was to be some forty five more days before I discharged myself but not without a nightmare or two in between! Whatever could possibly go wrong seemed to do just that culminating in septicaemia and endocarditis. I consider my life to have been saved at that time by the anaesthetist Keith Wilkinson and Graham Lloyd-Brandrick who revived me from at least two 'septic showers' when I apparently died for a while! I suppose it was just for a few moments on each occasion but I remember a big bright light in front of me and a feeling of relaxing peace and quiet! Not for long! Luckily I survived and seem to recall thinking "Hang on an 'effin minute I'm not ready yet!" Special thanks to Keith and his team for their care at that scary time are certainly due and I'm pleased to say that I managed to thank him some years later in Bushy's tent with a pint of Guinness! Thanks Boy!

An emotional trip home was to follow and after forty five 'black' days in hospital I couldn't get over just how blue was the sky, how fresh was the air or how white the flowers on the thorn bushes were on our route along the Scollag Road home! Simple things yes but not to be taken for granted ever again, I was so glad to be alive and back home at our lovely little farm Ballakissack with the woman I love so much, my Tricia.

I began a steady recovery with good food and exercise and gradually my strength returned under the care of my district nurses Mary Bregazzi and Denise Nelson and their team, all of whom were brilliant, with Mary sometimes recalling that I was the only patient ever in her long career, to be referred directly to her from the I.T.U. of Nobles Hospital! It was certainly a hard and painful period of our lives and one which I would never wish to repeat but I like to think that my physical strength and the love and strength of Tricia and our friends won the day, even if the month of May and indeed some of June as well, had been totally lost.

Onchan Stadium show had been and gone and once more I have to thank Dot Tilbury for taking my place on the night - the show must go on!

Although still very weak I continued to get better day by day and was helped along the way by many friends who came to visit, so much so that for many weeks afterwards the old teapot never cooled down. One day we even had a visit from none other than the 'Governor' himself, accompanied by his wife Sally and the A.D.C. Chris Tummon! A most enjoyable afternoon was to follow with some nice home made fruit cake, courtesy of our good friend Angela Whitlow and some good laughs and witty banter in a lovely unhurried atmosphere with truly good company and friendship that money just can't buy.

I was to be honoured yet again during the summer, this time by that wonderful band of young people in the Federation of the Young Farmers Clubs, as a guest speaker at their Summer Ball. Although I was still a bit shaky on my feet, Tricia and I were able to take up the kind invitation extended to us by the Chairman Philip (Combine) Corrin, via their lovely secretary Nicola Creer. We had a wonderful evening being treated like royalty and whilst I did my best to entertain with my speech, I hope I did OK as my contribution for the honour they bestowed upon us that evening.

I was also quite 'chuffed' to be invited to write the 'foreword' for the programme of my favourite event, the Manx National 2-day Trial for 2004. Thanks team for asking me!

Towards the end of October the world famous Purple Helmets were to be the star attraction at Donnington for a new concept called the No 1 Plate. The idea was that top riders from all the motorcycling disciplines would compete against one another in each and every one of those branches of the sport. It turned out to be a great idea with the eventual winner being our own hero David Knight the world Enduro champion. The only setback seemed to be that the gate receipts were insufficient when compared with the expenditure and even though large crowds were present at the event it was clear that the organisers were a bit worried and seemed a bit stressed. As usual we drew a large crowd to each show and for our own amusement the lads had a race of their own on the motocross track to fill in time between each performance. This also drew a large crowd and was possibly a bigger attraction than the official moto cross, the only setback being that the bikes were caked in thick mud. This mud was then splattered all over the show area in our next performance and as far as we were concerned it added to the fun but not so the official stunt riders who weren't too pleased with having to perform their high speed stunts on mud instead of clean tarmac! I feel that it would have been relatively simple to move our show to another area but by this time a real 'jobsworth' type of official had started to bawl and shout at me to "Tell your mates to sweep up this f...mess!". Well, the message I understood, but when he started to point his finger at my nose as well, then I thought he was being rather rude, so I gripped his finger and explained to him that if he had anything to say to the team then perhaps he would like to tell them himself! I think I may have gripped his finger a bit too firmly because by this time he had gone quite pale and stormed off saying something like "That's it! That's 'effin it! Where's Robbie!"

Robbie, of course, being our old friend Robbie Allan, who was running the show and by now quite stressed - he certainly didn't need this whingeing git crying in his ear about some mud scattered on the tarmac by crazy, out of control, madcap stuntmen in big coats! I think this must have been the last straw for Robbie and he sacked us, much to the delight of the Helmets who went back to the Red Gates bar instead of doing the last show! I am very pleased to say that Robbie calmed down again some time later and we remain the very best of friends! Up to now, this remains the one and only time we have ever been sacked and I have to say that we thoroughly enjoyed it! Thanks Robbie! I was also very pleased to have been able to do my part in the show, having by now regained enough strength and stamina for a very demanding weekend.

Mares and foals, our lovely wedding and Norman Wisdom

Some days later, Tricia and I travelled to Heysham with the Old Leyland horse wagon to collect two lovely brood mares for the farm and as such, spent all day on the Ben My Chree with just a brief turn around on land as we swopped the horses from the haulier's wagon to our own at the pub nearby. The two lovely grey mares, both in foal to the same coloured stallion, travelled really well and produced two coloured foals, Declan and Finuala. Both beautiful animals, we still have them at the yard along with a sister for Declan, born the following year, called Shannon, the mares however were sold on some three years later.

Despite all the setbacks of accident and illness, things at Ballakissack were ticking over nicely thanks to the efforts of Tricia and a lot of help from our old friend Phil Quayle and the good friends and neighbours that surround us. It goes without saying that this didn't include the dreadful family next door! But they were arrested soon after this anyway so maybe there is a God up there after all!

At the end of 2004 Tricia and I had a lovely wedding in Newbury in Berkshire, having decided in the previous summer that a small 'do' would be all I could manage during my convalescence. I was by this time stronger than I thought I would have been and was able to enjoy it very much, with just six close friends in attendance to celebrate. The following day we had a lovely time at Newbury Racecourse for the Hennessey Gold Cup and I have to say it was a superb package that I would thoroughly recommend to anyone - if they wanted to get married of course! A big surprise was to happen the following weekend when

Declan with his mum!

Declan   Shannon   Finuala

Sue Kirkpatrick organised a big party for us with friends from far and wide! It was a great party and quite emotional for us after all we had been through with the night flying by too quickly as good things do and with my sincere apologies to anyone of our friends who may have inadvertently been missed off the guest list!

Yes, things seemed to be looking up at last and we rounded the year off in Northern Italy with a skiing trip to see in the New Year. I hasten to add that skiing was out of the question for me although I was making good progress, a fall at this time would probably have finished me off! Instead, I took with me this very manuscript and contented myself each day with some nice strong expresso and good whisky, whilst I wrote my 'book'. The young barmaid, a lovely girl from Bosnia, was most attentive and kept an eye on my glass, topping up the coffee and whisky when needed and generally treating me like a V.I.P. as I wrote this humble list of memories down. I was alone in the hotel bar most mornings and was most impressed at the service bestowed upon me by this softly spoken young lady and it wasn't until close to the end of our stay that I found the reason why. It transpired that she thought I was some celebrity or famous novelist writing what was to be a best seller or something! Flattered though I was, I had to tell her the truth and we all had a good laugh about it later on! Ah well! The Tsunami happened while we were there but it had nothing to do with me!

With the mention of 'Celebrity' I was entertained one day by none other than Norman Wisdom himself and couldn't believe my eyes when I saw him approaching our back door at a fast walk only to stumble in comedy fashion, then right himself with the agility of a teenager, never mind a man in his eighties! He had come along for the ride one day with his housekeeper Sylvia when she was buying an antique chaise longue and rocking chair from me. Sylvia had been introduced to me by George Gelling and I was pleased to do business with her and honoured by the presence of this famous man sitting in my old chair and enjoying a cuppa with us at Ballakissack.

Moving into 2005 I had a couple of nice 'tasks' bestowed upon me, the first being asked to judge the wonderful Young Farmers Concert which I consider a great honour and I just hope I got it right, ably assisted by my old mate Phil Quayle - ok maybe not? They haven't asked me back!

The second of these jobs was 'gifted' to me by Dot Tilbury who normally compared the Marown Ploughing Match concert but she was unable to help due to a prior commitment and 'nominated' me in her absence. Well, I think it went reasonably well but I have to say that the last time I attended this very concert was some forty five years previously whilst taking part with the Youth Club under the expert guidance of the Gelling family. Indeed, George Gelling was by now their only representative with his brother Johnny and sister Joice both sadly gone and sorely missed for their contribution over many years. I think that the crowd must have known I was going to be there because the hall was only about half full! It was either that or as Ken Collister explained to me "There's a lot of other 'doos' on tonight Derry, so don't blame yourself, yes there's a whist drive on at Glen May!" Enough said! Anyway, thanks Dot, it was a good night and good to see old friends from years ago.

New D.V.D. and farewell to the Macfadyens

During the summer we were busy making a new D.V.D. of more Purple Helmet nonsense and it was decided to try and make something 'completely different'. Dave Rielly once again 'nailed' many bits of footage together and we decided to do one or two celebrity interviews as well to add a new slant onto the usual 'shite'! The first of these interviews was with famous bike racing commentator and former truck racer and superbike rider Steve Parrish. A great sport as ever, Steve answered my 'in depth' questions so well that we had to hold back the laughter between us while we went for a 'take' with the expert help of Greenlight T.V. camera men! Perhaps my biggest challenge however was to be set in the lovely lounge at none other than

Government House. Always a good sport and true gentleman, his Excellency Ian Macfadyen the 'Guv'nor' himself had agreed to be interviewed by me with the possibility of his becoming a Purple Helmet, if suitable, now that he was losing his job! His five year term as Governor of the Island was coming to an end and I would like to say that in my opinion, both he and his lovely wife Sally were without equal, before or since, in the warm friendly way they conducted themselves with such energy and opened up Government House as never before to the Manx people. Thank you both.

On a chance meeting one day with former Director of Tourism Terry Toohey, while we enjoyed a pint of Okells in the Railway Inn, he told me he was organising a 'Tattoo' at St Johns to celebrate the sixty years since the end of World War Two. "You need the Purple Helmets!" I suggested and he jumped at the chance of an appearance by our impeccably prepared military style display team! Unfortunately (for me) I was to be yet again in hospital on the evening of what was to be a wonderful and emotional show. I had however co-ordinated things by 'phone and once again asked Dot Tilbury to do her best in my absence. I believe it was good because the next day I had a phone call from an ecstatic Terry extolling the virtues of the 'wonderful Purple Helmets' and thanking me most sincerely! I received a similar call from the 'Guv' too, wishing me well and I must admit to feeling more than a little emotional and indeed proud to say the least!

It was common knowledge in the island that those fine people were to leave us on 27th September, which for me at least was yet again badly timed with another operation due on my leg that very day! With this in mind I said my own personal goodbyes some days before and it was whilst I was at 'Guv House' I met Chris Tummon who told me that the farewell was to be a rather low key affair with a goodbye from the house staff, followed by a simple drive to the boat, via the War Memorial and a salute from the British Legion. 'That's not much of a send off' I thought, 'we'll soon see about that!' I know! A Motor Cade, American style, to escort MAN 1 to the boat was what was called for!

Derry and Tricia!

156

Only one snag, most of the bikes and coats had not yet returned to the island from the 6 day in Slovakia, but several phone calls later from my hospital bed and we had the nucleus of an entourage of out riders! Chris Tummon has told me since that all was quiet at the house and the staff were lined up for a tearful farewell when who should roar up round the corner of the drive in perfect formation but the World Famous Purple Helmets! Most emotional! And this was followed by a 'right Royal' trip down the main drive with the leading outriders stopping the traffic in Governors Road for the car to sweep out onto the main road - American style! The outriders rejoining the Motorcade and covering each and every side road in turn as in a military operation, must have been a stirring sight and I only wish I had been there myself, but at least we were able in our own way to say our 'thank you' to the Macfadyens for all the happy times up there at Government House with the various dignitaries over the previous five years.

The year 2005 is where I will finish writing I think as it finished on a high with this sad but memorable farewell and soon afterwards we launched our D.V.D. called 'On Any Shite Sunday'! I am pleased to say that as I write this some three years on in 2008 I have despite the many set backs and 'close to death' experiences, reached the age of 60!

I am going to sit down and have a nice cup of tea and Penguin biscuit now, so to all my friends, I've got the kettle on at Ballakissack Farm!

So keep laughing boys! And I'll see you all of a sudden!

WANTED

*Above,
The Triumph TR6
used in the escape.*

NAKED TRUTH

It was on the bike in the top picture that Derek made his daring bid for freedom. Naked, except for his Ex-Army Trench coat, which had no buttons, Derek had been forced off the road at a Police blockade. He then careered down the steep rocky banking, bouncing up and down on the tank for 200yards. It is now understood why he thought he would not stand out amongst the Purple Helmets.

Good friend Trish Kilmartin, said "I have only seen him once since but I broke it off"

Poor Derek!

*Above,
Derek, posing as one of the
Purple Helmets. If only he had
paid more attention to detail the
bike's condition is a dead
giveaway.*

MANXMAN ESCAPES FROM ASYLYM

Police in Kirkby Lonsdale were alerted to the fact that one of the Isle of Man's most notorious outlaws may be at large in the town this weekend.

Known only as Derek to his friend, he has almost single-handedly brought the world of motorcycling into disrepute with his unprecedented bouts of drunkenness and debauchery.

Police were warning locals not to approach this man as it is suspected he somehow manages to corrupt all those who come into contact with him.

It was rumoured that Barge Poles had been placed at strategic points in the town in case he should approach any of the young women.

REWARD
OUTSTANDING

**Keith Moore & Derry Kissack
The Fun Run - Douglas promenade 1988**